upper intermediate

real life

WORKBOOK

GW00371781

contents

Vocabulary

Success and achievements

1 Complete the tables.

A

Verb	Noun
inspire	1 _inspiration_
satisfy	2 _____
achieve	3 _____
respect	4 _____
compete	5 _____
pressurise	6 _____
sacrifice	7 _____

B

Adjective	Noun
motivated	8 _____
dedicated	9 _____
disciplined	10 _____
challenging	11 _____

2 Complete the sentences with words from exercise 1.

1 My cousin goes to an alternative school because he can't stand any form of d_iscipline_ .

2 We're under a lot of p_____ at school these days because of the exams.

3 Jessica often takes up new activities, but she doesn't have the m_____ to keep practising.

4 My own s_____ with what I do is more important to me than gaining the r_____ of others.

5 If you want to be a champion, you have to make s_____ – you can't party every night!

6 My greatest a_____ so far has been learning to keep my room tidy!

7 I like sports, but I don't like the atmosphere of c_____ . I feel no need to show I'm better than others.

Grammar

Present tenses

3 *Underline* the correct verb form.

1 Is he tired already? He obviously *doesn't go/isn't going* running often enough!

2 I *take/am taking* a self-defence course these days. I need it, especially as I *live/have been living* in a dangerous part of the city.

3 Please don't disturb me, I *do/am doing* my piano practice.

4 More and more people *are passing/have passed* the school-leaving exam early these days.

5 We *are training/have been training* for the race for months now – we feel confident we can win.

6 I *have done/have been doing* all my exercises for today and now I can relax.

4 ** Complete the text with the phrases below.

[
almost every day   already
at the moment   for the last two years
generally ✓   more and more
]

FEBRUARY 23

I'm a Business Studies student at Sydney University, but the real passion in my life is surfing. I ¹ _generally_ spend all my free time out on the waves, so it is sometimes difficult to finish all my course work. My parents are worried that I don't study enough. ² _____ I'm training hard for the national surfing championships in Manly. I've been competing in the junior competitions ³ _____ , ever since I turned sixteen. This is the first year I'll be old enough for an adult competition. I've ⁴ _____ won three junior competitions, but I can't wait to compete at a higher level! I practise for four or five hours ⁵ _____ during the week and the whole of the weekend. I'm getting ⁶ _____ confident that I have a real chance of succeeding

5 (✻✻) **Complete the dialogues with the sentences below.**

a I do it every day.
b I don't normally do it.
c I'm doing it right now. ✓
d I've already done it.
e I've been doing it for the last half an hour.

1 A: Let's look for adventure holidays on the internet today, like we said.

B: Actually, _c_ Come and have a look with me.

2 A: Could you get our swimming things ready?

B: ___ They're waiting by the door. We can go.

3 A: Will you clear the table, please?

B: Oh, please. ___ I think it's Jack's turn now.

4 A: Could you please repair my bike?

B: ___ That's why I'm so dirty.

5 A: Could you lend me your guitar?

B: ___ But I'll make an exception if you promise to be careful with it.

6 (✻✻✻) **Complete the text with the correct form of the verb in brackets (present simple, present continuous, present perfect or present perfect continuous). If more than one form is possible, use the continuous form.**

Millie ¹ _goes_ (go) to tango lessons in her free time. The lessons ²_____ (take) place on Thursday afternoons. She ³_____ (learn) Argentine tango for five months. She ⁴_____ (already/ learn) the basic elements and now she and her partner ⁵_____ (begin) to improvise. Right now they ⁶_____ (prepare) for the carnival. Millie's friend Katie ⁷_____ (not understand) why she ⁸_____ (want) to learn such an old-fashioned dance. But Millie just loves it!

7 (✻✻✻) **Complete each pair of sentences with the forms of the verb in CAPITALS.**

1 I _know_ Chris well. After all, we _have known_ each other for fifteen years.   KNOW

2 This book is difficult. I _____ it for two hours and I _____ only seven pages. READ

3 I (*negative*) _____ these exercises every day. I _____ them today because I've got a competition tomorrow.   DO

4 Ann _____ the cello. She _____ since she was seven.   PLAY

5 I _____ of running a marathon.
I _____ it'll be a great adventure.   THINK

Grammar reference

Present simple

We use the present simple

- to talk about things that happen repeatedly (routines, habits):

*I often **go** to bed at 11p.m.*
*Owen **plays** football every Saturday.*

- to talk about things that are always true (general truths):

*We **start** work at nine o' clock every day.*
*It **snows** here every winter.*

Present continuous

We use the present continuous

- to talk about things that are happening now (at the time of speaking) or around the time when we speak:

*She's **talking** on the phone now.* (at the moment of speaking)
*They're **studying** algebra this semester.* (around the moment of speaking, not necessarily right now)

- to express current gradual changes:

*Her English **is getting** better.*
*Many young people nowadays **are leaving** their villages and heading towards the towns and cities.*

With state verbs, that is verbs that express emotions (*hate, like, love*), activities of the mind (*believe, know, need, remember, seem, think, understand, want*) or senses (*feel, hear, see*), we can only use the present simple, even though they are describing a situation happening now:

*He **doesn't believe** me.*
*I **hate** getting up early.*

Present perfect simple and present perfect continuous

We use the present perfect to talk about activities and events

- which happened in the past but have results/ consequences now:

*She **has failed** the entrance exam.* (consequence = she hasn't got a place at university)
*They **have won** a lot of money.* (result = they can afford to buy a new house)

- which started in the past and continue up to now:

*I **have been working** here for five months.* (I'm still working here.)
*They **have always liked** Chinese food.* (They still like it.)

We use the present perfect continuous to talk about continuing or repeated actions.

We only use the present perfect simple with state verbs (e.g. *like, believe, need, know*).

Vocabulary

Extreme adjectives and intensifiers

1 **Complete the sentences with the adjectives below.**

> exhausted   freezing   hilarious ✓   huge
> outstanding   starving   terrifying

1 We couldn't stop laughing – it was _hilarious_ . It's the funniest film I've seen for ages.

2 Kate forgot our sandwiches and all the shops were closed so we couldn't buy anything to eat. We were _____ by the time we arrived.

3 All the performances were good, but his was _____ . I've never seen such a talented actor.

4 We were all absolutely _____ because the central heating had stopped working.

5 Being lost in the jungle was a _____ experience. I've never been so frightened in all my life!

6 It was a simply _____ building. We walked around for hours before we found the right department.

7 I got up at six and we've been rehearsing non-stop all day – I'm _____ !

2 **Complete the dialogues with extreme adjectives.**

1 A: So, were you surprised?
   B: Surprised? We were absolutely _amazed_ !

2 A: So, was it hot there?
   B: Hot? It was absolutely _____ !

3 A: Did you get wet?
   B: You can say that again. We were absolutely _____ .

4 A: Do you think she's intelligent?
   B: Oh yes, she's absolutely _____ .

5 A: Were the exam results bad?
   B: Bad? They were absolutely _____ .

6 A: Did he get angry?
   B: You can say that again. He was absolutely _____ .

7 A: Were they worried?
   B: Worried? They were absolutely _____ !

Grammar

Past tenses

3 (**✲**) **Underline the correct verb form.**

1 Meryl Streep _has received/received_ sixteen Oscar nominations, which is more than any other actress, but she _has only won/only won_ twice.

2 As a boy, the director Martin Scorsese _watched/was watching_ several films a week.

3 Harrison Ford _was working/worked_ as a carpenter for George Lucas, the director of _Star Wars_, when Lucas _had offered/offered_ him a role in the film.

4 While he _was preparing/had prepared_ for the film _Fight Club_, Edward Norton lost thirteen kilograms, which he _put on/had put on_ before for _American History X_.

5 When Johnny Depp met Vanessa Paradis, it was love at first sight, even though he _was dating/had been dating_ the British model Kate Moss for almost four years.

6 Quentin Tarantino became interested in film after he _had dropped/had been dropping_ out of college because of bad grades.

4 (**✲✲**) **Match the sentence beginnings 1–6 with the endings a–f.**

1 He was a rich man
2 He was sent to jail
3 She trusted Adam
4 He finally became an actor
5 She stopped working for six months
6 She got the role in the musical

a after he'd tried many different jobs.
b because she had impressed everyone with her singing.
c after her son had been born.
d because his father had made a fortune in oil.
e because she'd known him since childhood.
f for something that he hadn't done.

5 (✳✳✳) Complete the text with the correct past tense forms.

In 1968, the actor Dustin Hoffman wanted to get the part of Ratso Rizzo, a homeless New York con man, in the film *Midnight Cowboy*. He [1] _made_ (make) an appointment to meet the film executive in charge of the casting on a street corner in Manhattan. Before he [2] _____ (go) to the meeting, he [3] _____ (put on) some dirty old clothes. When the film executive [4] _____ (arrive) on the corner, a poor beggar [5] _____ (stand) there and [6] _____ (ask) people for money. The executive [7] _____ (pay) no attention to him. After he [8] _____ (wait) for a long while, the beggar [9] _____ (walk) up to him and [10] _____ (introduce) himself as Dustin Hoffman. He [11] _____ (get) the part, and the film [12] _____ (win) Academy Awards for Best Picture, Best Director and Best Screenplay.

Grammar Plus: Question tags

6 (✳✳✳) Add question tags.

1 He's made about thirty films, _hasn't he_ ?
2 You haven't been here before, _____ ?
3 They talk too much, _____ ?
4 There are some good ideas in this book, _____ ?
5 Help me get dressed for the concert, _____ ?
6 Let's go to the cinema tonight, _____ ?
7 I'm getting better at singing, _____ ?

Grammar reference

Past simple and past continuous

We use the past simple to talk about completed actions in the past:

*They **bought** a house two years ago.*

We use the past continuous to describe actions in progress at a certain time in the past:

*At midnight yesterday we **were** still **finishing** the project.*

Past perfect simple and past perfect continuous

We use the past perfect tenses to describe an event or situation which happened <u>before</u> other past events (expressed in the past simple):

*On my way to work I realised I **had left** my laptop at home.*

(the second event happened before the first = first I left my laptop, then I realised.)

Form (past perfect continuous)

We form the past perfect continuous with *had + been + verb + -ing.*

	+	–
I/You/He/She/ It/We/They	**had ('d) been waiting.**	**had not (hadn't) been waiting.**

General questions			Short answers		
Had	I/you/he/she/ it/we/they	**been waiting?**	Yes, No,	I/you/he/she/ it/we/they	**had. hadn't.**

Wh- questions

*How long **had** you **been waiting** when she finally turned up?*

Use of past perfect

We use the past perfect simple when we answer the question *How much/How many?*:

*I **had written** <u>six pages</u> of my essay.*

We use the past perfect simple to talk about states:

*Before I met John, I **had known** his wife for over a year.*

We use the past perfect continuous to emphasise that the earlier action continued over a period of time or was repeated:

*When I met him, he **had been working** for our company for ten years.*

We use the past perfect continuous when we answer the question *'How long?'*:

*I **had been writing** my essay <u>for four hours</u>.*

Question tags

We use question tags to ask for agreement or to confirm something we already know. We usually form question tags with the auxiliary verb.

We use *do/does/did* for present and past simple when there is no auxiliary verb:

*Marek worked with you, **didn't he?***

For imperatives and requests, we use *will* as the auxiliary verb:

*Hurry up, **won't you**!*

For requests and suggestions, the question tag is always positive.

Vocabulary

Reaching the top

1 Complete the text with the words below.

> determination   luck   natural talent ✓
> self-confidence   skills   social network
> support

Norton School of Performing Arts

Are you good at acting? Have you got a ¹ _natural talent_ for performing? Then **Norton School of Performing Arts** is the perfect place for you!

At **Norton**, we:

★ give you all the ² _____ you need to help you develop your ³ _____ as an actor.

★ help you improve your ⁴ _____ so you don't feel nervous or frightened when you perform.

★ help you prepare for auditions for professional work – auditions are all about preparation, they're not just a matter of ⁵ _____ and being in the right place at the right time!

★ help you develop your ⁶ _____ to succeed – you can't give up at the first obstacle!

★ show you how building a ⁷ _____ of contacts through the internet and acting agencies can help you succeed.

★ and on top of all this, you'll get a first-class, all-round education too!

So what's stopping you?
Come to **Norton School** – you won't regret it!

2 Complete the table.

Verb	Noun	Adjective
confide	¹ _confidence_	confident
determine	² _____	³ _____
–	luck	⁴ _____
–	⁵ _____	talented
support	⁶ _____	⁷ _____
–	⁸ _____	exceptional
network	⁹ _____	–
succeed	success	¹⁰ _____

Listening

3 ② Listen to an extract from a radio programme about Warren Buffett. Choose the correct answers.

1 Warren Buffett is now
  a the richest man in the world.
  b a millionaire.
  c a billionaire.

2 Warren Buffett
  a has already given money to charity.
  b has never given money to charity.
  c is not well-known for giving money to charity.

3 Who is organising the $600 Billion Challenge?
  a Just Warren Buffett.
  b Buffett and Bill Gates.
  c Buffett and Bill and Melinda Gates.

4 Who is being asked to contribute to raise the money?
  a Ordinary Americans.
  b Rich people all over the world.
  c The 400 richest Americans.

5 People who contribute
  a can choose how their money is used.
  b can't choose how their money is used.
  c don't usually choose how their money is used.

4 ② Listen again and answer the questions.

1 How old was Buffett when he became a millionaire?

_____

2 What percentage of his money is Buffett giving away?

_____

3 Why did Buffett decide to give his money away now?

_____

4 How many charities will the money go to?

_____

5 What percentage of their money do people have to promise to donate?

_____

Reading

5 Look at the photo and read the text title and list of paragraph headings a–g in exercise 6. Choose the best answer.

The text is about

1 how you can improve your football skills.

2 a football school that has been very successful.

3 the places where football is most popular.

6 Read the text and check your answer to exercise 5. Match the headings a–g with the correct paragraphs 1–6. There is one extra heading.

a Great facilities   ____

b Small country, big success   _1_

c A different way of thinking   ____

d Top players all over the world   ____

e Life skills, not just coaching   ____

f Everybody loves football!   ____

g Finding the players of the future   ____

7 Read the text again. Tick (✓) true, cross (✗) false or write (?) if there is no information.

1 ☐ The Ivory Coast has always produced a lot of good footballers.

2 ☐ Guillou and Ouégnin started the academy because there weren't any good players in the ASEC Mimosa Football Club.

3 ☐ The academy students train for longer per day than students in many other countries.

4 ☐ The former manager of the England football team admires the ASEC Mimosa Academy.

5 ☐ The coaches and teachers at the school are all men.

6 ☐ Charles Silue doesn't have a clear idea of what he wants to do in the future.

'Football is my passion'

1 _b_

Until recently, the Ivory Coast, a small country in West Africa, did not have a high profile in international sport. It's a poor country – of the population of twenty million, 25 percent live below the international poverty line of US $1.25 a day – but over the last ten to fifteen years it has produced so many world-class football players that the world has started to notice. So what's the secret? How does the tiny Ivory Coast produce so many football giants?

2 ___

In 1993, Jean-Marc Guillou, a former French national footballer, became the new manager of ASEC Mimosa Football Club in Abidjan*. Guillou decided to start a training academy where talented young players would receive football coaching, as well as a more general education. So, he set up the ASEC Mimosa Academy with Roger Ouégnin, the club's chairperson, to train the players of the future.

3 ___

In addition to well-equipped classrooms, the school has two excellent football pitches and gardens. The boys live at the academy and learn maths, history, geography, physics, French, English and Spanish as well as training for at least four hours every day – something which is just not possible in many European countries because of the weather. They also get free healthcare.

4 ___

Now, nearly twenty years later, graduates of the ASEC Mimosa Academy play in professional football teams across the globe: Kolo Touré, Emmanuel Eboue, Salomon Kalou, Didier Zokora, Yaya Touré – the list of international stars who were trained in the school is astonishing. The talented young boys who enter the academy are transformed into the kind of skilled professionals every club wants. Sven-Goran Eriksson, the former manager of the England team, recently called it the 'most successful football academy in the world'.

5 ___

The academy director Walter Amman believes its success is because the football coaches and teachers try to help the boys develop as people, not just as footballers. 'We try to protect them, and to teach them responsibility, to help them become men,' he explains.

6 ___

For one of the students, fifteen-year-old Charles Silue, success – both his own and that of the other students in the school – is all about attitude. Silue is determined, focused and self-confident, and he is also extremely talented. After he leaves the academy he wants to play for Barcelona, then for Manchester United. 'Many young African players just think about money,' he says. 'They focus on that. But here we're taught to think differently – to be responsible and concentrate on our objectives. Football is my passion. The money will follow.'

*Abidjan – the Ivory Coast's biggest city

going to extremes

Writing

A narrative

1 In **paragraph 1**, set the context for the narrative. Say where and when it happened and who the main characters are. Try to get the reader's interest and make him/her want to read more, e.g. hint that something exciting or terrible is going to happen.

2 In **paragraph 2**, describe the events leading up to the main event. Give the reader a clear picture of the situation before an unexpected event happens.

3 In **paragraph 3**, describe the main events in detail. Use exclamation points to add drama to the story. Include information about the consequences of events and describe people's feelings. Use different sorts of adjectives, including extreme adjectives, to make your description more interesting.

4 In **paragraph 4**, say how the story ends. Try to finish in an interesting way, for example with a quote, a comparison or a comment about what happened.

Disaster on Kilimanjaro!

Three months ago I went on an expedition to climb Mount Kilimanjaro in Africa. I love climbing and for years my dream had been to get to the top of Kilimanjaro. I had been training for six months and I was sure I could do it. Little did I know that disaster was about to strike.

The first day passed without any incidents, but then my problems started. As we got higher, I found it more and more difficult to concentrate because there was less oxygen. I stopped looking at the ground, I could only think of reaching the summit.

All of a sudden, I heard a strange sound! I looked down – to my horror I was standing on a puff adder. I was absolutely terrified. These snakes kill many people each year and I had my foot on one! Fortunately, my foot was near its head so it couldn't bite me. I managed to jump onto a rock, thankfully, just out of reach. The snake tried several times to bite me, but then it disappeared. As I was climbing off the rock, I slipped and fell and shattered my ankle.

The other climbers managed to carry me down the mountain because they knew it would take rescuers a long time to arrive. I was in pain all the time and feeling sick and exhausted. At the bottom, a helicopter was waiting to take me to hospital. Thankfully, my leg was not permanently damaged and I am hoping to climb Kilimanjaro next year! My brother, who is an experienced climber, laughed at the story – once he stopped being worried about me. 'You forgot the second rule of climbing, Sarah,' he said, shaking his head. 'The first rule is "always find a good hold for your hands" but the second is "watch your feet!"'

Sarah

Useful language

Getting the reader's attention

Little did I know that it was going to be the best/worst/most frightening/most amazing day of my life.

Linking words

all of a sudden … slowly … immediately … in the end … meanwhile …

Describing feelings

I was absolutely/really/totally … amazed/terrified/delighted.

Describing the main event

To my horror/surprise/relief/amazement/despair …

Finishing the narrative

It was the best/worst/most exciting/most frightening day/night of my life!

1 Read the narrative and answer the questions.

1 Why didn't the snake bite her immediately?

2 How did she get to hospital?

2 Read the narrative again and <u>underline</u> the expressions the writer uses to:

1 hint to the reader that something unexpected is going to happen. (paragraph 1)

2 hint to the reader that something bad is going to happen. (paragraph 2)

3 introduce the main event in a dramatic way. (paragraph 3)

4 describe how she felt when saw the snake. (paragraph 3)

5 describe how she felt when she was going down the mountain. (paragraph 4)

6 comment on the story at the end. (paragraph 4)

3 Complete the adverbials table below. One of the adverbials can go in two groups.

> eventually   gradually   sadly ✓
> strangely   suddenly   surprisingly ✓
> thankfully   to my horror   unfortunately
> fortunately ✓   all of a sudden ✓

Describing something positive	Describing something negative
1 _fortunately_	3 _sadly_
2 _____	4 _____
	5 _____
Talking about time	**Saying how you feel**
6 _all of a sudden_	10 _surprisingly_
7 _____	11 _____
8 _____	12 _____
9 _____	

4 Rewrite the sentences using adverbials from the table in exercise 3. Pay attention to punctuation.

a Jane hit her head on the rock. (negative adverbial)

To my horror, Jane hit her head on the rock.

b She was unconscious. (negative adverbial)

_____

_____

c We heard a terrible noise – Jane's canoe had hit a rock in the river! (time adverbial)

_____

_____

d There happened to be a rescue station close by, so we carried Jane there. (feeling adverbial)

_____

_____

e Jane disappeared under the water, but she appeared again. (time adverbial)

_____

_____

f We pulled Jane out of the water. She was still breathing. (positive adverbial)

_____

_____

5 Read the beginning of the narrative about the canoeing expedition. Put the sentences a–f from exercise 4 in the correct order 1–6 to tell the main events of the story.

Last month I went canoeing with two friends, Jane and Simon. It was a beautiful day and the river was calm. We had no idea of the terrible adventure that was about to happen.

1 _c_   2 ___   3 ___
4 ___   5 ___   6 ___

6 Write the last paragraph of the story about the canoeing expedition. Include the information below. Use adverbials and expressions from the *Useful language* section.

1 what the people at the rescue centre did to help (helicopter → hospital)

2 what happened to Jane

3 how the writer and Simon felt

4 what happened afterwards/how the story ended

7 Complete the strategies box with the words below.

> punctuation   organise   information ✓
> improve   list

A narrative

- Read the task carefully. Think about the ¹ _information_ you need to include (*who, what, where, when, why, how*) and make notes.

- Make a ² _____ of useful words and expressions and decide where you can use them.

- Write your first draft making sure you ³ _____ it correctly into four paragraphs.

- Read your draft. Can you ⁴ _____ it by using more interesting vocabulary, linkers or idioms? Can you vary the tenses more?

- Check the number of words and then check your ⁵ _____ , grammar and spelling.

8 Choose one of the tasks below and write a narrative. Use the essay structure on the opposite page and the strategies in exercise 7 and ideas in the exercises to help you. Write 200–250 words.

> **1** You are one of the other people in the group of climbers on Kilimanjaro. Rewrite the story from your point of view.
>
> **2** Write about an unexpected event, real or imaginary, that happened to you.

Talking about photographs

1 Look at the photos and complete the text with the words and phrases below.

> have in common   seem   look like
> makes me   related to the topic ✓

These photos are [1] _related to the topic_ of success and happiness. What they [2] _____ is that they both show teenagers who [3] _____ happy. The photo on the right shows a group of teenagers. They [4] _____ they're friends. It looks as if they are having a good time. They seem very happy. They're standing close together and they've got their right hands all piled together. For me, the photo shows how important having friends is for being happy and successful. In the other photo a teenage girl is smiling and holding a piece of paper. I think she's got good exam results. It [5] _____ think about the importance of getting a good education. In my opinion, the aspect of happiness the photo shows is doing well at school. So, these two photos illustrate two different ideas of what makes people happy and what it means to be successful.

Expressing an opinion

How would you define success in life?

	Asked of US teens aged 13–17	
Happiness/Content	★★★★★★★★★★★★★★★	15%
Having goals	★★★★★★★★★★	10%
Good job/Having a job	★★★★★★★★★	9%
Having a good relationship with family	★★★★★★	6%
Rich/making good money/ having enough money	★★★★★★	6%
Hard work/trying your best	★★★★★	5%
Being educated	★★★★★	5%

2 Look at the survey results and complete the dialogue. Put the words in order to make sentences which express opinions.

A: How would you define success in life? What do you think makes a person successful?

B: being happy./my mind/is/To/thing/ the most important

[1] _To my mind, being happy is the most_
   important thing.

A: Why is that?

B: successful/unhappy./I see it/The way/ not really/is that you're/if you're

[2] _____

   _____

A: I don't think anyone disagrees with that!

C: a good relationship/If you/with your family/ is most/important./ask me

[3] _____

   _____

A: Do you think so?

C: the most./the people who/Don't/they are/ can support you/forget that

[4] _____

   _____

A: Do you agree?

D: important./opinion/education/In my/is more/ a good

[5] _____

   _____

C: Why do you think that?

D: without a good education./get a good job/ bear in mind that/You have to/it's difficult to

[6] _____

   _____

examtrainer 1

Use of English

Recognising parts of speech

1 Write *noun, verb, adjective* or *adverb* for each word below. <u>Underline</u> the word suffixes which show what part of the speech the word is.

1 arrange<u>ment</u>   *noun*   4 amazingly   _____

2 furious   _____   5 dedication   _____

3 sympathise   _____   6 responsibility   _____

2 Match the nouns below to the word formation patterns 1–8.

> partnership   ability   brotherhood
> boredom   encouragement ✓   happiness
> exhaustion   importance

1 Verb + *ment*: *encouragement*

2 Verb + *tion, sion, ition* or *ation*: _____

3 Adjective + *-ity*: _____

4 Adjective + *-ness*: _____

5 Adjective ending in *-ant* or *-ent*
 → noun ending in *-ance* or *-ence*: _____

6 Noun + *-ship*: _____

7 Noun + *-hood*: _____

8 Noun, verb or adjective + *-dom*: _____

3 Complete the tables.

Verb	Noun
improve	1 *improvement*
advertise	2 _____
move	3 _____
motivate	4 _____
compete	5 _____
prepare	6 _____

Adjective	Noun
real	7 *reality*
creative	8 _____
kind	9 _____
polite	10 _____
confident	11 _____
free	12 _____

4 Complete the definitions of the <u>underlined</u> nouns.

1 <u>Membership</u> of this club is very expensive.
 – being a *member*

2 My mum had a very good <u>childhood</u> in the countryside.
 – the time of life when one is a _____

3 The documentary shows the actor's rise to <u>stardom</u>.
 – the status of a _____

Exam task

5 Complete the text with the correct form of the words in brackets.

Summerhill school

Summerhill is an unusual school: in the words of its famous founder, A.S. Neill, a school where students have '[1] *freedom* (free) to be themselves'. Neill, who created the school in 1921, believed the most important [2] _____ (achieve) in life is finding [3] _____ (satisfy) and [4] _____ (happy) rather than getting high exam results or a well-paid job. The school does not force students to follow a programme of study. Instead, it aims to support each student's [5] _____ (develop) by helping them discover and follow their own interests. By being free to make their own choices, students build the [6] _____ (motivate) to learn and the [7] _____ (self-confident) they need to succeed in their chosen areas. The school doesn't encourage intense [8] _____ (compete) among students. Some people have criticised Summerhill, claiming its students don't receive a proper [9] _____ (educate). But one thing is certain: A.S. Neill's ideas have been an [10] _____ (inspire) to educators around the world for nearly a century.

Exam TIP

In word formation exercises, think about the part of speech and the meaning. You can use the context of the sentence to help you decide whether a noun, a verb or an adjective is required.

Vocabulary

Flat sharing

1 Match the sentence beginnings 1–6 with the endings a–f.

Six tips on how to avoid rows with flatmates!

1. Share
2. Set clear
3. Behave
4. Communicate
5. Treat others with
6. Have a

a respect.
b about important issues.
c household rules.
d chores and responsibilities.
e chat and a laugh.
f reasonably.

2 Complete the advice with words and expressions from exercise 1.

question from: tensor91

Some friends have suggested renting a flat together. I'd really like to do it, as I feel I'm too old to live with my parents but I'm worried. Will we get on all right? Won't we end up falling out over things like chores?

reply from: flatAid

I think you're absolutely right to think about these issues in advance. This should help you to avoid conflict in the future. So, for example, if you don't want to argue about ¹ _chores_ , you have to make sure you ² _____ responsibilities fairly. Also, set clear ³ _____ rules about things like noise or leaving your things in the shared spaces. But also consider what kind of people your future flatmates are. Will you be able to ⁴ _____ a chat and a laugh together after six months in the same flat? And even more importantly, will you be able to communicate about important ⁵ _____ before you get to the stage of a row? If you communicate and ⁶ _____ each other with respect, you should be able to solve all problems.

Grammar

Present perfect simple and continuous

3 (*) Underline the correct verb form.

1 I'm afraid Sarah's not in. She*'s gone*/*'s been going* out.

2 I*'ve waited*/*'ve been waiting* for a reply to one of my job applications for months now. I feel really depressed.

3 We*'ve bought*/*'ve been buying* a dishwasher. We*'ve argued*/ *'ve been arguing* for ages about who does the washing-up!

4 Jack's *decided*/*'s been deciding* to move back in with his parents.

5 How long *have you lived*/*have you been living* away from home? Do you miss your family?

6 How many times *have you avoided*/*have you been avoiding* a discussion about household chores because you don't want us to have a row?

4 (*) What have they been doing and what have they done? Complete each pair of sentences with the present perfect and present perfect continuous tense of the verbs below.

[paint   dance   write   tidy up ✓]

1 He*'s been tidying up* all afternoon. She*'s tidied up* the whole house and is going into town now.

2 I _____ thirty job applications this week and I'm exhausted. She _____ job applications all summer.

3 They _____ the wall in the hot sun. I _____ the wall and I'm going to start the doors now.

4 She _____ with him. We _____ with him a few times, but we prefer to dance with each other!

5 (**✱✱**) **Match the sentences that go together.**

1 I've been washing the dishes.
2 I've washed all the dishes.
3 Mum's been marking students' essays all night.
4 Mum's marked all the essays.
5 I've been revising History and Geography since Friday.
6 I've revised History and Geography.

a Be quiet. She's very tired.
b Could you dry them up now?
c I can go out and party.
d I'm taking a break because I want a glass of milk.
e She can come to the cinema with us now.
f What a dreadful weekend!

6 (**✱✱**) **Complete the sentences with the correct tense (present perfect simple or continuous) of the verb in brackets.**

1 I *'ve been sending* emails since lunch. I think I *'ve sent* about twenty. (send)
2 Mike _____ all weekend. He _____ three essays! (write)
3 Chris _____ since this morning. He _____ lunch for twelve people! (cook)
4 I _____ for three hours. I _____ already _____ the living room. (clean)
5 He _____ to get a job for ages now. He _____ every local company. (try)

7 (**✱✱✱**) **Complete the pairs of sentences with the verbs in brackets in the correct tense (present perfect simple or continuous).**

1 A: I *'ve been thinking* about the problem you mentioned.
   B: And *have you come up* with a solution? (think/come up with)
2 A: What _____ recently? I _____ you for ages.
   B: I _____ in France for six months. I'm here on a short visit. (do/see/be)
3 A: _____ ? Millie and Sam are going out together!
   B: They _____ since Christmas! Where _____ ? (hear/go out/be)
4 A: I _____ a flat with James for six months and we don't get on.
   B: Why? _____ discussing your problems? (share/try)

Grammar reference

Present perfect simple

We use the present perfect simple to talk about single complete actions

- which happened not long ago and have results now:

I've passed my driving test! (I'm happy and I can drive now.)

- which happened in the past, but we don't know or are not interested in exactly when:

They've studied medicine. (It is not important when.)

We can also use the present perfect when we specify the number of repeated actions which happened in the period of time leading up to the present:

We've visited grandma in hospital three times.
How many times have you seen this film?

Present perfect continuous

We use the present perfect continuous to talk about continuing or repeated actions which happened over a period of time leading up to the present.

We use the present perfect continuous to talk about

- actions which are still going on and which are not finished:

Mr Smith's been teaching in our school since October. (He's still teaching in our school.)
I've been learning French for four years. (I'm still learning French.)

- actions which have ended just before the present and have consequences in the present:

I'm exhausted. I've been painting all day. (I feel exhausted because of the painting.)

Comparison of uses

We use the present perfect continuous to focus on the continuing activity or situation itself and the present perfect simple to focus on the result:

He's written twenty Christmas cards. (result)
He's been writing Christmas cards all morning. (activity)

We use the continuous form when answering the question *how long?* and the simple form when answering the question *how much?* or *how many?*:

How many miles have they run? They've run ten miles.
How long have they been running? They've been running all afternoon.

State verbs

With state verbs (e.g. *know, have, understand, believe, like*) we can only use the present perfect simple, even though they are describing a continuing situation:

I've known Mark for over ten years.
They've always liked football.

2

Vocabulary

Behaviour and relationships

1 Match the captions a–e to the cartoons 1–5.

a I'll just ignore him. ___

b Please stop nagging? _1_

c He's always showing off in front of his mates. ___

d Oh dear. I've mislaid my glasses again. ___

e Please don't interrupt! ___

2 Complete the sentences with the verbs below in the correct form.

> interrupt keep leave
> make have ✓ take

I'm so fed up with my family!

1 I'm getting on really badly with dad at the moment and we're always _having_ rows.

2 Mum _____ forgetting where she put her car keys.

3 My sister _____ ages to have a shower and I have to wait!

4 My brother is always _____ a mess in the bathroom.

5 And he keeps _____ everyone when they're trying to say something.

6 And they say I _____ a drama out of everything!

Grammar

Present and past habits

3 ⊛ Match the sentences 1–6 with the habits a–f.

1 Ellen's very reliable.

2 My aunt's very generous.

3 Alice is obsessed with keeping fit.

4 Kate's memory is not very good.

5 I think Ann's a bit of a workaholic.

6 You can't really trust Joanna.

a She spends hours in the gym every day.

b She keeps telling lies – it really gets on my nerves.

c She's always working late.

d She never forgets arrangements we've made or breaks her promises.

e She's always buying me presents.

f She keeps forgetting everyone's birthdays.

4 ⊛⊛ Complete the sentences with the correct form of *used to* using the words in brackets.

1 Mike _used to mislay_ (mislay) things a lot and forget arrangements when he was younger. He's more reliable now!

2 _____ (you/make) a drama out of tiny things when you were a teenager?

3 He _____ (not/show off) so much but now he's always trying to impress the girls.

4 We _____ (spend) hours gossiping with our friends after school.

5 Where _____ (you/live) before you moved here?

6 You _____ (not/nag) me like this before we got married!

5 ⊛⊛ Complete the sentences with the correct form of the words in brackets.

The Blog Site

The neighbours from hell!

Our neighbours [1] _keep having_ (keep/have) noisy parties until late at night. Their guests [2] _____ (constantly/block) our drive with their cars. They [3] _____ (keep/leave) rubbish on the pavement in front of the house and their dog [4] _____ (constantly/get into) our garden and frightening the cats. My sister says I shouldn't get so upset because at least they are friendly. The neighbours we had before were much worse. They [5] _____ (used to/phone) the police every time we had a few visitors. When the police started ignoring their calls, they [6] _____ (would/come) round to the house to complain and refuse to leave. Worst of all, they [7] _____ (always/gossip) about us: they [8] _____ (keep/tell) everyone how unfriendly we were!

6 (✱✱) Tick (✓) all the verb forms that can complete the sentences below. One, two or three answers may be correct.

1 My brother Peter ___ long hair when he was a little boy.
   a ☑ had
   b ☑ used to have
   c ☐ would have

2 When we were six, we ___ outside every afternoon.
   a ☐ played
   b ☐ used to play
   c ☐ would play

3 Our neighbour ___ at us.
   a ☐ would shout
   b ☐ used to shout
   c ☐ was always shouting

4 I ___ olives when I was younger.
   a ☐ wouldn't like
   b ☐ didn't use to like
   c ☐ didn't like

5 My brother used to get on my nerves. He ___ my model aeroplanes without asking.
   a ☐ was always taking
   b ☐ would take
   c ☐ kept taking

6 When I was seven, I ___ doing my homework!
   a ☐ enjoyed
   b ☐ used to enjoy
   c ☐ would enjoy

Grammar Plus: *be/get used to*

7 (✱✱✱) <u>Underline</u> the correct form of the verb.

1 I *am used/am getting used* to travelling on my own. I've been doing it ever since I remember.
2 The woman sitting next to me on the plane *wasn't used to/didn't use to* flying and she was afraid.
3 After a year in Morocco we gradually *used to/ got used to* functioning in a hot climate.
4 In my previous school we *didn't use to start/ didn't get used to starting* lessons until nine o'clock.
5 I've only had a driving licence for two months. I'm not quite *used to driving/drive* yet.
6 I've just finished school and started my first job. I'm gradually *used to/getting used to* the new routine.

Grammar reference

Habits in the present and in the past

To talk about habits in the present, we use

- the present simple:

*She always **tells** me the truth.*

- the present continuous + *always/constantly* when a habit is annoying or surprising:

*They**'re constantly finding** problems with everything.*

- *keep* + verb + *-ing* to emphasise that an action happens very often (especially a bad habit):

*They **keep asking** ridiculous questions.*

To talk about habits in the past, we use

- the past simple:

*He **shouted** at his dog all the time.*

- the past continuous + *always/constantly* when a habit is annoying or surprising:

*My sisters **were constantly falling** out.*

- *kept* + verb + *-ing* to emphasise that an action happened very often (especially a bad habit):

*Tom and Paul **kept distracting** each other during the test.*

- *used to* for states (e.g. *be, have, believe, like*) and actions which were true or happened regularly in the past but are not true or don't happen regularly now:

*Matthew **used to read** every day.* (He doesn't do it any more.)

- *would* for repeated actions in the past:

*My grandfather **would** often **criticise** me for wasting money on sweets.*

NB *Used to* can be used for both actions and states, whilst *would* is used only for actions.

*I **used to be** (NOT ~~would be~~) afraid of dogs.* (state)
*I **would often run away** in tears when our neighbour's dog tried to play with me.* (action)

be/get used to + *-ing*

be used to

We use *be used to* + *-ing* to talk about things which are familiar to us:

*I**'m used to** sharing things with others – I've got four siblings. When I started work in the bakery, I **wasn't used to** getting up at 4 a.m.*

get used to

We use *get used to* + *-ing* to talk about the process when new things are becoming more familiar:

*With time I **got used to** driving on the left.* (It became familiar to me.)
*He's slowly **getting used to** living on his own.* (He's becoming accustomed to it.)

Vocabulary

1 Match 1–7 with a–g to make collocations.

1 be in charge of   a down with someone
2 start   b family finances
3 have a   c property
4 settle   d relationship
5 bring   e dating
6 inherit   f someone out
7 ask   g up your children

2 Complete the sentences with the correct form of the collocations from exercise 1.

1 In many countries, it is still the man who decides how to spend the money in a household. Men earn the money and so they _are in charge of family finances_ .

2 I think you and your husband should discuss your ideas about how to _____ before you have a baby.

3 When Tim's grandparents died, he _____ a house from them.

4 I don't think you should get married until you are ready to _____ and live the rest of your life with one person.

5 John and Katie have just _____ . They're going to the cinema together for the first time tonight.

6 I know you really like Mark. Why don't you invite him to the party? I don't think it always has to be a boy who _____ .

7 I think communication is very important when you _____ with someone.

3 Complete the text.

To work or not to work?

A survey has revealed that 52 percent of women would rather be full-time [1] _housewives_ (ohsiweuevs) but they go back to work because they need the money. But even when women work, men still regard themselves as head of the [2] _____ (lohdohesu). This is true even when the woman earns more or is the only [3] _____ (adinnerwerb). Many people believe that this is one reason why more marriages are ending and the [4] _____ (ivcerod tera) is going up. Perhaps we should all have [5] _____ (rargedna ramiresga) like they do in countries such as India, where the parents choose the husband or wife for their children!

Reading

4 Read the introduction and look at the words below. Choose the best answer.

These extracts are probably about

a Indian culture in general.
b the family and relationships in Indian culture.

> husband   got married   engagement
> stay single   an arranged match   romance

When the love of her life, Jonathan, is sent to Delhi (India) for his job as an international news reporter, Sarah Macdonald leaves her dream job as a radio presenter in Sydney (Australia) and they go to live in Delhi.

Sarah finds many things different about life in the two countries but she makes friends with some Indian women, Padma, Aarzoo and Billie, and starts to find out more about Indian culture.

5 Read Extract 1 on page 17. Tick (✓) true or cross (✗) false for the statements below.

1 ☐ It's the first time Sarah has met Surinder.
2 ☐ Padma didn't like Surinder the first time she saw him
3 ☐ Padma and Surinder weren't in a relationship for a long time before they decided to get married.
4 ☐ Padma is worried that her mother won't like Surinder.
5 ☐ Surinder's parents are very happy when they hear the news.

6 Read Extract 2 and choose the correct answers.

1 How does Jonathan feel about having a *rakhee*?
   a He's happy because he thinks it will be easy to find a husband for Aarzoo.
   b He's nervous because he doesn't think Aarzoo and Sunil will get engaged.
   c He's worried because he will have to find someone for Aarzoo to marry.
   d He's flattered because Aarzoo wants to marry him.

2 Aarzoo doesn't want to marry an Indian man because
   a an Indian man will expect her to stop working and not have a career.
   b she doesn't want to make tea for her husband.
   c she has a career in movies.
   d she prefers Western men to Indian men.

3 What does the author say about arranged marriages?

   a She has always thought they were a good idea.

   b She has a different opinion about them since she moved to India.

   c She says it's the only way couples can get married in India.

   d She thinks all couples are happy.

4 Billie

   a will blame herself if she doesn't get married.

   b thinks her parents will find her a suitable husband.

   c thinks she could find a better husband for herself than her parents.

   d thinks her parents are to blame for the fact she isn't married.

5 It hasn't been easy for Billie's father to find a suitable husband for her because

   a Billie didn't like any of the men he has found.

   b there aren't many men who aren't divorced.

   c there aren't many acceptable men who meet all his conditions.

   d they all drink.

6 What does Billie say about the family of whoever she might marry?

   a The family aren't important as long as the man is nice.

   b She only wants to marry someone who isn't too close to their family.

   c It's really important that she likes the man's family.

   d She wants to marry someone who doesn't have a big family.

Extract 1

There is a knock at the door. It's Padma – and a tall cute Indian guy. She introduces him as, 'Surinder, my husband.'

Rachel and Mary, friends who have come round for a chat, make us some *chai** and stay on to hear the story.

'Well, so, I was at the Thai conference and on the last day I looked up and saw Surinder. My heart almost stopped beating, I couldn't breathe, I felt dizzy, the whole lot. He walked over and we just knew. We talked, we walked out of the seminar, got on a boat, went to an island and got married in the local church.'

They hold hands and look lovingly into each other's eyes. I nearly fall off my chair. Rachel drops the teapot and Mary freezes.

India is in love with the idea of romance. On TV, men woo women with romantic songs, flowers and heart-shaped balloons. And then there's reality. Sons and daughters do not fall in love and marry without their parents' agreement or permission.

I shriek, 'Padma, what did your mum say?'

Padma looks down.

'You haven't told her?'

'No. Surinder is perfect. Mum'll be happy. He's Indian, he's a doctor, he must be the most suitable boy in the country. He's perfect.'

Surinder smiles sweetly. He also hasn't told his parents and he leaves to tell them. I can't sleep with worry, but he rings in the morning. His parents are cool – upset and hurt, but accepting. Padma and I celebrate with a cup of chai. Padma goes to break the news to her mum.

chai – Indian tea

Extract 2

When Jonathan finally returns from Nepal, I pick him up at the airport. He's arrived home when all the men of Delhi are wearing bracelets. Once a year, girls who have a brother put a special bracelet or *rakhee* around his wrist to show their affection and to ensure that he will look after her and help her get married. At a nightclub, my friend Aarzoo ties a *rakhee* on Jonathan. He is flattered but nervous about this. Aarzoo has called off her engagement to Sunil and this bracelet means Jonathan is now responsible for finding her a new mate. He doesn't know many single guys Aarzoo would possibly want. She's off Indian men altogether.

'They just want a slave. I want a career, I want to make movies. I can't give it up for a man who wants me to make *chai* all day.'

The problem is, she's also doubtful about Western men. Aarzoo decides to stay single and Jonathan wipes his brow.

Billie is under pressure to get married soon but she'll accept an arranged match. My feelings on arranged marriages have changed since I've lived here and seen that organised matches can often work. Most couples really are very happy. Besides, finding someone in a culture where there's not that much girl–boy mixing can be difficult, if not impossible. Billie doesn't have much experience with boys and she trusts her parents to know what she wants and needs. In any case, Billie says if she doesn't get married she won't feel like a loser – her parents will take the blame.

Because Billie is an extremely high-caste Brahmin*, her father will only consider very elite men. They're unacceptable if they have a relative who's divorced, if they drink, if they have the wrong job or salary or if the parents are showy. So far, he's only found a few suitable boys and Billie dismissed them quickly; one because he wanted to talk to her alone and the other because she didn't like his parents.

'Sarah, I want someone who is from a pleasant family. I'm not getting married to him, I'm getting married to his family. They have to be nice.'

*In traditional Hindu society, people belong to different classes or castes. Of these, the Brahmin caste is the highest 'most elite' class.

A formal phone conversation

1 Choose the best response.

1 Could I speak to the manager, please?

  a Why do you want to speak to him?

  b Can I ask what your call is concerning?

2 I'll put you through now.

  a Hold on a minute.

  b Thank you.

3 Good afternoon. HN Hotels.

  a Who's calling, please?

  b Could I speak to the manager, please?

4 Can I take a message?

  a Yes. Could you ask Mr Smith to call me?

  b Yes. Could you tell me when to call Mr Smith?

5 Who's calling, please?

  a I'm calling to speak to the manager.

  b My name's Lucy Lewis.

2 Put the sentences in the phone conversation a–k in the correct order 1–11.

a ☐ Can I ask what your call is concerning, Ms Stone?

b ☐ Hello. Could I speak to the manager, please?

c ☐ … I'm sorry. I'm afraid Mrs Stein's not available. Can I take a message?

d ☐ It's Lisa Stone from the *Daily Star* newspaper.

e ☐ Yes, please. Could you ask her to call Lisa Stone from the *Daily Star* on 0799 783529?

f ☐ I'd like to interview him or her about the opening of the new Mattison factory next month.

g ☐ *1* Good morning, Mattison Limited. How can I help you?

h ☐ Thank you.

i ☐ Certainly. Who's calling, please?

j ☐ *11* OK, no problem. I'll ask her to call you as soon as possible. Goodbye.

k ☐ OK. It's Sylvia Stein you need to speak to. Hold the line, please. I'll put you through.

A formal letter

3 Match the parts of the letter 1–8 with the descriptions a–h.

```
                                        Flat 2,
                                        Castle Mill House,
                                        Jericho Street,        ( 1 )
                                        Oxford
                                        OX2 7EN

   3967 Miramonte Avenue,               1 January 0000        ( 2 )
( 3 ) Oakland,
   CA 92483

( 4 ) Dear Mr Edwards,
                         ( 5 )



                         ( 6 )


( 7 ) I look forward to hearing from you.
      Yours sincerely,
( 8 ) Anita Scherer
      Anita Scherer
```

a ☐ The date

b ☐ Explanation of who you are and why you are writing

c ☐ *1* Your address

d ☐ The opening, for example *Dear Mr Hill,*

e ☐ The address of the person you are writing to

f ☐ Closing the letter and saying you expect a reply

g ☐ Your signature with your name printed underneath

h ☐ The main part of the letter, including the questions you want to ask and the reasons you are asking them

4 Put the words in the correct order.

1 am/your advert./I/in/writing/to/response

  I am writing in response to your advert.

2 look/from/hearing/forward/you/I/soon./to

  _____

3 would/I/know/like/how/to/the course costs./much

  _____

4 like/know/I/more/would/the extra activities./about/to

  _____

5 am/interested/I/living with a family./in

  _____

6 My/and/I/a student/name's/Pawel Adamicz/ at secondary school./am

  _____

exam trainer 2

Use of English

Phrasal verbs

1 Complete the sentences with the verbs below.

[fall   get   tidy   split ✓   switch]

1 Have you heard? Mary and Jim have _split_ up. They're no longer together.
2 Could you please _____ the light off when you leave?
3 I don't often _____ out with my boyfriend, and if I do, we both say sorry very quickly.
4 I don't _____ on with my brother's girlfriend. In fact, I don't like her at all.
5 Will you help me _____ up after the party?

2 Complete the sentences with the correct preposition.

1 I must give these books _back_ to the library.
2 In my country, it's not very common for a woman to ask a man _____ .
3 Hello? Please hold on. I'll put you _____ to Mr Dobson in a second.
4 Eva doesn't want to get married and settle _____ yet.
5 I'm looking forward _____ meeting my boyfriend's cousins.

3 Circle the correct option. Sometimes both are correct.

1 Could you please ___ ? I can't hear my own thoughts.
   a turn down the music
   b turn the music down
2 Jo's going to ___ when we're away.
   a look after our dog
   b look our dog after
3 The robbers forced the bank employees to ___ .
   a hand the money over
   b hand over the money
4 Paul's got my mp3 player. I must ask him to ___ .
   a give it back
   b give back it

Exam tasks

Sentence transformations

4 Complete the second sentence so that it means the same as the first. Use the word in CAPITALS.

1 When I first asked Ruby on a date, the weather was horrible.   OUT
   When I first _asked Ruby out_ , the weather was horrible.
2 I'm trying to calculate how much money we need for our trip.   WORK
   I'm trying to _____ how much money we need for our trip.
3 My great-aunt had five children and she had to raise them on her own after her husband died.   UP
   My great-aunt had five children and she had to _____ on her own after her husband died.
4 I had to stop playing the piano because I didn't have enough time.   GIVE
   I had to _____ playing the piano because I didn't have enough time.

Open cloze

5 Complete the text with one word in each gap.

The education of women in my family

My great-grandmother was one [1] _of_ the first women in my country to study law. She loved it and was looking [2] _____ to a career as a lawyer. Then she met my great-grandfather. After she graduated, they got married and settled [3] _____ in his home. At the time it was considered obvious that she would [4] _____ up her career, but I think it's sad that such an intelligent woman had to stay at home, with no intellectual activity other than playing bridge. She did one unusual thing though: she looked [5] _____ her daughters herself. Most family friends handed [6] _____ the care of their children to nannies and governesses, but my grandma and her sister were brought [7] _____ by their highly educated mother. When they [8] _____ up they both went to university. My grandma became a doctor and she continued working after she was married and after her children were born.

Reading

Multiple matching – short texts

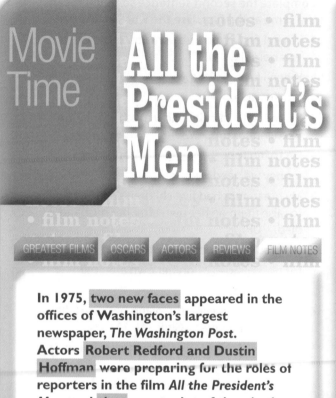

Movie Time

All the President's Men

GREATEST FILMS | OSCARS | ACTORS | REVIEWS | FILM NOTES

In 1975, two new faces appeared in the offices of Washington's largest newspaper, *The Washington Post*. Actors Robert Redford and Dustin Hoffman were preparing for the roles of reporters in the film *All the President's Men*, and they spent a lot of time in the newsroom, observing journalists at work and attending staff meetings. They blended into the newsroom environment so effectively that one day the science reporter told Hoffman to go and bring some office supplies. He'd mistaken the actor for an employee.

1 Read the text. Choose the correct answers a, b or c.

1 Who do all the highlighted words refer to?
  a the actors
  b the reporters
  c other employees

2 Look at the underlined phrases. What do they all demonstrate?
  a That everyone in the office was very busy.
  b That the actors started behaving like reporters.
  c That the actors cared about the environment.

2 Answer this exam question about the text in exercise 1. Choose the correct answer a, b, c or d.

What is the text supposed to show?
a What work was like at *The Washington Post*.
b That *The Washington Post* is an important newspaper.
c How carefully Redford and Hoffman prepared for their roles.
d How employees were treated at *The Washington Post*.

Exam TIP

In the exam you may be asked about the purpose of a text or its main point. A correct answer to such a question is based on the text as a whole, not on one particular sentence.

3 Read the texts 1–3. Choose the correct answers a, b, c or d.

1 What is the purpose of this text?
  a To encourage children to do housework.
  b To give advice to parents.
  c To analyse children's behaviour.
  d To teach people life skills.

① Why should you teach your children to do household chores?

The simple answer is, because it's good for them and it's good for you. It's good for them because they learn skills they'll need in adult life; and by 'skills' I mean not only cleaning or washing up, but sharing duties and not expecting others to do everything for you. They learn to be tidy, organised and not afraid of a bit of physical work. And why is it good for you? Obviously, because you have less housework to do. But also, you have fewer reasons to be annoyed with your children – and that's good for everyone!

2 What is the title of Sylvia Plath's poem?
  a *Mirror*
  b *Eye*
  c *Ring*
  d *Glasses*

(2)

_____

I am silver and exact. I have no
  preconceptions.
Whatever I see, I swallow immediately.
Just as it is, unmisted by love or dislike
I am not cruel, only truthful –
The eye of a little god, four-cornered.

by Sylvia Plath

3 What is the main point of this passage?
  a If you have fewer friends, it's more difficult to find a partner.
  b If you start a new relationship, you gain new friends.
  c If you start a relationship, you spend less time with your friends.
  d If you can't go to your friends when you're in trouble, they're not true friends.

(3)

A recent study suggests that starting a romantic relationship may come at the cost of losing some friends – two, to be exact! According to research by Robin Dunbar from Oxford University, single people have on average five close friends, that is, people who they trust and who they would go to if they were in trouble. People in romantic relationships have four, and one of those four is their partner. In other words, they only have three platonic friends. Why does that happen? Because dating someone takes up a lot of time and attention, which you then don't have for your friends.

Listening

True / False / No information

4 (3) Listen to the beginning of a radio conversation about how to prepare for a marathon. Tick (✓) true, cross (✗) false or write (?) if there is no information.
  1 ☐ Windermere Marathon always takes place on 17 May.
  2 ☐ If you're unfit, you can't run a marathon.
  3 ☐ Running is not the only form of exercise you will need.

5 (3) Complete the sentences. Listen again if you need to.
  1 The speaker says that '_____ Windermere Marathon will take place on 17 May', but we don't know if it takes place on that day _____ year.
  2 The speaker says, 'Unless you've got serious _____ , you're probably _____ to run a marathon.'
  3 The speaker says, 'You should do _____ exercises every day.'

6 (4) Listen to the rest of the interview about marathons. Tick (✓) true, cross (✗) false or write (?) if there is no information.
  1 ☐ You should start by running five to six kilometres a day.
  2 ☐ Shortly before the marathon you should run about twenty kilometres every day.
  3 ☐ Some kinds of fruit are especially good for runners.
  4 ☐ Many runners need more than eight hours of sleep.
  5 ☐ You should run faster in the second half of the marathon than in the first.

Exam **TIP**

A statement is **true** when the recording says the same thing in other words.

A statement is **false** when the statement and the recording contradict each other (say opposite things).

We can say there is **no information** when the statement *could* be true, but the recording does not say so.

self-assessment test 1

Vocabulary & Grammar

1 <u>Underline</u> the correct words to complete the sentences.

1 Have you got what it *makes/<u>takes</u>/reaches* to become a successful journalist?
2 I think all parents should be given some advice on how to *look/bring/grow* up children.
3 The building was absolutely *huge/big/large*.
4 I did everything I could, but I guess it's *up/over/down* to luck right now.
5 She keeps *interrupting/nagging/gossiping* me about getting a better job.
6 Let's grab something to eat first. I'm absolutely *starving/soaked/boiling*.
7 I'm living with three other students and I have to *treat/share/avoid* chores with them.

/6

2 Complete the sentences with one word in each gap.

1 It *takes* her ages to get ready in the morning.
2 In my country, the divorce _____ for first marriage is about 40 percent.
3 I was not angry with her, I was absolutely _____ !
4 When are you going to _____ down and get married?
5 How much money do I owe you? I can't work it _____ myself.
6 Gina is the main _____ while her husband stays at home and looks after their children.
7 I hope the price of petrol won't _____ up again next month.

/6

3 Complete the sentences with the correct present or past form of the verbs in brackets.

1 My grandmother lives in Brazil but she originally *comes* (come) from Argentina.
2 Ian felt exhausted because he _____ (dig) in the garden for two hours.
3 It should be warmer now. I _____ (turn) up the heating.
4 Fiona _____ (stay) with her cousin until she finds somewhere to live.
5 We _____ (watch) a documentary on TV when suddenly all lights went out.
6 It's your turn now. I _____ (iron) for over an hour.
7 Did Paul and Jane really split up? How long _____ (they/be) together?
8 He snatched the woman's handbag and _____ (run) away.
9 It shows that Ann's a novice driver. How long _____ (she/learn) to drive?

/8

4 Correct the mistakes in the sentences.

1 When we arrived, everyone has been dancing.
   When we arrived, everyone was dancing.
2 I can't work because my computer always crashing.

   _____
   _____
3 As a child, I would feel often lonely.

   _____
4 My new book is ready – I've been writing nine chapters.

   _____
   _____
5 Why did you keep to ask her the same question over and over again?

   _____
   _____
6 How many miles have you been driving in your lifetime?

   _____
   _____

/5

5 Complete the text with the correct form of the words in brackets.

Happily Married in the New Millennium

To all bloggers

Would you like to take part in a writing
[1] _competition_ (compete)? Here is your chance!

You don't have to be a proficient writer – it's enough to be able to write [2] _____ (reason) well to enter. Our topic this time is 'Happily Married in the New Millennium.'

Why is the marriage institution failing miserably nowadays? Are [3] _____ (arrange) marriages better than love marriages? What are your views? What makes a good marriage? Is it [4] _____ (dedicate), trust or equally shared [5] _____ (responsible)? Give it a go whether you're married, about to marry or anti-marriage altogether. Get your [6] _____ (inspire) from your own life or the lives of others.

Prizes for best entries. 300 words max. The deadline for receiving entries is 31 March. Email us for more information.

/5

Listening

6 (5) Listen to the interview with four recipients of The Duke of Edinburgh's Award. Answer the questions with their names Helena (H), John (J), Bethany (B) or Matthew (M).

Who:

1 was in charge of a group of children as part of the programme? ____

2 wanted to give up several times? ____

3 at some point felt under a lot of pressure to complete his/her programme? ____

4 has received a lot of support from other people? ____

5 thinks the key to success is determination? ____

6 has gained some self-confidence? ____

7 believes now she/he can reach the top? ____

/7

Communication

7 Complete the dialogues with one word in each gap.

Dialogue 1

A: Could I [1] s_peak_ to Mr Chambers, please?

B: Who's [2] c_____ , please?

A: My name's John Laughton.

B: Can I ask what your call is [3] c_____ ?

A: I'm calling about tomorrow's meeting.

B: [4] H_____ the line, please. I'll put you [5] t_____ .

A: Thank you.

Dialogue 2

A: Hello. Is Mrs Howard [6] t_____ , please?

B: I'm afraid she's not [7] a_____ at the moment.

A: Could you ask her to call me back?

B: Yes, of course. Can I have your name and telephone number, please?

Dialogue 3

A: Can I speak to Jessica, please?

B: I'm afraid she's just [8] p_____ out somewhere.

A: Could you tell her to give me a [9] r_____ ?

B: Sure, no problem.

/8

8 Underline the correct words to complete the text.
There are two photographs [1] *of/off* people at a roller skating rink. The photo [2] *in/on* the left shows a couple holding hands and skating together. They [3] *seem/might* quite pleased with themselves in spite of the fact that they are both struggling to keep on their feet. The woman looks [4] *like/as though* a beginner skater. She's obviously not doing very well but is still willing to give it a go. [5] *In/To* my mind, it's important to try new, challenging things and enjoy the process of learning. Roller skating is not easy, as the couple in the picture are finding out. And you have to bear in [6] *mind/opinion* that it may take a lot of time and patience to master it.

/5

Marks	
Vocabulary & Grammar	/30 marks
Listening	/7 marks
Communication	/13 marks
Total:	/50 marks

Vocabulary

Communications

1 Label the pictures with the words below.

> text message   flexible screen
> handset   social networking site
> handheld games console

2 Which two-word noun goes with all of the words below?

1 _____ _____ addiction
2 _____ _____ handset
3 _____ _____ network

3 Complete the sentences with words from exercises 1 and 2. Sometimes you need to change the form.

1 I need a new mobile phone _handset_ . This one's in terrible condition.

2 A: My phone's got no signal here.
   B: Mine has. Which _____ do you use?

3 A: I'm worried. I think my brother is _____ to his mobile phone.
   B: I don't think he is. He actually left it at home when he went to football practice last night!

4 A: I want to get in touch with Mo, but I can't find her on Bebo or any other _____ .
   B: I think I've got her mobile number. Why don't you send her a _____ ?

Grammar

Future forms

4 (*) Underline the correct form.

1 'Hello? Mum? I'm stuck in a traffic jam. I'*ll be*/*'m going to be* late for dinner. Sorry!'

2 'I have no idea how to use this new handset.' 'Don't worry. I'*ll show*/*'m going to show* you.'

3 The library *opens*/*is opening* at 10.30.

4 *Will you do*/*Are you doing* anything special on Saturday?

5 Look at this crowd. We'*ll wait*/*'ll be waiting* for hours to get into the club.

5 (**) Complete the sentences with the correct future form of the verb in brackets. Sometimes more than one answer is possible.

1 The performance _starts_ at seven p.m. (start)

2 Dave _____ a website design course during the holidays. (do)

3 He _____ home next week. (come)

4 I _____ you when I know the exam results. (text)

5 Hurry up! Our bus _____ in half an hour. (leave)

6 (**) Read the situations. What would you say? Complete the sentences with the correct future form of the verbs in brackets.

1 Someone asks you about your plans for the winter holidays.
   'Don't ask. _I'm going to be studying for my exams_ (I/study/exams)!'

2 You're waiting for someone at the station. You don't know the exact arrival time.
   'What time _____ (the train/get in)?'

3 Your computer is acting strangely.
   'Oh no. _____ (it/crash/again).'

4 You decide to finish some work that you've been putting off.
   '_____ (I/do/it/today).'

5 Your friends want to go out. You've got a medical appointment.
   'I'm sorry. _____ (I/see/doctor/five). Maybe later?'

7 (**) **Complete the dialogue with the correct future form of the verbs below.**

> be back   check   take   pick up   arrive
> be late   come ✓   go   do   not be able

A: Mathieu and Julie [1] _are coming_ from Sydney this afternoon. Who [2] _____ them [3] _____ from the airport?

B: What time [4] _____ their flight [5] _____ ?

A: Four thirty this afternoon.

B: I can't make it then. I [6] _____ the dog to the vet at four o'clock.

C: OK. I [7] _____ it, then.

A: The flight [8] _____ probably [9] _____ , though. Lots of flights are delayed today.

C: Hang on. I [10] _____ the airport website. Yes, the flight is two hours late. And that means I [11] _____ to go.

B: I [12] _____ then. I'm sure I [13] _____ from the vet's by that time.

Grammar Plus: *be about to, be on the point of, be likely to* and *be unlikely to*

8 (***) **Complete the second sentence so that it means the same as the first. Use the words in CAPITALS.**

1 The weather will probably improve at the weekend.   LIKELY

The weather _is likely to improve_ at the weekend.

2 Peter's going to win this chess game in a moment.   POINT

Peter _____ this chess game.

3 The concert is going to begin very soon. ABOUT

The concert _____ begin.

4 More people will probably have internet access in the future.   LIKELY

More people _____ in the future.

5 The situation of the world's poor will probably not improve very soon.   UNLIKELY

The situation of the world's poor _____ very soon.

Grammar reference

Future forms

Present simple

We use the present simple for timetables, schedules, routines, dates, etc:

*Her train **leaves** at 5.40 a.m. tomorrow.*

Present continuous

We use the present continuous to talk about future events we have already arranged. We often specify the date, time, etc:

*We**'re flying** to Australia in July.*

be going to

We use *be going to*

- to talk about general intentions and plans for the future which may still change:

*My sister **is going to become** an actress.*

- to talk about predictions based on something we know or can observe now:

*Look out! We **are going to crash!** (We can see another car.)*

will/won't

We use *will/won't* + infinitive without *to*

- to express a prediction based on opinions, beliefs or experience:

*I'm sure my mother **will be** furious when she sees this mess.*

- to talk about a decision about the future made at the moment of speaking:

*Is that the phone? I**'ll answer** it.*

- to make threats and promises:

*I promise I**'ll give** you the money back tomorrow.*

be about to/be on the point of

We use *be about to* + infinitive and *be on the point of* + -*ing* to talk about something which is going to happen in the immediate future:

*It looks like the Democrats **are about to** win the election. I've had enough. I**'m on the point of** leaving.*

be likely/unlikely to

We use *be likely/unlikely to* + infinitive to express the probability of something happening or not happening in the future:

*The vocalist is sick – they**'re likely to** cancel the concert. Tom**'s unlikely to** propose to Sue.*

Vocabulary

Talking about technology

1 **Match words 1–5 with a–e to make compound nouns.**

1 internet   a life
2 desktop   b engine
3 battery   c console
4 search   d connection
5 games   e computer

2 **Mary wants to buy a new laptop. The shop assistant is showing her a new model. Complete what he says with the words below.**

> browser   drive   games   high-definition
> internet   life   projector   touch-screen
> system   wireless

The hard ¹_____ is 250 GB. This model's got a ²_____ screen: just look at the wonderful picture quality. Most importantly, it's got a battery ³_____ of ten hours. Of course, it comes with the latest operating ⁴_____ installed. If you like, we'll also install your favourite web ⁵_____ for you.

And you get a ⁶_____ mouse as a bonus. Or, if you prefer, you can choose the offer of a high-speed ⁷_____ connection for a year. And if you buy the premium version, you have a choice of a ⁸_____ phone or a digital mini-⁹_____ with it … No, I'm afraid the handheld ¹⁰_____ consoles are not available as free-gift items.

3 **Match the sentence beginnings 1–5 with the endings a–e.**

1 You can browse
2 You can transfer
3 You can download
4 You can upload
5 You can update

a your profile on a social networking site.
b various files onto the internet.
c the web in search of information.
d files from one digital device to another.
e apps, videos and other files from the internet.

Grammar

Second conditional

4 (✱) **Underline the correct forms.**

1 If I _were/would be_ you, I _got/would get_ a new battery for that phone.
2 What if you _had/would have_ to live without modern technology for a year?
3 If it _wasn't/wouldn't be_ so cold, we _would feel/felt_ more like going out.
4 If we _hadn't/didn't have_ so much electronic equipment, we _might speak/spoke_ to each other more often.
5 I might agree to meet an online friend provided that we _met/would meet_ in a public place and I _would have/had_ a friend with me.

5 (✱✱) **Put the words in the correct order to make sentences. Add commas where necessary.**

1 memory/could/graphics/my computer/it/create/had/I/on/more
If _my computer had more memory,_
I could create graphics on it .
2 write/a/went/blog/a long trip/I/on/would/I
If _____
_____ .
3 do/I/a/homework/the library/I could/my/had/in/laptop
If _____
_____ .
4 might/provided/a/buy/battery life/had/it/new/long/laptop/that/a.
I _____
_____ .
5 angry/our neighbours/were/noisy/yours/as/as/I'd/really/get
If _____
_____ .
6 another/even/free/wouldn't/digital gadget/if/was/it/want
I _____
_____ .

6 (✱✱) **Complete the second conditional sentences with the correct form of the verbs in brackets.**

1 If I _____ (find) someone's mobile phone, I _____ (call) the first number in their phone book to tell them.

2 What if all the computers in the world _____ (fail) at the same time?

3 Supposing your best friend _____ (tell) you a lie, how _____ (you/react)?

4 If I _____ (not surf) the internet so much, I _____ (not keep up with) the latest games.

5 If you _____ (not spend) so much time chatting to strangers online, you _____ (have) more time for your real friends.

7 (✱✱) **Underline the correct option.**

1 *Supposing/Even if* your mobile broke down on holiday, what would you do?

2 *Even if/Provided that* I wanted a handheld games console, my parents wouldn't buy me one.

3 I might let you use my new laptop *provided that/supposing* you were a bit more careful.

4 I wouldn't join a social networking site *even if/supposing* a hundred people invited me! It's a waste of time.

5 We could invite Steve to the party *provided that/even if* he promised not to play games on his phone all the time.

6 *Supposing/Provided that* you designed a new piece of software, would you sell it or make it available for free?

8 (✱✱✱) **Use the prompts to write second conditional sentences.**

1 know how to install this application → not ask you for help

If I _knew how to install this application, I wouldn't ask you for help_ .

2 have a faster internet connection → download more videos

If I _____

_____ .

3 move to another country → keep in touch with my friends online

If I _____

_____ .

4 be ten years old → love this new game

If I _____

_____ .

5 spend more time reading → know more words

If I _____

_____ .

6 live in Japan → probably have even more electronic gadgets

If I _____

_____ .

Grammar reference

Second conditional

We use the second conditional (*if* + past simple, *would* + infinitive without *to*) to talk about unreal, impossible or unlikely situations in the present or in the future:

*If Mike **were** taller, he **could play** volleyball much better.* (but Mike is not taller)
*If I **had** your figure, I **would become** a model.* (but I don't have your figure)
*We **wouldn't be** late for work if you **got up** ten minutes earlier.* (but you stay in bed)

be

In the second conditional sentences after *I*, *he*, *she* and *it*, we can use either *was* (the standard past form) or *were*. *Were* is more common than *was* in written and formal language:

*If he **was/were** more outgoing, he **would have** more friends.*
*If I **was/were** wealthy, I **would donate** part of my income to charity.*

could and might

Instead of *would* in the main clause, we can use the modal verbs *could* or *might*:

*If you **asked** Tom for a loan, he **might** agree to lend you some money.*
*If we **earned** more, we **could** go on a Mediterranean cruise.*

even if, provided that and supposing

Instead of *if* in conditional sentences, we can also use *even if*, *provided that* and *supposing*:

***Even if** you **apologised** profusely for your comment, it **wouldn't be** enough.*
***Provided that** she **completed** her essay on time, she **might get** quite a good grade for it.*
***Supposing** he **asked** you out, **would** you **turn** him down?*

What if … ?

Instead of *What would happen if … ?*, while asking a question we can simply say *What if … ?*

***What if** he **insisted** on moving to Australia?*
***What if** all Web advertisements **were** blocked?*

What slanguage* do you speak?

Teens and slang

Slang is fun – it's always been part of English, making the language richer and more diverse. Teenagers in particular tend to use slang like their own private language. ¹___ So is teenagers using slang something we should worry about? The real question is not whether teens should use slang or not but if they know when and how to use it. ²___ They claim that young people are increasingly unable to distinguish situations in which it's acceptable to use slang from situations where they should use more formal language.

'Young people can't speak properly'

For some time now, teachers and educators have been complaining that teens don't know how to express themselves in writing. They are so used to sending texts with abbreviations and no punctuation that they barely remember what standard written English is like. What is more, researchers have noticed that many young people are finding it difficult to communicate without using slang in formal contexts, such as the classroom or at work.

Banning slang in the classroom

In order to overcome the problem, one school in Manchester took the radical step of banning slang completely from the classroom. 'It was clear that many students found it difficult to get through a sentence without saying "innit" or "know what I mean?"' explains Maria Nightingale, the school principal. Nightingale and the teachers in the school were worried about their students' inability to use 'normal' English. ³___ Since the school banned slang, exam results have improved dramatically.

Studying slang

St Francis Xavier School in London has taken a different approach – they've put slang on the curriculum. A-level** students learn to analyse slang and research its origins. ⁴___ Slang expert Tony Thorne believes that talking about slang helps people to develop a sense of 'appropriacy' with regard to language use. Appropriacy means using the right variety of language in the right context – for example, business jargon in business meetings, formal English in exams and slang with your friends.

Slang – our new language?

However, many people feel that the way teens are using slang is part of a new social trend. They believe the profile of slang is changing. It is not that slang has become more popular but that it has become more public. Ten years ago, serious newspapers never printed slang, now it's everywhere – in the press, on TV, in music. ⁵___ Will slang take over and become part of standard English? Only time will tell.

---

* slanguage – an invented word, a combination of slang + language

** A-level – exams that you take when you are 18 years old before you leave school or go to university.

Reading

1 Look at the title and paragraph headings in the text. What do you think the text is about? Choose the best answer.

    a slang in different countries   **b** teenagers using slang at school   **c** the function of slang in society

2 Find and <u>underline</u> the words 1–5 in the text. Match the words with the correct definitions a–e.

    1 diverse   **a** extreme, new and very different

    2 distinguish   **b** to recognise and understand the difference between things

    3 radical   **c** special words and phrases that are only understood by people who do the same job

    4 banning   **d** with many different parts, varied

    5 jargon   **e** forbidding or stopping something

3 Read the text and match the sentences a–f to the gaps 1–5 in the text. There is one extra sentence.

a They investigate the various functions of slang and its connection to identity, particularly for minority groups.

b For them, talking in slang is part of growing up and establishing a sense of identity.

c Slang is used as a form of protest.

d Some experts believe that they don't.

e It's almost impossible to avoid it.

f They believed it could stop their students from getting a good job or from doing well in exams.

4 Read the text again and tick (✓) true, cross (✗) false or write (?) if there is no information.

1 ☐ Experts are worried because teens are using slang as a private language.

2 ☐ A lot of people think that teenagers today don't know how to write English.

3 ☐ The principal of the Manchester school said students found it hard to communicate using slang.

4 ☐ Students at the Manchester school are doing better in exams since slang was banned.

5 ☐ Some students in London are now studying slang at school.

6 ☐ Studying slang has helped the London students to improve their language skills.

7 ☐ Most people now believe that slang will soon become standard English.

5 Answer the questions.

1 Is slang a new thing? _____

2 Why do people think teens find it difficult to write formal English?

_____

_____

3 How did Maria Nightingale and the teachers in the school in Manchester feel about the students' use of slang?

_____

_____

4 Who is Tony Thorne? _____

5 Where can you see slang now that you didn't ten years ago?

_____

_____

Listening

6 ⑥ Listen to five short recordings about communication. Number the text types a–e in the order you hear them.

a ☐ a recorded message

b ☐ a description of a film

c ☐ a conversation between two friends

d ☐ an extract from a TV interview

e ☐ a presentation

7 ⑥ Listen again and choose the correct answers.

1 Sally says that
   a she is angry because Jake didn't make a copy of a CD for her.
   b Jake laughs at her because she has problems using technology.
   c Jake is going to help her install a new computer program.

2 Kate thinks that
   a communication is the most important thing in relationships.
   b Sally should tell Jake she doesn't like him making fun of her.
   c Sally should learn to use all her computer programs.

3 Which is NOT true about the Seattle Museum of Communications?
   a You don't have to pay to visit the museum.
   b You can take an online tour of the museum on their website.
   c The museum is open five days a week from 8.30 a.m. to 2.00 p.m.

4 What is the museum phone number?
   a 206-767-3022
   b 206-676-3012
   c 206-767-3012

5 Professor Skye thinks that communicating in person is particularly problematic for
   a older people.
   b young people.
   c people in their thirties.

6 In *The Black Balloon*, Luke and Charlie are
   a two teenage brothers who have problems communicating.
   b two friends who have grown up together.
   c two teenagers who fall in love with the same girl.

Writing

A 'for and against' essay

1 In **paragraph 1**, briefly introduce the topic in one or two sentences.

2 Explain that there are arguments on both sides. Do NOT give your own opinion here.

3 In **paragraph 2**, make it clear that the paragraph supports the topic or proposition in the essay. It contains the ideas 'for' it.

4 Write two or three points in favour of the topic and support your ideas with evidence and/or examples. Use linking words to add ideas, give reasons and contrast ideas.

5 In **paragraph 3**, make it clear that the paragraph argues against the topic or proposition in the essay title. Write two or three points 'against' and support your ideas with evidence and/or examples. Use linking words to add ideas, give reasons and contrast ideas.

6 In **paragraph 4**, sum up the arguments for both sides and draw a conclusion. Give your own opinion on the issue.

What are the advantages and disadvantages of cars to society as a whole?

Many people today could not imagine life without a car. However, although car ownership obviously has many benefits, the increasing number of cars on the road also creates considerable problems. So, are cars good for society in general?

One of the greatest advantages of car ownership is the freedom it gives you. If you have a car you can travel when and where you want to without having to rely on anyone else. What is more, cars help older, less physically fit people keep their independence. In remote areas without public transport, cars help people to stay in touch with the wider world and have a better quality of life. finally, many people are employed to produce cars, repair them or serve customers in petrol stations. This creates jobs which is a further benefit for society.

On the other hand, using cars has some serious disadvantages. firstly, cars are bad for the environment. They use petrol and cause pollution. Unrecycled rubbish from old cars is responsible for mountains of toxic waste. Secondly, the roads are becoming more and more crowded. Traffic jams are causing many cities to come almost to a standstill whilst exhaust fumes poison the air. finally, using our cars too much could be making us less fit and less sociable. Many of us drive everywhere instead of walking even short distances which means we get less exercise and talk to each other less.

In conclusion, there are strong arguments on both sides of the debate. In my opinion, the benefits of using cars outweigh the disadvantages. However, I strongly feel that we need to develop more ecological cars and better traffic systems so that we can continue to enjoy the benefits of cars without damaging the environment and our overall quality of life.

Useful language

1 Introducing arguments
The first/One advantage/disadvantage is …

2 Listing ideas
Firstly, …   Secondly, …   Thirdly, …   Finally, …

3 Adding information
What is more, …   Besides this, …

4 Contrasting information
However, …   Although …   On the other hand, …

5 Explaining consequences and giving examples
Due to …   As a result, …

6 Concluding the essay
To sum up, …   To conclude, …   In conclusion, …
To summarise, …

7 Giving your opinion
In my opinion, …   I think …
I firmly/strongly believe that …

1 Read the essay and answer the questions.

1 What are the writer's arguments in favour of cars?

2 What points does the writer make against cars?

3 What conclusions does the writer come to? Do you agree?

4 Can you think of any points for or against cars that are not mentioned in this essay?

2 Read the essay again and <u>underline</u> the phrases the writer uses to express the ideas 1–5 below.

1 There are more good things than bad things about using cars.

2 The roads are filling up with cars.

3 One of the best things about owning a car is …

4 Traffic jams are stopping traffic in the cities almost completely.

5 Of course there are many advantages to owning a car.

3 (Circle) all the linking words and expressions in the essay.

4 Join the ideas with the linking words and expressions below.

[due to   as a result   although   however]

1 _____ car ownership has many benefits, cars are seriously damaging the planet.

2 There are too many cars on the road these days. _____ , traffic in the cities is coming to a standstill.

3 _____ the fact that it can cause accidents, it is illegal to use mobile phones whilst driving.

4 Mobile phones are now quite cheap to buy. _____ , they are manufactured using child labour.

5 Read the notes for an introduction to a 'for and against' essay about having a lot of television channels. Tick (✓) the four best sentences to include.

☐ There used to only be a few channels on TV in most European countries.

☐ Most people have at least one TV in their house.

☐ Having many channels has advantages and disadvantages.

☐ In many countries TVs now have many channels because of cable.

☐ I think it's positive to have a lot of channels because then you can choose which one to watch.

☐ So, is having more channels beneficial on the whole?

☐ Television was invented around 1925, so it's existed for almost 100 years.

6 Write the introduction to the essay. Use the introduction in the essay on page 30 to help you.

7 Look at this draft for the second paragraph of the essay. Tick (✓) three ways to improve it.

A lot of channels means there is more variety. If you have a lot of channels, you can always find something worth watching. If you have a lot of channels, you will probably have a lot of speciality channels. Speciality channels are good for people with hobbies or interests.

1 ☐ Avoid repetition where possible.

2 ☐ Give two or three advantages.

3 ☐ Use linking words and other expressions to help the reader to follow the arguments.

4 ☐ Use an appropriate phrase to introduce the arguments in favour.

5 ☐ Give her opinion.

8 Rewrite the second paragraph of the essay. Make the improvements you decided on in exercise 7.

9 Look at the notes for the third paragraph and choose two or three arguments against having a lot of television channels. Decide how you could link ideas together and what order you would write them in. Write the paragraph.

– you can waste a lot of time looking for something to watch

– doesn't necessarily mean quality programmes

– many programmes and films repeated when lots of channels

– too much choice can make it hard to choose!

– often things on two or more channels at the same time that you want to watch

– evidence that people watch more television if more channels

10 Complete the strategies box with the words below.

[four   structure   order   arguments ✓]

A 'for and against' essay

- Make a list of [1] _arguments_ for and a list of arguments against.

- Choose the best two or three ideas for and the best two or three ideas against. Decide which [2] _____ to write your ideas in and what reasons or examples you can add.

- Write your first draft making sure you organise it correctly into [3] _____ paragraphs.

- Read your draft. Do you need to use any other useful words/expressions to [4] _____ the essay clearly?

- Check the number of words and then check your punctuation, grammar and spelling.

11 Read the task and write a 'for and against' essay. Use the structure on the opposite page and the strategies in exercise 10 and ideas in the exercises to help you. Write 250–300 words.

What are the positive and negative aspects of low-cost international air travel?

real time 3

Giving a speech

1 Complete Charlie's speech with the words and expressions below.

> some people say   in my opinion   like
> sum up   began   I'd like to talk about ✓
> Lastly   What's more   To my mind
> for example   First of all   let me finish
> explain why   Secondly

Good morning! [1] *I'd like to talk about* social networking sites being a waste of time. Social networking sites only [2] _____ a few years ago – [3] _____ , Facebook only started in 2004 and MySpace in 2003. However, they are already extremely popular. Now, [4] _____ that young people use them too much and don't communicate face-to-face enough. Well, [5] _____ , social networking sites are a good thing. Let me [6] _____ . [7] _____ , they are an easy way of keeping in touch with a lot of people. [8] _____ , you don't have to spend a lot of time every day on the site – five minutes is enough. This means you can keep in touch with your online contacts quickly and easily and still have plenty of time to spend with your friends. [9] _____ , that is time well spent. [10] _____ , you can find friends that you have lost touch with through these sites. They are [11] _____ huge phonebooks, but without numbers, where you can find anyone you need to. [12] _____ , they make it easy for you to share photos with your friends. So, to [13] _____ , it's clear to me that social networking sites have many advantages. And [14] _____ by saying that you can enjoy the benefits of these sites and still have plenty of face-to-face contact with friends.

2 <u>Underline</u> the four points that Charlie makes in favour of social networking sites.

Answering simple questions about a speech

3 Match questions 1–3 from the audience to the answers a–c.

1 *What was your point about social networking sites being a quick and easy way to keep in touch?* ☐

2 *Why do you think that social networking sites are like phonebooks?* ☐

3 *Why did you mention sharing photos as a benefit?* ☐

a You can use them to look for contact details of people. For example, if you've lost your phone or someone's number, you can find them through Facebook.

b I think it's because it's an easy way to show your pictures to your friends. You don't have to carry them with you, you just post them. For me, that's great.

c It only takes a minute to post your status or a comment, but that way you can communicate with a lot of people at the same time.

4 Prepare a speech about television. Use as many of the expressions from exercise 1 as possible. Use the ideas below or your own ideas.

Television is bad for society.

- TV was first invented around 1925 and the first broadcasting service began in 1936.
- Now there are millions of TVs and many channels to choose from.
- Many people watch over four hours of TV a day – too much!
- Many violent films, too much reality TV, silly shows and series. Not enough good programmes e.g. documentaries or well-made dramas.
- Better to have other hobbies, e.g. sports or social activity groups.

examtrainer 4

Use of English

Compound nouns

1 Write compound nouns for the definitions 1–6.

1 A person who plays the violin: _violin player_
2 A person who trains dolphins: _____
3 Rules which people follow in a household: _____
4 A connection to the internet: _____
5 A console used to play games: _____
6 A computer that stands on top of your desk: _____

2 Complete the sentences with the words below.

> back   communication   film
> landline   lead ✓   networking

1 In 1997, Day-Lewis played the _lead_ role in the film *The Boxer*. (Unit 1)
2 In 1979, an unknown Australian actor arrived at a _____ audition looking bruised and exhausted. (Unit 1)
3 The animal trainer Max Lungren was teaching a dolphin to do a _____ flip. (Unit 2)
4 Mobile phones have huge benefits for people in developing countries where there are no _____ telephones. (Unit 3)
5 Around a billion people worldwide have joined social _____ sites in the last few years. (Unit 3)
6 What does the future hold in terms of _____ technology? (Unit 3)

3 Match words 1–6 with a–f to make compound nouns.

1 pocket	a rate
2 native	b labour
3 divorce	c browser
4 child	d life
5 web	e money
6 battery	f speaker

Exam tasks

Multiple-choice cloze

4 Choose the correct answer a, b, c or d to complete the text.

> The last two or three decades have seen incredible advances, especially in ¹ _a_ technology. Billions of people have ² ___ phones. To get in touch with a friend who's far away, you can now email them, phone them, send a ³ ___ message, or even send a photo taken a few seconds earlier. However, a lot of the gadgets we enjoy are produced in developing countries by badly-paid workers or even by ⁴ ___ labour. And even in the rich countries all is not well. Family bonds are weaker, people have fewer children and in many countries the divorce ⁵ ___ is going up. Perhaps worst of all, ⁶ ___ warming is threatening the whole planet.

1 **a** communication ✓ **b** communicating
  c connecting **d** social
2 **a** portable **b** handy **c** move **d** mobile
3 **a** texting **b** text **c** phone **d** electronic
4 **a** cheap **b** wage **c** slave **d** illegal
5 **a** number **b** amount **c** problem **d** rate
6 **a** world **b** global **c** earth **d** climate

Banked cloze

5 Complete the text with the words below. There is one extra word.

> browser   connection   drive   engines
> games   life   system ✓

> My boyfriend is into technology. I'm not, and going to a party at his friend's house last weekend was a mistake! When we arrived, his mates were discussing the features of the latest operating ¹ _system_ . Then one of them started asking me questions about my laptop. When I told him it had a battery ² _____ of six hours he declared it was rubbish. Another one told me which web ³ _____ I should use. A third told me about the effective use of search ⁴ _____ . When they all sat down at a ⁵ _____ console and started playing I was able to go to the kitchen with three other girlfriends. We had some tea and a chat about boyfriends and then suddenly all the boys joined us. Why? The internet ⁶ _____ had stopped working!

4 happy & successful

✱ revision
✱✱ average difficulty
✱✱✱ extra challenge

Vocabulary

Life skills

1 Match the words 1–4 with their opposites a–d.

1 positive   a happy
2 miserable   b weakness
3 mental   c negative
4 strength   d physical

2 Complete the text with the words below.

> thankful   support   strengths
> positively   well-being
> physically   objective ✓

Happiness and Well-being

LIFE SKILLS COURSE FOR SECONDARY SCHOOL STUDENTS

The most important [1] _objective_ for any school is to teach its students how to live and how to relate to the world around them. Teachers, like parents, want the children in their care to be mentally and [2] _____ healthy, and that is what teaching happiness and [3] _____ is all about.

Here are some of the things participants will learn:

★ Thinking [4] _____ : Learn to look at your experiences in a less negative way.

★ Being [5] _____ : Make lists of all the things you feel grateful for and stop thinking about the things you're not happy with.

★ Understanding your own individual [6] _____ : Know what you're good at as a person and feel better about yourself.

★ Wishing other people well: People who help and [7] _____ others are happier people themselves.

Grammar

Modals

3 ✱ Match the sentences 1–6 to the explanations a–f.

1 You must check this essay one more time.
2 You should check this essay one more time.
3 I must learn another foreign language.
4 I have to learn two foreign languages.
5 You should have read this chapter.
6 I needn't have read this chapter.

a I'm advising you to do it.
b It's a pity you didn't do it.
c I'm obliged to do it.
d I'm ordering you to do it.
e It was unnecessary.
f I want to do it.

4 ✱✱ Complete the sentences with *must, have (got) to* or *should*.

1 You _____ learn to think more positively! Otherwise you're never going to succeed in life.

2 I think you _____ try and talk this over with your parents. I'm sure they'll understand your point of view.

3 You know you _____ to fill in these forms. It's boring, but that's how you get into university.

4 I'm thinking of giving up music and taking a life skills course instead. Do you think I _____ ?

5 I _____ finish my project by the end of the week. The deadline is on Friday.

6 I really _____ improve my computer skills. They're so important in any kind of work.

5 ✱✱ Tony had an unsuccessful job interview and his friends are giving him advice. Complete the sentences with *should have/shouldn't have* and the correct form of the verbs.

1 You _shouldn't have spilt_ (spill) coffee on the application form.

2 You _____ (wear) dirty jeans to the interview.

3 You _____ (say) more about your strengths.

4 You _____ (take) an IT course last year.

5 You _____ (lie) about your language skills.

6 You _____ (tell) them you learn new skills quickly.

6 (**⁎⁎**) **Complete the sentences with _needn't have_ and an appropriate verb.**

1 I solved twenty maths problems, because I thought that was our homework for today. I was wrong.

   I _needn't have solved_ all those problems.

2 Bill arrived at the airport three hours before the flight, but there were no queues at all.

   He _____ so early.

3 We were visiting some friends abroad. We didn't know what present was appropriate so we bought an expensive vase. All the other visitors only brought flowers or sweets.

   We _____ such an expensive gift.

4 Mary took a taxi to get to the concert on time. The concert started thirty minutes late.

   She _____ a taxi.

7 (**⁎⁎⁎**) **Complete the email with _must, have (got) to, should, should have/shouldn't have, needn't have_ and the correct form of the verbs in brackets. Sometimes more than one answer is possible.**

❌

To:	ali28@gmail.com
From:	katie15@hotmail.com
Subject:	Team-building expedition

Hi Ali

The team-building expedition some of our class went on was not as good as I hoped. We made so many mistakes. First of all, we ¹ _shouldn't have started_ (start) so late. If you set off at midday, you ² _____ (walk) in the hottest weather. Secondly – this is really embarrassing – we ³ _____ (bring) a map. Sam had said he knew the way perfectly. Well, he didn't and I ⁴ _____ (believe) him! I really ⁵ _____ remember to pack a map the next time. Finally, we ⁶ _____ (buy) so much food. We didn't manage to eat it all and we had to carry it back. I hope we do better next time. We ⁷ _____ (do), after all the mistakes we made this time!

See you soon
Katie

Grammar Plus: _ought to_

8 (**⁎⁎⁎**) **Complete the sentences with _ought to/ought to have_ and the correct form of the verbs below.**

[thank   give up   feel ✓   tell   choose]

1 We _ought to feel_ more grateful for all the good and positive aspects of our lives.

2 You _____ me that you were leaving the course. I could have offered your place to another student.

3 I _____ Mrs Graham for her help or she may think I'm ungrateful.

4 They _____ subjects they were interested in. They would have got better exam results.

5 We _____ Latin and studied another modern language instead. It would have been much more useful!

Grammar reference

Obligation, suggestions and advice

Obligation

To express obligation, we use

- _must_ if we talk about obligation imposed by the speaker:

I **must** call her and explain what happened yesterday. (my own internal obligation)
You **must** work harder or you'll never pass the exam. (I'm telling you.)

- _have (got) to_ if we talk about external obligation imposed by rules or other people:

We all **have to** obey traffic laws. (These are the rules.)
I've **got to** stop smoking. (That's what the doctor told me to do.)

Suggestions and advice

To make suggestions or give advice, we use

- _should_ or _ought to_ (they are not as strong as _must_):

You **should** apologise to him immediately.
I think everybody **should** put some money towards the present.
We **ought to** pack some food for the picnic.

To say that something was a good idea but the person didn't do it, we use

- _should_ or _ought to_ + _have_ + past participle:

She **should have** studied medicine instead of business administration.
Your girlfriend **ought to have** come to my party. It was great!
They **ought to have** done it themselves.

To say that someone did something but it wasn't a good idea, we use

- _shouldn't_ + _have_ + past participle:

You **shouldn't have** sold your car so cheaply.
They **shouldn't have** eaten so many sweets before dinner.

To say that someone did something which was unnecessary, we use

- _needn't_ + _have_ + past participle:

You **needn't have** brought so much food. We've got everything.
My parents **needn't have** worried about me because I was perfectly safe.

4

Vocabulary

Skills and ambitions

1 Complete the interviewer's comments about candidates for a job with the phrases below.

> ability to work in a team   enthusiastic ✓
> highly motivated   proven experience
> sound IT skills   willing to learn

I'm really excited about this job! I can't wait to start!

1 This candidate is very _enthusiastic_ .

I can use a variety of software without difficulty.

2 She's got _____ .

I'm always happy to learn new skills.

3 This candidate is _____ .

I've worked for a government project in the same field. Here are my references.

4 He's got _____ .

I'm good at working together with people.

5 She's got the _____ .

I really want this job. I'm prepared to work very hard to prove I'm suitable.'

6 This candidate seems _____ .

2 Complete the text with one word in each gap.

How did you get the job? We asked six successful job applicants this question and here's what they told us ...

● 'My qualifications were not ideal, but I impressed the interviewers with my [1] _positive_ attitude!'

● 'They wanted someone with sound IT [2] _____ , and you know I've always been into computers.'

● 'I suppose I'm very well [3] _____ . I've got a university degree and I've also completed a few specialist courses related to this job.'

● 'I said I'm [4] _____ to learn. That's always a good thing to say if your qualifications aren't brilliant.'

● 'They did some psychological tests and decided I had good [5] _____ skills – perhaps because I really like people!'

● 'They thought the group project we did at school showed my ability to work in a [6] _____ .'

Grammar

Future continuous and future perfect

3 (✻) Complete the sentences with the future continuous form of the verb in brackets.

1 Holidays at last! This time tomorrow I _'ll be lying_ (lie) on the beach!

2 You can take my motorbike. I _____ (not/use) it tomorrow.

3 By the time you get up, I _____ (drive) down the motorway.

4 This is your captain speaking. We _____ (fly) over the Sahara desert shortly.

5 I _____ (not work) in my study all day tomorrow, so you can use the computer.

6 In a few years' time, Nigel _____ (work) for an international corporation.

4 (✻) Complete the sentences with the future perfect form of the verbs below.

> achieve   become   build ✓   buy
> graduate   finish

1 I hope the government _will have built_ one more underground line in five years' time.

2 The climate _____ much warmer by 2050.

3 We _____ (*not*) building our boat by June.

4 In a few more days I _____ all the Christmas presents I need.

5 What _____ (I) by the time I'm my parents' age?

6 My friend's gone to Australia for five years. By the time we meet again, we _____ from university.

5 (✻✻) Underline the correct option.

1 My dance lesson *will be finishing/will have finished* by six, so we can go out then.

2 We'll *be playing/'ll have played* basketball on Saturday. Would you like to play?

3 My younger brother *will be growing/will have grown* at least another ten centimetres by the time he's eighteen.

4 By next month, Chris and I *will be knowing/will have known* each other for ten years.

5 I probably *won't be going/won't have gone* to the disco. I'm not feeling well.

6 *Will they be using/Will they have used* the projector tomorrow?

36

6 (✱✱) **Complete the sentences with the correct form of the verb in brackets (future perfect or future continuous).**

1 This time next week, we _____ (travel) to Paris. What shall we do on the train?

2 By my next birthday, I _____ (have) this watch for eight years. I got it for my tenth birthday.

3 I _____ (not/finish) this essay by the deadline. I started too late.

4 We _____ (not/go) bowling tonight. Ann's got a cold and I've got to study.

5 I _____ (think) of you when I get on the plane this time next week.

6 _____ (they/invent) a cure for AIDS in ten years' time, do you think?

7 (✱✱✱) **Complete the sentences with the correct form of the verb in brackets (future perfect or future continuous). Put the adverb in the correct place.**

24 APRIL

What will have happened to my classmates in ten years' time? What will they be doing?

1 *Carol* <u>*will hopefully have found*</u> *(found) a job in Spain.* *(hopefully)*

2 *Charlie _____ (work) abroad.* *(also)*

3 *Mike _____ (start) several new bands.* *(definitely)*

4 *Dan and Jessica _____ (not/go out) together any longer.* *(probably)*

5 *Andy _____ (design) software, just as he is now.* *(still)*

6 *Monica _____ (not/win) an Oscar yet.* *(probably)*

Grammar reference

Future continuous

Form

We form the future continuous with *will/won't + be + -ing* form of the main verb.

	+	–
I/You/He/She/It/We/They	**will ('ll) be waiting.**	**will not (won't) be waiting.**

General questions			Short answers		
Will	I/you/he/she/it/we/they	**be waiting?**	Yes, No,	I/you/he/she/it/we/they	**will.** **won't.**

Wh- questions *Where exactly will you be waiting for me?*

Use of future continuous

We use the future continuous

• to talk about activities which will be in progress at a certain time in the future:

Tomorrow at five p.m. I will be flying to Paris.

• to talk about future events which are very likely to happen:

I'll be going to the supermarket on Saturday.

• to ask about people's plans, often if we want something:

Will you be using your iPad today? (because I'd like to borrow it.)

Future perfect

Form

We form the future perfect with *will* or *won't + have + past participle* of the main verb.

	+	–
I/You/He/She/It/We/They	**will ('ll) have finished** by ten.	**will not (won't) have finished** by ten.

General questions			Short answers		
Will	I/you/he/she/it/we/they	**have finished by ten?**	Yes, No,	I/you/he/she/it/we/they	**will.** **won't.**

Wh- questions *How long will you have been married by February 2020?*

Use of future perfect

We use the future perfect to talk about activities which will be complete before a certain time in the future:

By the time we get home the children will have gone to sleep.

Adverbs

The position of adverbs with these tenses is different in affirmative and negative sentences:

Affirmative → adverb goes after *will*:

This time tomorrow they will <u>probably</u> be sunbathing on the beach.

Negative → adverb goes before *won't*:

She <u>probably</u> won't have arrived by tomorrow night.

Time expressions

this time (tomorrow/next week), at (five o'clock) tomorrow, (twenty years) from now, in a few (months'/years') time, by then/ by the time I'm fifty/the end of next year/January 2020

Reading

1 Read the text on page 39 quickly and choose the best answer.

a The text describes new types of careers that could exist in the future but don't exist now.

b The text is about the skills that young people need to develop to get the best jobs today.

2 Find the words in the text and choose the correct meaning.

1 *evolves*
   a gets bigger
   b becomes more difficult and complicated
   c changes and develops over a period of time

2 *transform*
   a carry something heavy
   b change a lot
   c move a long distance

3 *healthcare*
   a the services that look after people's health
   b the study of people's health and different illnesses
   c the people who look after other people's health

4 *administer*
   a give
   b accept
   c understand

5 *media-savvy*
   a likes watching TV
   b has a good knowledge and understanding of the world of media
   c can program in different visual media

6 *personalising*
   a changing something so that it has more personality
   b making something more interesting
   c making or changing something so it is especially suitable for one person

7 *source*
   a a person, place or thing that provides something you need or want
   b a type of liquid food that contains a lot of protein
   c a variety or type of something

3 Match the jobs in paragraphs 1–6 to the people a–f below.

a ☑ I'm really good at science. I've always wanted to be a doctor, but I also love technology.

b ☐ I'm very concerned about the environment. I want to find solutions for problems like pollution.

c ☐ I'm a creative person with good IT skills. I don't want to be a computer programmer. I want to use my communication skills to do something fun.

d ☐ I've always been interested in Biology but I know I don't want to be a doctor. I'm more interested in doing something more specialised where I can work with people.

e ☐ I'm practical and love being outside. I'm good at environmental science but I don't want to sit in a lab all day.

f ☐ Computers are my passion! I definitely want to work in IT. I'm very organised and I'd like to help people.

4 Read the text again and choose the correct answers.

1 According to the writer, in the future
   a there will be new jobs in which people can use the skills they have now.
   b people will need skills that don't exist at the moment for new sorts of jobs.
   c there probably won't be many new jobs, most people will do the same jobs as now.
   d people won't do any of the jobs they do now as all jobs will have changed.

2 In the future
   a most people will be growing body parts to replace their old ones.
   b it will only be possible to produce new legs or hearts, not other body parts.
   c there will be special factories which produce body parts.
   d people might be able to create replacement body parts that are alive.

3 Scientists believe nanotechnology
   a won't change the way we treat illnesses very much.
   b will only change the way we treat some illnesses.
   c will change the way we treat all illnesses.
   d will mostly be used in surgery.

4 A virtual manager
   a will probably do only one or two different types of task.
   b won't need to be organised because computer programs will do the work.
   c won't exist for a long time yet, it's a job people will be doing in many years time.
   d is a career that could exist very soon for someone with good IT skills.

5 At the moment, personalised entertainment
   a doesn't exist.
   b isn't usually done by people.
   c is done by specialists.
   d is not important for advertisers.

6 Vertical farms
   a will go up the outside of tall buildings.
   b won't be able to produce much food.
   c won't need much technology.
   d will be the only type of farms in the future.

The world of work

Future jobs

Have you ever thought of being a tour guide in space or an internet lawyer? Or maybe you would prefer to be a virtual teacher? These are just some of the new jobs and careers that experts believe people will be doing in ten or twenty years. As technology evolves, the job market will evolve with it and the world will need people with new and different sets of skills to take up new, different kinds of jobs. We've done some research into just some of the new job opportunities that might be waiting for you in the future.

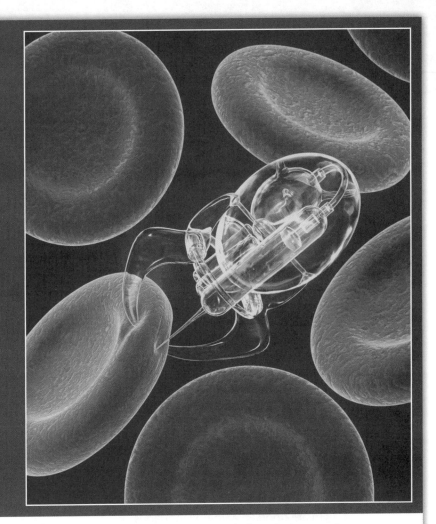

Health

1 Science will probably have advanced so far that it will be possible to create or clone living body parts, such as a new leg or heart. These body parts will be grown in laboratories, so we'll need people to create them, attach them and then work with patients in helping them adapt to their new bodies. This would be a great career for someone who is strong in science but has good interpersonal skills too.

2 If you don't fancy that, then how about 'nano-medicine'? Scientists believe advances in nanotechnology* will transform healthcare – for example, nanorobots** will be able to deliver medicines to specific areas of the body or repair the body from inside. We'll need well-qualified specialist doctors to administer these treatments.

Climate

3 The problem of climate change is getting worse and we'll need engineer-scientists to reduce the effects and solve the problem. Researchers predict these specialists will be doing amazing things such as building giant umbrellas to reflect the sun. We're going to need creative people who can come up with good ideas for fighting climate change and who have the skills in engineering and science to deliver solutions.

> * nanotechnology – the skill of building very small machines using computer technology (1 nanometre = 1 billionth of a metre)
>
> ** nanorobots – tiny robots made using nanotechnology

Entertainment and the internet

4 There will be lots of opportunities for people with sound IT skills. For example, we'll probably need virtual managers. In just a few years' time, these virtual managers will be helping people with their electronic lives by looking after their email, storing data correctly, updating profiles and passwords and so on. Organisational skills will be the key to this job!

5 Another IT career will be personalising TV, radio and the internet – that means for example, when you switch on your TV, the programmes will have been chosen just for you by creative, media-savvy people who have the technical skills to work with a range of visual and interactive media. Personalisation of entertainment is already happening. At the moment, it's mainly done by computers but no doubt there will be specialists who will work with producers and advertisers to create news, entertainment and information for each person.

Food

6 It is already possible to grow gardens on the sides of buildings. By 2020, vertical farms growing on the sides of skyscrapers in our cities could be an important source of food. Vertical farmers will need to be skilled in engineering as well as agricultural science. They will have to enjoy working outdoors but will need the technical skills to work with the complex technology for growing food in artificial environments.

Writing a CV

1 Look at the job advert and Milán's notes for his CV. Tick (✓) the seven things he should include and cross (✗) the three things he should leave out.

> **We are looking for childcarers, male and female.**
> - **Must be over 18 years old and available full time.**
> - **Excellent English, written and spoken is essential.**
> - **You should have good communication skills and enjoy working in a team.**
> - **Previous experience with children useful.**
>
> **To apply send your CV to Maria at mariagarcia@parkchildcare.co.uk**

1 ☐ My date of birth is 27 April 1993.
2 ☐ I speak and write English very well.
3 ☐ I have just left school and I am looking for a full-time job.
4 ☐ I am good at learning languages.
5 ☐ I can use a computer and I know all the programs well.
6 ☐ I am able to work well with other people.
7 ☐ My interests are travelling and music.
8 ✓ I have worked in a childcare centre every summer for the past three years.
9 ☐ I don't like jazz music or war films.
10 ☐ I studied at the *Szent László Gimnázium in Budapest* 2006–2010. I passed my Matura (equivalent of A-levels) in English with the top grade.

2 Rewrite the seven sentences from exercise 1 in the style of a CV. Use the words in the box to help you.

> language skills   personal interests   DOB ✓
> considerable experience   education
> school-leaver   ability to

1 *DOB 27/04/1993* _____
2 _____
3 _____
4 _____
5 _____
6 _____
7 _____

3 Write a full CV for Milán to apply for the job.

A job interview

4 Complete the extracts from a job interview with the expressions below.

> What are your strengths
> Sorry, I don't follow
> What I meant was
> Why do you want this job
> What are you weaknesses
> What do you mean ✓
> Where do you see yourself
> What I'm trying to say

A: So are you available immediately?
B: I will be soon.
A: [1] *What do you mean* when you say 'soon'?
B: Well, I'm just about to graduate from university.

A: [2] _____ ?
B: Because it's a great company to work for.

A: Do you have any experience?
B: Not exactly …
A: [3] _____ .
B: Well, I've done design work on my course, but I don't have any professional experience yet.

A: [4] _____ in ten years' time?
B: Sorry, I'm not with you.
A: [5] _____ what job do you imagine you'll be doing in ten years' time?

A: Do you speak any languages?
B: I studied French at school, but I haven't spoken it since then. [6] _____ is that my language skills need improving.

A: [7] _____ ?
B: I have great computer skills and I'm up to date with the latest programs.

A: [8] _____ ?
B: Probably my lack of experience.

exam trainer 5

Use of English

Verb + noun collocations

1 Match the phrases in the box to the correct verbs 1–4.

> decisions ✓   a relationship   homework
> a pay rise   sense   a headache   the sack
> a mess   housework   a chat   a noise
> the cooking   good marks at school

1 make _decisions_ , _____ ,
  _____ , _____ ,
2 do _____ , _____ ,
  _____
3 get _____ , _____ ,
  _____
4 have _____ , _____ ,
  _____

2 Complete the sentences below with the collocations from exercise 1. Sometimes you have to change the form of the verb.

1 I'm afraid I can't _make sense_ of these instructions. I don't understand them at all.
2 Daniel is going to _____ for the party. He knows how to make a great pizza.
3 Our neighbour _____ last month and now he's unemployed.
4 I don't think you can _____ with someone if you don't respect them.
5 Let's sit down and _____ . It's been ages since you told me any of your news.

3 Match the verbs 1–6 with the nouns a–f.

1 play   **a** the bill
2 achieve   **b** ages
3 solve   **c** weight
4 pay   **d** a goal
5 take   **e** a role
6 lose   **f** problems

Exam tasks

Open cloze

4 Complete the text with one word in each gap.

Sharing a room with my brother

I have shared a room with my brother Mike ever since I remember. The problem is, he can't do anything without ¹ _making_ a mess – and he won't tidy up afterwards. I had to ² _____ some rules about not leaving things on the floor in the middle of the room. It's also interesting to watch Mike when he finally decides to ³ _____ his homework. First he ⁴ _____ ages to prepare his desk, get himself something to eat, turn on some music and so on. And then it's almost time to go to bed. How he ever manages to ⁵ _____ good marks is a really puzzling question. Don't get me wrong though: I complain a lot about Mike, but I like him. It's great to be able to ⁶ _____ a chat and a laugh together after we come back from school.

Banked cloze

5 Complete the text with the words below. There is one extra word.

> achieve   do   feel   improve ✓
> make   solve

The tyranny of positive thinking

These days, many lifestyle gurus and authors of self-help books are telling us to 'think positive'. Looking at the bright side of everything can make us happier, more successful, and even ¹ _improve_ our health. The 'tyranny of positive thinking' is so powerful that some people may actually ² _____ guilty about being angry or sad. But is uncritical optimism always such a good thing? When you need to ³ _____ a difficult decision, it is better to have a true picture of the situation rather than a rosy one. Before you set out to ⁴ _____ all your goals with the obligatory confidence, you may want to ask yourself if those goals are what you really want and how realistic they are. And most importantly, if you want to ⁵ _____ problems effectively, you have to be able to admit that there is a problem first. Negative thinkers – speak out!

Reading

Multiple matching

1 Read the first part of an article about the effect of technological inventions on people's lives. Tick (✓) true or cross (✗) false.

The person in the text

1 ✓ experienced something he was unfamiliar with thanks to this new technology.

2 ☐ mentions a childhood dream.

3 ☐ refers to the way in which the invention increased people's access to culture.

4 ☐ wanted to own the device he describes.

5 ☐ comments on the proportions of the object.

Impressed by Inventions

We interviewed five members of the same family about the technological inventions that have made the greatest impressions on them.

Grandpa, 74

I remember the first TV set I ever saw, back in the 1950s. It was a wooden box the size of a fridge, but the screen was not much bigger than a postcard. I clearly remember the programme that was on: it was a ballet performance, and there was a male dancer in a sort of a bird costume with lots of feathers. I had never seen anything like it. Today it's hard to imagine, but before television the only way you would ever see a ballet dancer was if you actually went to the theatre.

2 <u>Underline</u> the parts of the text that helped you identify the correct answers.

Exam TIP

In this type of task, it helps to identify the specific place in the text which contains the same information as the statement. Note that the statements do not appear in the same order as the corresponding information in the text.

3 Read the rest of the article. Answer the questions with A, B, C or D.

Which person or people

1 wanted to have the device before it was invented? *C*

2 was pleased with the effects he/she was able to achieve using the new object? ____

3 is accustomed to new gadgets being invented all the time? ____

4 compares the invention he/she used with more modern versions of the same device? ____

5 likes a certain device because of its many functions? ____

6 mentions a childhood fantasy? ____

7 says using the invention required quite a lot of effort? ____

8 mention things that were important to them as children? *B* and ____

9 talk about the communication devices they like? ____ and ____

10 found an activity easier to do than it had been before? ____ and ____

A Grandma, 74

The most amazing invention? The first washing machine I had. An old-fashioned kind, where you still had to do a lot of work yourself: pour in hot water, start and stop the machine at the right time and wring the laundry out using a device called a 'wringer' that was attached to it. It may sound like a lot of bother if you're used to the modern fully automated washing machines, but after washing everything by hand it was just marvellous. I've been a fan of washing machines ever since.

B Dad, 47

The thing that impressed me more than anything in the world was the first set of felt-tip pens I got when I was about eight or nine. I loved drawing and painting; I always had crayons, coloured pencils, paints, but this was revolutionary: you held it like an ordinary pen but the colours were fantastically bright, the lines wider or narrower, whichever way you wanted to make them – it was like painting without all the bother of preparing brushes and cloths and water.

C Mum, 42

My favourite tech device is nothing very original: the mobile phone. But there's a special reason why I'm so fond of them. When I was a little girl, I dreamed of a phone that I could always carry with me, so I'd always be able to get in touch with my parents or my friends, which was very important to me. But it was a dream of the same kind as having a magic wand or a goldfish that gives you three wishes: I knew very well it was impossible. And then when I was thirty it was suddenly there. I'm still impressed!

D David, 18

To tell you the truth, I don't get that impressed by new technologies. I like them and I use them a lot but I'm not especially surprised when a new one appears. OK, I was impressed when iPhones first came out, because they really do everything. But in general, there is always something new, every year. You get used to it; you expect things to be this way. I've also got used to the thought that, as far as technology is concerned, everything is possible.

Listening

Short recordings

4 You are going to hear a father talking to his daughter about her career. Before you listen, note down any words or phrases you associate with the jobs below.

1 a summer camp counsellor: _____
_____

2 a nurse: _____
_____

3 a secretary: _____
_____

5 ⑦ **Listen twice. Which of the jobs a–c does the daughter want to do? Which of the words and phrases you wrote did you hear?**

a a summer camp counsellor

b a nurse

c a secretary

6 ⑦ **Listen again and complete the sentences.**

1 If I got a job as a _____ , I'd be working hard too, only I feel it would be less useful.

2 I worked at that _____ , remember?

Exam TIP

The recording is likely to contain words which appear in the wrong answers. Hearing an individual word is not enough to decide which answer is correct. Listen for several words or phrases associated with the answer.

7 ⑧ **Listen to four conversations in different situations. Choose the best answer.**

1 Two managers are discussing a job candidate they have just interviewed. They decide to employ the woman because of her
   a positive attitude.   b qualifications.
   c experience.

2 You will hear a woman leaving a message on voicemail. She is calling to
   a confirm a meeting.   b cancel a meeting.
   c change the date of a meeting.

3 You will hear two people discussing the jobs they were interested in as children. The man's choice of future job was influenced by
   a his parents.   b his friends' parents.
   c his teachers.

4 Listen to a businesswoman talking about a problem. Who is she talking to?
   a her boss   b an IT specialist
   c a customer

self-assessment test 2

Vocabulary & Grammar

1 Match the verbs 1–6 with the phrases a–f.

1 surf
2 upload
3 transfer
4 develop
5 download
6 update

a sound IT skills
b your profile on Facebook
c a video to the web
d apps from the internet
e the net
f music to your iPod

/5

2 Complete the sentences with one word in each gap.

1 The job offers good _career_ opportunities.
2 I've got Maths and Science A-levels and a degree in accountancy, so I'm well _____ for the job.
3 She'll work very well in a team – she's got good _____ skills.
4 We currently have job opportunities for highly _____ people who are hungry for success.
5 He has proven _____ of team working.
6 He needs to develop his IT _____ – he hasn't had much experience with computers.
7 Previous experience isn't necessary, but you need to be _____ to learn.

/6

3 Choose the best option a, b or c to complete the sentences.

1 What time _b_ the concert start on Saturday?
   a will   b does ✓   c is
2 Would he give me a hand with the move if I really ___ someone to help?
   a need   b needed   c would need
3 I hope I ___ my first house by the time I'm thirty.
   a buy   b will be buying   c will have bought
4 You ___ have spent so much money on flowers.
   a oughtn't   b mustn't   c shouldn't
5 If this iPad were cheaper, I ___ buy it.
   a might   b will   c can
6 I can't stay – I ___ to pick up Jo from work.
   a 've got   b must   c should
7 What ___ happen if nobody turned up?
   a can   b will   c would

/6

4 Complete the sentences with a correct future form of the verbs in brackets.

1 There's somebody at the door. Don't worry, I _I'll open_ (open) it.
2 By the time I'm thirty, I _____ (make) my first million dollars.
3 It's a long flight. Our plane _____ (arrive) in New York at 4.30 p.m. tomorrow.
4 Tim _____ (throw) a party to celebrate the end of the exams on Sunday.
5 I think Paul _____ (never/ask) her out. He's just too shy.
6 This time tomorrow we _____ (get ready) to go to the airport for our flight.
7 Tonight? Of course, I can come – I _____ (not do) anything important.
8 George, slow down! You _____ (crash) into the car in front!
9 By the end of next year, my grandparents _____ (be) married for fifty years.

/8

5 Complete the second sentence so that it means the same as the first. Use the word given in CAPITALS.

1 I'm not tall so I don't play basketball well.   WERE
   If I _were taller, I could play_ basketball better.
2 It was a better idea to go hiking instead of lying on the beach all day.   SHOULD
   We _____
   _____ lying on the beach all day.
3 Uniforms are obligatory in Al's school.   PUPILS
   All _____ school uniforms.
4 Julia is my best friend because she always stands by me.   IF
   Julia _____ stand by me.
5 I took a laptop with me but it proved completely unnecessary.   NEEDN'T
   _____ with me.
6 The winner gets promoted but I don't think they will win.   WOULD
   Provided _____ .

/5

44

Reading

6 Read the article. Choose the correct answers.

RECRUITMENT

RECRUITMENT TODAY is all about shouting. Employers shout about brands and jobs; jobseekers shout about CVs and skills. But the adage of 'the one who shouts loudest …' simply doesn't work any more. Everyone just stops listening. Wouldn't structured, informed recruitment conversations be better?

Social media is a fast, free and highly effective route to work when used correctly. Simply being a member of the right online communities gets conversations started, while engaging in them enables you to stand out.

At the moment, social media is being used more for entertainment than recruitment but using the web in the right way can make you stand out among other candidates hunting for the same jobs. It is therefore important that you look at your existing online brand and check for areas of concern. Start by Googling yourself and see what comes up.

Deciding where to invest energy is also important. Professional networks (LinkedIn) and mass-market propositions (Twitter and Facebook) seem the most obvious choices. What you do with your social media profiles will increase your chances of being found, considered and hopefully selected. So make sure that you keep them up to date, blog or comment on other's musings, make friends with people in your field, join the right groups, sign up to relevant mailing lists and take an active role in these activities. Be seen to be knowledgeable about your specialist area and others will draw that conclusion too.

People are today finding work through these powerful online networks. However, never underestimate the power of you leading the search. There are new and innovative means to present yourself online such as YouTube videos, industry blogs and online networks.

Employers are getting much better at searching and tracking social media content relating to their business or prospective employees. This makes it even more important to ensure your social media presence does you justice. It's time to build your own online brand.

1 According to the author of the article, current methods of recruitment
- **a** seem very demanding.
- **b** are not effective enough.
- **c** focus too much on brands.
- **d** are simply too loud.

2 You're more likely to get noticed by a prospective employer if you
- **a** only use social media for entertainment.
- **b** become a member of a social networking site.
- **c** make sure you appear on Google search.
- **d** get involved in suitable online communities.

3 Which piece of advice below is NOT mentioned in the article?
- **a** Sign up for all professional and social websites.
- **b** Use your own initiative while looking for a job.
- **c** Demonstrate your expertise in your field.
- **d** Update your profile once in a while.

4 What are employers' attitudes to social media?
- **a** They want each prospective employee to have an online brand.
- **b** They think it might be a fairer way of recruiting employees.
- **c** They're becoming more skilful at using it as a recruitment tool.
- **d** They consider it one of the most important methods of recruitment.

5 The best title of this article is
- **a** 'The demise of old recruitment methods.'
- **b** 'Social media is the new way to secure work.'
- **c** 'What can Facebook and Twitter do for you?'
- **d** 'Social networking websites' rapid growth.'

/5

Communication

7 Complete the speech with one word in each gap.

Today, I'd ^{1} _like_ to talk about arranged marriage. Some people ^{2} _____ , especially in the west, ^{3} _____ it is old-fashioned. I ^{4} _____ . ^{5} _____ me explain why. ^{6} _____ of all, people often confuse arranged marriage with forced marriage. But in my ^{7} _____ these two are completely different. In arranged marriages you have a choice. What I ^{8} _____ is that you can say 'no'. ^{9} _____ more, your parents look in places you wouldn't even consider looking for a partner. ^{10} _____ a good partner is exactly the ^{11} _____ as finding a good job. It requires time and effort. And ^{12} _____ more thing, love marriages are not necessarily any happier. ^{13} _____ at the divorce rate, for ^{14} _____ . It's been constantly ^{15} _____ in many countries. So, to ^{16} _____ up, arranged marriage is not such a bad idea and might offer a good alternative in today's divorce-ridden society.

/15

Marks	
Vocabulary & Grammar	**/30 marks**
Reading	**/5 marks**
Communication	**/15 marks**
Total:	**/50 marks**

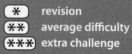

* revision
** average difficulty
*** extra challenge

Vocabulary

A performance

1 Complete the sentences with the verbs below.

> bow cheer clap costumes curtain
> discuss go up put on set stage
> stalls take ✓

1 Before the performance the audience _take_ their seats in the _____ and wait for the curtain to _____ .

2 Meanwhile, the actors _____ their _____ and make-up.

3 The actors appear on _____ .

4 During the interval the audience _____ the production.

5 The _____ goes up after the interval and sometimes there is a new _____ .

6 After the performance the cast _____ and the audience _____ and _____ .

2 Complete the sentences with one word in each gap.

1 The preparations for a performance take place _backstage_ .

2 Actors put on make-up and costumes in their _____ rooms.

3 The audience sits in the stalls or the _____ .

4 After the curtain goes up, the first _____ begins.

5 At the end of the performance, all the members of the _____ come on stage to take their bows.

6 The audience _____ their appreciation by clapping and cheering.

7 After the _____ , the audience take their seats again.

8 If the play is long, it's good to be able to buy _____ between the first and second act.

9 The _____ was really fantastic. The set, the cast, the story … everything was outstanding.

Grammar

The passive

3 (*) Underline the correct form.

1 Van Gogh's 'Café Terrace at Night' *painted/ was painted* in 1888.

2 Several of the museum's most valuable paintings *have damaged/have been damaged* in a fire.

3 Even though the concert *had cancelled/ had been cancelled,* the fans were still waiting outside the building.

4 A new concert hall *is building/is being built* in our city.

5 We *are expecting/are being expected* the actors to arrive soon.

6 The sets for our play *will paint/will be painted* by professionals.

4 (**) Complete the sentences with the passive form of the verb in brackets using the correct tense.

1 The original Globe Theatre in London _was built_ (build) in 1599.

2 Tickets for the concert _____ (sell) at the Student Council's office from next Monday.

3 Have you heard? An unknown painting by Rembrandt _____ (discover).

4 The old cinema in our town _____ (renovate) at the moment. It will open again around Christmas.

5 This film should _____ (watch) on a big screen.

6 It _____ (believe) that the play *The Two Noble Kinsmen* _____ (write) jointly by William Shakespeare and John Fletcher.

5 (✱✱✱) Put the verbs in the correct tense (sometimes there is more than one possible answer) and the correct form, active or passive.

Jane Grant's latest film [1]_____ (probably/surprise) her fans when it comes to the cinemas next week. The director, who [2]_____ (know) for heartwarming children's comedies, such as the 2009 hit *Daisy Jones in America*, [3]_____ (decide) to tell a dark fantasy tale this time. *Midnight Moon* [4]_____ (already criticise) by some reviewers for being unnecessarily violent. It [5]_____ (believe) that the film's star, nine-year-old Lily Thomson, was shocked by some of the scenes in which she [6]_____ (ask) to appear. Thomson's parents [7]_____ (refuse) to comment on her work for the film. The director, who [8]_____ (nominate) for Academy Awards three times, hopes this film [9]_____ (award) a long-awaited Oscar. *Midnight Moon* is beautifully shot and the special effects are outstanding. However, despite the film's visual appeal, it [10]_____ (not recommend) for family entertainment.

Grammar Plus: *get something done*

6 (✱✱✱) Rewrite the sentences using the structure *get something done.*

1 We're taking the costumes to the dry cleaners.
We' *re getting the costumes cleaned* .

2 Alice paid someone to frame her best friend's photo.
Alice _____
_____ .

3 Your car is filthy. You should take it to the carwash.
You should _____
_____ .

4 The theatre is employing someone to install new lighting.
The theatre _____
_____ .

5 Sally's flat has been redecorated for her by someone she employed.
Sally _____
_____ .

6 My neighbour employs someone to cut the grass for him every two weeks.
My neighbour _____
_____ every two weeks.

Grammar reference

Passives

Form

To form the passive we use the verb *to be* in the correct tense and add the past participle of the main verb. If we want to mention the agent (the 'doer' of the action), we use a phrase beginning with *by*.

Present simple passive	It *is* widely **believed** that the best opera singers are Italian.
Present continuous passive	He believes he **is being watched by** the police.
Present perfect passive	The floors **have been washed** and are still wet.
Past simple passive	'The Piano' **was directed by** Jane Campion.
Past continuous passive	They **were being followed by** crowds of fans.
Past perfect passive	All the letters **had been written by** the same person.
Future simple passive	The meeting **will be postponed** until tomorrow.
Modal passive	A promise of that kind **could/might/should be broken.**

Use of the passive

We use the passive when we don't know or care who does the action, when the agent is obvious or when we are more interested in the action itself than the person who does or did it:

*She realised her theatre tickets **had been stolen**.*

We use the passive to describe processes:

*Many of the old buildings **are being renovated**.*

We use the passive in newspapers and academic writing for an impersonal, objective style:

*Two men **were charged** with attempted murder last Friday.*

We use the passive in formal reports to report what people generally believe or say is true and when it is not important to mention who the people are. This structure is commonly used with verbs like *say, think, believe, know, claim, expect*:

***It is expected that** the next conference will be held in Sweden.*

get something done

We use the structure *get* + object + past participle to say that we arranged for something to be done:

*We **got** the front door lock **changed** last week.*
*I'm going to **get my car serviced**.*

Get something done can be used instead of *have something done* but it is slightly more informal and mainly used in informal spoken English.

Vocabulary

Music and entertainment

1 Match the verbs 1–6 with the nouns a–f.

1 post   a an album
2 have a   b a TV talent contest
3 play   c on a world tour
4 release   d music on the internet
5 go   e gigs
6 win   f number one hit

2 Complete the texts with the words below.

> gig hits label album posting
> released signed singles talent
> tour venues ✓

Four of my mates have formed a band. They're playing in small local ¹ _venues_ and they're also ² _____ their music on the internet. They actually seem to get a lot of ³ _____ . They'd like to win a TV ⁴ _____ contest, but I'm not sure that'd be good for them! They might stop making music and start appearing in commercials.

Green Day played their first ⁵ _____ in a restaurant called the Hickory Pit in Vallejo California on 17 October 1987. One of the band member's mothers was working there as a waitress. At the time, the band were calling themselves Sweet Children. In 1989 they ⁶ _____ up with the record ⁷ _____ Lookout and changed their name to Green Day. They didn't become really successful until their third full-length ⁸ _____ Dookie came out in 1994. In 1995 Dookie was nominated for nine MTV Video Music Awards including Video of the Year.

Grammar

More complex question forms

3 ✱ Complete the questions with the words below.

> advice director frequently
> long soon ✓ sort

1 How _soon_ do you think they'll start playing?
2 What _____ of entertainment should we organise?
3 How _____ are concerts organised in your city?
4 What _____ would you give to young people interested in making films?
5 Which _____ has had the greatest influence on 21st century cinema?
6 How _____ did the concert last?

4 ✱ Match the questions 1–6 with the sentences a–e.

1 Aren't they brilliant?
2 Didn't you notice anything?
3 Hasn't she tried looking on the internet?
4 Haven't you heard about the space mission?
5 Isn't it a beautiful day?

a I love autumn weather.
b It's been in the news all day.
c The robbers must have run past your window.
d I can listen to this song over and over again.
e You can buy any album there.

Beyoncé began her singing career with the group Destiny's Child, but she ⁹ _____ her first solo album Dangerously in Love in 2003. Dangerously in Love sold 317,000 copies in its first week and two of the songs Crazy in Love and Baby Boy became hit ¹⁰ _____ in the same year. In 2004, Beyoncé went on her first solo ¹¹ _____ to promote Dangerously in Love in Europe. She finished the year by winning five Grammy Awards, including best R&B song and best contemporary R&B album.

5 (✶✶) Write questions to find out the missing information in the sentences below.

1 I went to the mall with _____ last night.

Who did you go with ?

2 We looked at some _____ in the shops.

_____ ?

3 You know, I got some money for my birthday from _____ .

_____ ?

4 Would you believe it? I paid £50 for a _____ .

_____ ?

5 We also talked to some _____ we met there.

_____ ?

6 We talked about _____ .

_____ ?

6 (✶✶) Complete the indirect questions.

1 Did they know anyone in the music industry?

I wonder _if they knew anyone_ in the music industry.

2 Where did you lose the tickets?

Do you remember _____ the tickets?

3 How long does it take to prepare for a tour?

I'd like to know _____ to prepare for a tour.

4 Is it difficult to succeed in the film world?

Do you think _____ in the film world?

5 What do you think of this play?

Tell me _____ of this play.

6 Did they give out any back-stage passes?

Would you mind telling me _____ any back-stage passes?

7 (✶✶✶) Complete the questions with one word in each gap.

1 Who did you go bowling _with_ ?

2 _____ expensive do you think the tickets will be?

3 What are we all waiting _____ ?

4 Do you happen to know where the venue _____ ?

5 _____ kind of instruments do you play?

6 Can you tell me _____ the album will be released soon?

Grammar reference

Questions

Compound questions

Compound questions combine the question words *What* or *Which* with a noun or *How* with an adverb:

What suggestion would you make to improve working conditions?
Which article was more comprehensive?
How quickly does hair grow?

Negative questions

We use negative questions to express surprise, in exclamations or when we expect the listener to agree with us. In such questions, we use contracted negative forms:

Didn't you *hear* me? I called you several times.
Isn't he a clever boy!
Haven't we *met* before?

Answers to negative questions:

Haven't we met before?
Yes. (= yes, we have met before)
No. (= no, we haven't met before)

Questions with prepositions

When a verb or an adjective used in a question is followed by a preposition, the preposition comes at the end of the question:

Who did you go *with*?
What are you afraid *of*?

In such questions, the preposition can't be omitted.

Indirect questions

In indirect questions we use the same word order as in statements (the subject comes before the verb):

*What time **does** the coach **leave**?* (direct question)
*Do you know what time the coach **leaves**?* (indirect question)

The question auxiliary *do/does/did* is not used in the past and present simple:

*When **did** the concert **start**?*
*Could you tell me **when** the concert **started**?* (not did start)

In indirect *Wh-* questions we use the same question word as in the direct question:

Where is the post office? (direct question)
*Can you tell me **where** the post office **is**?* (indirect question)

In indirect *Yes/No* questions we use *if* or *whether*:

Do you play football every weekend?
*I'd like to know **if/whether** you **play** football every weekend.*

Some opening phrases often used for indirect questions are:

Can/Could you tell me … ?   Do you know… ?
Do you think … ?   I wonder … ?   Have you any idea … ?

Vocabulary

Writers and writing

1 Complete the text with the words and phrases below.

> plots   location   original angle
> publishing deal   constructive feedback
> research   budgets   worldwide
> point of view   agent ✓

Writer's Weekly

Jill Law talks to publishing professional Simon Coe about working with some of our most talented writers, the Harry Potter phenomenon and advice for the next generation of would-be authors.

Jill: Simon, you know some of our best contemporary poets and authors but you're actually an ¹ _agent_ , aren't you?

Simon: That's right. I help authors by contacting different publishers about their books. I try to get them a ² _____ .

J: What tips have you got for would-be authors?

S: Well, you should do a lot of ³ _____ . It makes the story more realistic. After you've written it, let different people read it, get some ⁴ _____ and rewrite it.

J: The Harry Potter books have been released ⁵ _____ and are very popular. So, why do you think JK Rowling's books have been so successful?

S: I think it's because she came up with an ⁶ _____ . I mean, stories set in schools aren't new but a story set in a school for magic, that was new at the time. And she told the stories from the ⁷ _____ of a teenage boy.

J: And what about the ⁸ _____ of the books?

S: Well, the stories are great fun! A lot happens. You never get bored!

J: And did the films all have a big ⁹ _____ ?

S: Oh yes. The one for the last film was estimated at £150,000,000!

J: Wow! I suppose it's expensive to shoot them on ¹⁰ _____ .

S: Yes, but most of the budget was for special effects.

Reading

2 Look at the events from the life of teenage author Christopher Paolini. What order do you think they happened in?

1 ☐ He went on a book tour.
2 ☐ A famous author read his book and liked it.
3 ☐ His got his first publishing deal.
4 ☐ He finished school.
5 ☐ His parents read his book.
6 ☐ His first book was made into a film.
7 ☐ He wrote his first book.
8 ☐ His second book was released.

3 Read the text on page 51 quickly and put the events in the correct order. Were your guesses correct?

4 Match the questions 1–6 to the paragraphs a–f where you can find the answer. Answer the questions in 3–5 words.

1 How old was Paolini when his first book came out?   _c_
_____

2 What kind of stories did he like when he was growing up?   ___
_____

3 Which two countries did Paolini tour in 2003 to promote his book?   ___
_____

4 What was the name of his first book?   ___
_____

5 What does Paolini intend to do after he finishes the series of books he is working on?   ___
_____

6 When did the film of his first book come out?   ___
_____

5 Read the text again. Tick (✓) true or cross (✗) false or write (?) if there is no information.

1 ☐ Paolini read a lot when he was young.
2 ☐ Author Bruce Covill gave Paolini some good advice about writing.
3 ☐ Paolini's family helped him to get his book noticed by people.
4 ☐ After his first book was published by Knopf, Paolini spent all his time writing.
5 ☐ Most of Paoloni's fans are in Europe.
6 ☐ Paolini hasn't yet decided what to call his fourth book.
7 ☐ Paolini doesn't have any ideas for future books.

Making it big ...

A Most teenagers only dream of having a book published or being a successful author but Christopher Paolini did more than dream. He wrote his first book when he was just fifteen. Today, teenagers all over the world are fans of *Eragon*, his bestselling novel, which has also been made into a successful Hollywood film.

B Paolini was born in 1983 in Southern California, America. As a child, he often wrote short stories and poems and read widely. He especially loved science fiction and fantasy authors such as Bruce Covill, Raymond Feist, Anne McCaffrey and Ursula K Le Guin. Covill in particular inspired him to write. He and his sister Angela were homeschooled by their parents, Kenneth Paolini and Talita Hodgkinson, and he gained his high school graduation diploma when he was just fifteen years old.

C After finishing school, Paolini started to write a book as a personal challenge. He wanted to write a story that he would enjoy reading and tell it from a teen boy's point of view. The plot centres round a boy growing up and becoming a dragon rider in a magical world called Alagaesia. The book he wrote was *Eragon*. After revising it, he gave the book to his parents to read. They were so impressed they decided to publish the book themselves. It came out in 2001, when Paolini was just eighteen. The family spent the next year promoting* the book in libraries, bookshops and schools.

D In 2003, Paolini got a lucky break**. When author Carl Hiaasen read the book, he loved it so much that he contacted his publisher, Knopf Books, and suggested they might be interested in publishing it. After reading the book, Knopf got in touch and offered Paolini his first publishing deal. The book was released in 2003 and Paolini went on a tour around Britain and America to promote it.

E In 2004, he started work on the second book in the *Inheritance Cycle* series, *Eldest*. It came out in 2005 and the third book, *Brisingr*, came out in 2008. Paolini is now working on the fourth and final book of the series. It hasn't got a title yet. Meanwhile, in 2006, the film of *Eragon* came out. So far, over twenty million copies of his books have been sold worldwide and fans are eagerly awaiting his next book.

F When he finishes the *Inheritance Cycle*, Paolini plans to take a long holiday and think about which of his many story ideas he will write about next. We hope he won't take too long!

* promote – to attract people's attention to a product by advertising, talking or writing about it
** lucky break – something lucky that happens unexpectedly and that can help you succeed

Listening

6 (9) Read the list of books by American author S.E. Hinton. Listen to the interview and write the order the books are first mentioned.

- [ ] *Big David, Little David*
- [ ] *Tex*
- [1] *The Outsiders*
- [ ] *Some of Tim's Stories*
- [ ] *Taming the Star Runner*
- [ ] *Rumble Fish*
- [ ] *Hawkes Harbor*
- [ ] *The Puppy Sister*
- [ ] *That Was Then, This Is Now*

7 (9) Listen and complete the sentences.

1 Hinton's first novel was published while she was *at university* .

2 People all over the world have bought over _____ copies of her first book.

3 To help her recover from writer's block, her _____ made sure she wrote every day.

4 _____ of her books were made into films.

5 Hinton worked as a _____ scout to find suitable places to make the films.

6 *Big David, Little David* came out in _____ .

8 (9) Listen again and choose the correct answer.

1 *The Outsiders*
   a was written when she was fifteen.
   b didn't immediately make her famous in America.
   c became the most popular novel for young people ever.
   d is still a popular book nowadays.

2 Hinton got the idea to write *The Outsiders* from
   a two teachers at her school.
   b her publisher.
   c two groups of students at her school.
   d a famous pop group called *The Greasers*.

3 She published under the name of S.E. Hinton
   a because she preferred it to her full name.
   b so that reviewers wouldn't know she was female.
   c because there was another writer called Susan Hinton.
   d she didn't want people to know her full name.

4 What do they say about the film versions of her books?
   a There weren't any big Hollywood stars in any of the films.
   b Francis Ford Coppola directed all four of the films.
   c They were 'indie' or independent films.
   d Hinton appeared in small parts in three of the films.

5 Her book of short stories was published in
   a 1995   b 2004   c 2006   d 2009

5

Writing

A film review

FILM REVIEW

1 In **paragraph 1**, introduce the film, giving details about the storyline, the setting, the main actors and the director.

2 In **paragraph 2**, describe the plot in more detail, but don't give away too much. Don't describe the ending!

3 In **paragraph 3**, describe the good/bad/best/worst things about the film and give your opinion.

4 In **paragraph 4**, write your conclusion. Say if you recommend the film or not, and who you recommend it to.

The Blind Side

The Blind Side is the latest offering from Texan director John Lee Hancock whose other recent films include *King Arthur* and *Midnight in the Garden of Good and Evil*. It's a feel-good sports drama and true-life story based on the book of the same title by Michael Lewis about Michael Oher, the American football star. Set in Memphis, Tennessee, the film stars newcomer Quinton Aaron as Michael Oher and Sandra Bullock, who won an Oscar for best actress for her role, as Leigh Anne Tuohy, the woman who changed his life.

African-American teenager Michael Oher, has grown up in poverty with a mother who is a drug addict and he ends up homeless. His luck changes when he meets Leigh Anne and Sean Tuohy, a wealthy white couple who rescue him from the streets and eventually end up adopting him. The Tuohys support Michael through his difficulties at school and help him to develop his talent as a football player. Central to the film, which touches on issues such as social class and racism, is the relationship between Michael and Leigh Anne and the transformative effect he has on the privileged Tuohy family's life. When Leigh Anne's friends congratulate her for changing Michael's life, she replies: 'No, he's changing mine.'

The Blind Side has been criticised for being over sentimental and simplistic and some consider the sports scenes to be disappointing. Although the climax of the film involves Michael fighting for a place to play football at university, there is no 'big game' to conclude the film. For me, however, the best thing about the film was the fact that it relies on the portrayal of the relationships between the main characters to keep the viewers engaged. Although Bullock is outstanding, all the lead characters give great performances and I found the story gripping and very moving.

Overall, despite missing an opportunity to be more political or more dramatic, *The Blind Side* is still an enjoyable and inspirational film. If you like a good heart-warming drama, then it's especially well worth seeing, but it's a film which I would recommend to almost anyone.

Useful language

Introducing the film

The film stars …/The main characters are played by …/ It takes place/is set in …/The setting is …

Describing the plot

The film/story starts/opens/begins …

Talking about the good points

The best thing about the film is …

It was a feel-good film/heartwarming.

It was thoroughly enjoyable/inspirational.

Talking about bad points

The worst thing about the film is …

It's disappointing.

Giving a recommendation

I definitely would recommend this film …
I definitely wouldn't recommend going to see this film …

It's well worth going to see.

It's not worth going to see.

1 Where would you find the following information in a film review – the beginning (B), the middle (M) or the end (E)?

1 ☐ information about the plot and the characters
2 ☐ who wrote the book the film is based on
3 ☐ who the film was directed by
4 ☐ overall evaluation of the success of the film

2 Read the review of the film *The Blind Side* above and check your answers to exercise 1. Were your predictions correct?

3 Read the review again. Answer the questions.

1 What are the weaknesses of the film?

_____

2 Who was the film directed by?

_____

3 Who are the three main characters?

_____

4 Who wrote the book the film is based on?

_____

5 What is the best thing about the film in the reviewer's opinion?

_____

6 How could the film be better?

_____

4 Find the underlined words in the text and choose the best definitions.

1 *The Blind Side* is an underlined{inspirational} film.
   a something that makes you feel hopeful or encouraged
   b that makes you want to cry

2 a true-life story
   a a story that seems very realistic
   b a story that is based on a real person's life

3 The story was really gripping.
   a very exciting and interesting
   b rather boring and predictable

4 The story was very moving.
   a made you feel emotional
   b had lots of events in a short time

5 The lead characters give great performances.
   a play their parts very well
   b overact

6 The portrayal of the relationships.
   a the story behind the relationships
   b the way relationships are represented by the actors

7 Michael's presence has a transformative effect.
   a makes things more complicated
   b changes things a lot in a positive way

8 It's well worth seeing.
   a It isn't a good idea to see it.
   b It is a good idea to see it.

5 Read the sentences from a review of the film, *The Last Station*. Rewrite the review using the words below.

[portrayal   gripping   true-life ✓   moving
inspirational   performance   well-worth]

1 *The Last Station* is about the writer Tolstoy's life. The film really inspired me and made me think.

2 The story was set in Russia. It was about marriage – Tolstoy's relationship with his wife – and death and it made me feel emotional.

3 The plot wasn't very exciting, but it was beautifully filmed. The main actors played their parts well.

4 For me, the best thing about the film was the way Christopher Plummer played Tolstoy.

5 I recommend going to see the film.

'The Last Station' is the true-life story of the writer Tolstoy. The film ...

_____
_____
_____
_____

6 Complete the strategies box with the words below.

[expressions   notes ✓   logical   ending]

A film review

• Read the task carefully. Make [1] *notes* and decide what information to include in each paragraph.

• Write each paragraph, making sure the sentences are in a [2] _____ order. Remember not to give away the [3] _____ of the film when you describe the plot.

• Use a variety of adjectives and [4] _____ to make your writing more interesting.

• Check the number of words and then check your grammar, spelling and punctuation.

7 Choose one of the tasks and write your own film review. Use the structure on the opposite page and the strategies in exercise 6 and ideas in the exercises to help you. Write 200–250 words.

1 Write a review of a film you enjoyed.
2 Write a review of a film you did not enjoy.

Talking about statistics

1 Look at the bar chart and complete the sentences with the words below.

> a tiny   most   eighteen percent
> a fifth ✓   five percent   least   minority
> majority   thirteen

Cinema earnings by film genre

- Comedy
- Animation
- Action
- Horror and Sci-Fi
- Documentary
- Crime
- Drama
- Thriller and Adventure
- Musical
- Other

0%   5%   10%   15%   20%   25%

1 Comedies earned _a fifth_ of the total.

2 Documentaries earned _____ percentage of the total.

3 Crime films earned a little under _____ of the total.

4 The _____ of the money was earned by horror and sci-fi, and comedy films.

5 _____ out of every hundred people went to see action films, which earned thirteen percent of the total.

6 A _____ of people went to see documentary films which only earned one percent of the total.

7 The statistics show that the _____ money was earned by musicals and documentaries.

8 What the statistics prove is that the _____ money was earned by comedies, closely followed by horror and sci-fi films.

Talking about trends

2 Complete the table with the verbs below. Add the noun forms where possible.

> rise ✓   increase   go down ✓   decrease
> fall   go up   double   halve

+ Words meaning more		− Words meaning less	
Verb	Noun	Verb	Noun
rise 1 _____	a rise	go down 4 _____	–
2 _____		5 _____	
3 _____		6 _____	

3 Look at the graph and complete the description. <u>Underline</u> the correct answers.

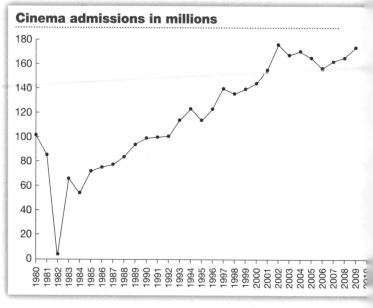

Cinema admissions in millions

180
160
140
120
100
80
60
40
20
0

1980 1981 1982 1983 1984 1985 1986 1987 1988 1989 1990 1991 1992 1993 1994 1995 1996 1997 1998 1999 2000 2001 2002 2003 2004 2005 2006 2007 2008 2009

Between 1980 and 1981 the number of people who went to the cinema [1] *rose/fell*. Between 1981 and 1982 the number went down [2] *slightly/sharply*. Between 1980 and 1984 the number of viewers roughly [3] *halved/doubled*. However, between 1985 and 1988 the number went [4] *up/down* steadily. Between 1990 and 1992, the number of cinema goers [5] *stayed pretty much the same/fluctuated a lot*. Between 1992 and 2002, the number of viewers steadily [6] *increased/decreased*. Since 2002, the numbers have fluctuated [7] *a little/ a lot* although in general they have [8] *risen/fallen* [9] *slightly/dramatically*. What the information shows is that the number of people who go to the cinema has nearly [10] *doubled/halved* since 1980.

examtrainer7

Use of English

Easily confused words

1 Complete the sentences with the correct form of the verbs below. Use each verb once only.

> discuss say ✓ speak talk tell

1 I _said_ thank you and left.
2 The film _____ the story of a young street dancer trying to escape from gang life.
3 Chris can _____ four languages.
4 We sat in a café and _____ about the concert.
5 We _____ the play and its film version in class last month.

2 Complete the sentences with the correct word below. Use each word once only.

> break interval pause

1 During the _____ the audience talked about the unexpected ending of the first act.
2 We met during the lunch _____ , after my double Maths lesson.
3 There was a slight _____ when nobody said anything.

> chair place seat

4 The action takes _____ in nineteenth-century London.
5 I had an expensive _____ in the stalls, so I could see the actors really well.
6 There was nowhere left to sit but the attendant was very kind and brought a _____ for me.

> audience spectators viewers

7 Many TV _____ are annoyed by commercial breaks in the middle of films.
8 The _____ loved the play and they clapped for a long time.
9 Five hundred _____ came to watch the match.

Exam Tasks

Banked cloze

3 Complete the text with the words below. There is one extra word.

> acting place plays tells says
> scene stars

25th Hour ★★★★★

Spike Lee's film *25th Hour* [1] _____ the story of one day in the life of a young Irish-American who is about to go to prison for drug dealing. The action takes [2] _____ in New York, and there are some beautiful shots of the city. Edward Norton [3] _____ the main role. His [4] _____ is really impressive. There is an amazing [5] _____ in which the character talks to himself in the mirror. He feels so bitter that he [6] _____ something insulting about every social and ethnic group in New York before he finally admits that he is really angry with himself.

Multiple-choice cloze

4 Circle the best option.

Last Saturday my sister Anna, who is studying to be an actress, appeared on [1] _a_ in a real theatre for the first time. She [2] ___ the role of Eliza in *Pygmalion* by G.B. Shaw. We arrived at the theatre and found our [3] ___ . When Anna said her first line I could hardly breathe. During the [4] ___ we went to see her in the dressing room, but she wanted to concentrate and she [5] ___ us to come after the show. At the end, the [6] ___ clapped and cheered! And one review in the local paper said she 'gave a terrific [7] ___ '!

1 **a** stage   **b** act   **c** scene
2 **a** played   **b** acted   **c** starred
3 **a** rows   **b** seats   **c** chairs
4 **a** break   **b** interval   **c** pause
5 **a** said   **b** spoke   **c** told
6 **a** audience   **b** viewers   **c** spectators
7 **a** acting   **b** play   **c** performance

Vocabulary

Food and tastes

1 Complete the table with the foods a–f below. Write the names of the food categories.

	Food	Category
1 chilli	*d garlic*	*herbs and flavourings*
2 liver	___	___
3 mango	___	___
4 ice cream	___	___
5 tuna	___	___
6 turnip	___	___

2 Complete the sentences with the food words below.

> beans ✓ garlic liver powder
> prawns tuna

1 If you're vegetarian, you should eat _beans_ as a source of protein.

2 You can use curry _____ or paste to make chicken curry.

3 _____ is a meat that contains a lot of vitamins.

4 I like food with lots of _____ in it but I never eat it before I go out.

5 We went deep-sea fishing last summer and I caught a beautiful _____ .

6 I'm semi-vegetarian. I eat _____ and other seafood.

Grammar

Quantifiers

3 ✱ Complete the table with the quantifiers below.

> a few   a great deal of ✓   very little
> a large number of   a little   a couple of
> very few   a bit of

Tea	Biscuits
A great deal of	

4 ✱ Number the quantifiers below from the smallest (1) to the largest (5).

> very little   a great deal   hardly any
> a little   quite a lot

1 _hardly any_   4 _____

2 _____   5 _____

3 _____

5 ✱✱ Underline the correct words to complete the sentences.

A: We need to buy [1] *plenty of/a bit of* food for the garden party. Fifty people are coming.

B: Right. What shall we buy?

A: First of all, we need [2] *a lot of/very few* vegetables for the different salads. They will be the main dishes. And [3] *quite a lot of/very little* bread to go with the salads.

B: And [4] *a large number of/a great deal of* fresh fruit. We've got pineapples and strawberries, but maybe we could also get [5] *a couple of/a little* watermelons, what do you think?

A: OK. Now about the snacks … I think we should get [6] *a little/a few* large packets of nuts and maybe [7] *a little/a few* bags of crisps.

B: How about drinks?

A: Don't worry, there's [8] *very little/quite a lot of* mineral water.

B: And there are [9] *very few/plenty of* cartons of juice!

6 (✱✱) Complete the text with phrases a–e below.

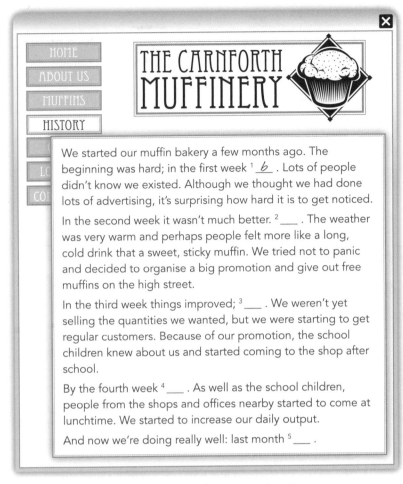

THE CARNFORTH MUFFINERY

HOME
ABOUT US
MUFFINS
HISTORY

We started our muffin bakery a few months ago. The beginning was hard; in the first week ¹ _b_ . Lots of people didn't know we existed. Although we thought we had done lots of advertising, it's surprising how hard it is to get noticed.

In the second week it wasn't much better. ² ___ . The weather was very warm and perhaps people felt more like a long, cold drink that a sweet, sticky muffin. We tried not to panic and decided to organise a big promotion and give out free muffins on the high street.

In the third week things improved; ³ ___ . We weren't yet selling the quantities we wanted, but we were starting to get regular customers. Because of our promotion, the school children knew about us and started coming to the shop after school.

By the fourth week ⁴ ___ . As well as the school children, people from the shops and offices nearby started to come at lunchtime. We started to increase our daily output.

And now we're doing really well: last month ⁵ ___ .

a people bought a few muffins every day
b we hardly sold any muffins at all ✓
c we sold a really large number of muffins
d we still sold very few
e we were selling quite a lot

7 (✱✱✱) Complete the text with the words below.

> a little   a few   few   hardly any
> a great deal ✓   a large number   little

Here's what we got for our picnic. According to the weather forecast, it's going to be very hot, so we've got ¹ _a great deal_ of bottled water. I'm going to take ² _____ lemonade for the children, but not too much because they won't drink it all. We've got ³ _____ of different sorts of sandwiches because Jane and I both made some. I hope we finish them all! There's very ⁴ _____ room in the basket and they take up most of the space. Unfortunately, we've got ⁵ _____ fruit because I forgot to buy any. There were ⁶ _____ apples left in the fruit bowl so I put those in. We have got lots of cake, though! As you know, there are very ⁷ _____ sweet things I can eat because I'm on diet, but there's diet carrot cake for me and muffins and brownies for the rest of you.

Grammar reference

Quantifiers

Large quantities

To talk about large quantities, we use *a great deal of, loads of, plenty of, a lot of, quite a lot of* and *a large number of*.

We use *loads of, plenty of, a lot of, quite a lot of* with both uncountable nouns and countable plural nouns:

a lot of luggage   *a lot of* students
quite a lot of milk   *quite a lot of* countries
loads of time   *loads of* toys
plenty of food   *plenty of* chips

loads of is informal. It is often used in speech but should not be used in formal written language:

*The President received **a lot of** (**NOT** loads of) criticism for his handling of the crisis.*

We only use *a large number of* with countable plural nouns:

*a large number of **buildings***
*a large number of **people***

We only use *a great deal of* with uncountable nouns:

*a great deal of **money***
*a great deal of **time***

Small quantities

To talk about small quantities, we use *very little, a little, a bit of, hardly any, a couple of, a few* and *very few*.

We use *very little, a little, a bit of* with uncountable nouns:

***very little** perfume*
***a little** sugar*
***a bit of** luck*

a bit of is a more informal expression, but is often used in speech and writing.

We use *a couple of, a few, very few* with countable plural nouns:

***a couple of** days*
***a few** problems*
***very few** projects*

NB *a couple of* is a more informal expression, but is often used in speech and writing.

We use *hardly any* with uncountable nouns and countable plural nouns:

***hardly any** bread*
***hardly any** books*

Vocabulary

Describing dishes

1 **Match the sentences 1–5 with the replies a–e.**

1 I don't really like such hot and spicy food.

2 Will the fish be fried?

3 This is too rich for me. I'm on a diet.

4 What's that French cheese like?

5 Some people think this dish is disgusting.

a It's soft and runny with a strong smell, but it's delicious.

b Yes, I prefer milder tastes, too. Shall we order something different?

c You can have it grilled if you prefer.

d Really? Personally, I think it's delicious.

e Well in that case, I can offer you lean meat and boiled vegetables.

2 **Complete the conversation with the words below.**

> exotic   flavour   protein
> pickled   raw ✓   tender
> mashed

Mike: Is the meat cooked yet?

Chris: No, it's still [1] _raw_ . But look, it's excellent quality. The steaks will be delicious and [2] _____ .

Mike: … and full of [3] _____ . And the garlic will give them a strong [4] _____ .

Chris: Are we going to serve them with [5] _____ potatoes?

Mike: Yes, and with vegetables. What are these little white round things?

Chris: They're [6] _____ onions. They go with the cheese course.

Mike: What about dessert?

Chris: We'll just have a big plate of [7] _____ fruit.

Mike: Mmm. This is going to be a lovely meal.

Grammar

Relative clauses

3 (*) **Underline the correct words to complete the sentences.**

1 Sushi is a Japanese speciality _that_/who often contains raw fish.

2 The meal was OK except for the potatoes, _which/that_ were overcooked.

3 I think the person _which/who_ invented pizza was a genius!

4 Finland is the country _which/where_ people drink the most coffee.

5 The person _who/which_ does the most to make the school a cheerful place is the lady in the canteen.

6 Tea first appeared in Europe in the seventeenth century, _when/which_ sailors brought it from China.

4 (**) **Complete the sentences with the correct relative pronouns. Where no pronoun is needed, write Ø. Add commas where necessary.**

1 Bruges, _where_ I first tried Belgian food, is a beautiful old town.

2 The sixteenth century was a time _____ many new foods were brought to Europe from the Americas.

3 The chef Jamie Oliver _____ TV programme is watched in many countries has run several campaigns to promote healthy eating in the UK.

4 The food _____ I like best is fresh fruit salad.

5 We tried to cook the dish _____ had tasted so good at the party, but it just didn't have quite the same flavour.

6 My great-grandma, _____ used to bake delicious cakes, had learned all her recipes from her mother and aunts.

5 (**) **Complete the sentences with relative clauses.**

1 This is the chef. He made that fantastic prawn salad.
This is the chef _who/that made that fantastic prawn salad_ .

2 I've found the book. It contains the best pasta recipes I know.
I've found the book _____
_____ .

3 We've discovered a restaurant. They serve Bulgarian food there.
We've discovered a restaurant _____
_____ .

4 I've met the woman. You admired her cooking.
I've met the woman _____ .

5 I'll phone you in September. The course begins then.
I'll phone you in September _____
_____ .

6 This is the man. You wanted to see him.
This is the man _____ .

6 (✶✶) **Choose the best words, a, b or c to complete each gap. Sometimes two options are possible.**

The Weird Festivals Project
posted by Shelley – Year 12

We were supposed to find information about weird festivals and celebrations in England. Here's the most peculiar one [1] ___ I've found …

The Egremont Crab Fair, [2] ___ has been celebrated since the thirteenth century, is one of the oldest fairs in England. The small town of Egremont in Cumbria, [3] ___ it takes place, was granted the right to hold a market and a fair by King Henry II in 1266.

The fair got its name from crab apples, and an Apple Cart Parade, [4] ___ apples are thrown into the crowd, is still part of the celebrations. There are other traditional events, such as greasy pole climbing and a pipe smoking contest, but the event [5] ___ has made Egremont famous is the World Gurning Championships. 'Gurning' means something like 'making ugly faces'. Participants, [6] ___ come from all over the world, try to make the ugliest, most ridiculous faces they can manage. The person [7] ___ face impresses the judges the most is the winner. In 2002, BBC presenter Michaela Strachan, [8] ___ went to Egremont to report on the fair, took part in the competition as a joke and won.

see all Culture Projects

1 a ☑ that b ☐ whose c ☑ –
2 a ☐ which b ☐ that c ☐ –
3 a ☐ which b ☐ where c ☐ when
4 a ☐ when b ☐ which c ☐ that
5 a ☐ that b ☐ which c ☐ –
6 a ☐ which b ☐ who c ☐ that
7 a ☐ who b ☐ whose c ☐ that
8 a ☐ which b ☐ who c ☐ that

Grammar Plus: reduced relative clauses

7 **Cross out the unnecessary words to make reduced relative clauses.**

1 Paella is a traditional Spanish dish ~~which is~~ made with rice and seafood.

2 The people who have been invited to the picnic will bring their own food.

3 I can see something black that is lying across the road.

4 There are apples on the tree which was planted two years ago.

5 Do you know the girl in the white dress who is standing by the window?

6 The tomato is one of the fruits which were brought to Europe from the Americas.

Grammar reference

Defining relative clauses

Defining relative clauses identify or define which person or thing we are talking about and are essential to the clear understanding of the described noun. We begin relative clauses with relative pronouns:

• *who* or *that*, when we talk about people:

*She is the person **who/that** turned down my invitation.*

• *which* or *that*, when we talk about things:

*Have you got a book **which/that** is about global warming?*

• *whose*, when we talk about possession/belonging:

*I was talking to a man **whose** daughter I know from school.*

• *where*, when we talk about place:

*This is the café **where** I met your mother.*

• *when*, when we talk about time:

*She stood by me **when** I most needed encouragement.*

In defining relative clauses, relative pronouns *who*, *which* or *that* can be left out if they are followed by a personal pronoun or noun:

This is the tax form (~~which/that~~) I misplaced yesterday.
*Meryl Streep is an actor (~~who~~) **Jon** looks up to.*

Non-defining relative clauses

Non-defining relative clauses do not identify a noun we are talking about but add more information about it. They can come in the middle or at the end of the sentence and are always separated from a noun by commas:

*Mark, **who is studying art**, lives in Madrid.*
*They came after midnight, **which annoyed me**.*

In non-defining relative clauses, relative pronouns can't be left out.

Reduced relative clauses

Relative clauses can be reduced by omitting:

• the relative pronoun *who*, *that* or *which*

Full relative clause: *Do you know the girl **who is arguing** with Professor Jones?*

Reduced relative clause: *Do you know the girl ~~who is~~ **arguing** with Professor Jones?*

• the auxiliary verb *be* (*is/are/was/were/have been*):

Full relative clause: *The **students that have been chosen** for the competition are our best sportsmen.*

Reduced relative clause: *The **students** ~~that have been~~ **chosen** for the competition are our best sportsmen.*

Vocabulary

Travel

1 Complete the table with the words below.

> package holiday ✓   five-star city break
> take a guided tour   the locals   eat out
> beach resort   sunbathing   hiking holiday
> go sightseeing   travel rep   tour guide
> self-catering apartment   chilling out

Types of holiday	Activities/ things to do	People	Places to stay
package holiday			

2 Complete the sentences with the words and phrases below.

> beaten track   room service   landmark
> nightlife   set off   hitchhike   full board
> backpack ✓

Top holiday complaints!

→ The airline lost my ¹ _backpack_ so I didn't have any clothes for a few days.

→ The restaurant was OK but ² _____ was very slow. The food arrived two hours after we ordered it!

→ We paid for ³ _____ but we didn't eat all our meals in the hotel because the food was terrible!

→ The ⁴ _____ was awful – there weren't any good nightclubs and the restaurants all closed early! And there were no taxis late at night back to the resort so we had to ⁵ _____ . We had to wait ages for someone to give us a lift in their car.

→ The brochure said the hotel was off the ⁶ _____ but it was near the town. It wasn't in a remote place at all!

→ The hotel was so far from the airport we had to ⁷ _____ a day early. We lost half a day of our holiday travelling to it.

→ The guidebook was out of date! The museum didn't exist anymore and the clock tower, which used to be the most important local ⁸ _____ , had been knocked down.

Reading

3 You are going to read an extract from a travel book about a journey to India. Match the words from the text 1–3 with the definitions a–c. Now read the introduction and check.

1 trader (n)

2 full tilt (adv)

3 caravan (n)

a to go as fast as you can

b a person who buys and sells things as a job

c a group of people travelling together, especially in a desert or dangerous area

4 Read the introduction again. Complete the sentences with one word in each gap.

1 Dervla Murphy is a travel _____ .

2 She is from _____ .

3 She always travels by _____ on her trips.

4 *Full Tilt* is a book about a journey she made in 1965 from _____ to _____ .

5 Roz is the name of her _____ .

FULL TILT – DUNKIRK TO DELHI BY BICYCLE

INTRODUCTION

Most people's idea of the perfect holiday is chilling out at a good beach resort or perhaps going on a tour and doing some sightseeing. Not Irish writer Dervla Murphy. Murphy went travelling all over the world alone starting in the 1950s and wrote about her experiences. She is still travelling and having adventures! Murphy loves to get off the beaten track and meet the locals, and often makes friends with them. Luckily, she doesn't mind roughing it and she's slept in some pretty amazing places!

On this trip in 1965, she travelled thousands of kilometres from Dunkirk (France) to Delhi (India) on her bicycle, Roz. At this point in the trip, Murphy is in the mountains in Pakistan and she is with a group of Afghan traders who are travelling by camel caravan.

5 Find and <u>underline</u> these food and drink words in the text on this page. What do they mean? Write the words under the correct pictures.

[chicken stew   goat's meat   lentils   thyme]

1 _____

2 _____

3 _____

4 _____

6 Read the text and match the sentences 1–7 to the gaps in the story a–g.

1 After lunch of bread and chicken, I left my friends.

2 I was wakened by the sun coming over the mountain tops – such beauty!

3 Then the rain came so forcefully that you can't imagine it if you haven't seen it.

4 I met another Afghan camel caravan this evening and am staying with them tonight.

5 Fortunately the animal's owner expected it and caught me.

6 They told me they came from Delhi and were camping on the banks of the River Kaghan.

7 At last I'm really back to civilisation.

7 Read the text again and tick (✓) true, cross (✗) false, or write (?) if there is no information in the text.

1 The author slept near a fire with a group of people from Afghanistan.

2 The Afghans thought it was very funny when she fell off the camel.

3 When she met the English people they were more astonished than she was.

4 In her experience, most people she has met have not been very kind or generous.

5 The author and the Afghans both tried out the tips they were given.

6 In Abbottabad, after she had had a bath, the author went to arrange for some new clothes to be made.

7 She took her bicycle to have the brakes checked because she had used them a lot recently.

NARAN, 23 June

We had an excellent supper of goat's meat grilled over a wood-fire and lentils and bread. I slept well, in a circle of Afghans around a fire which we kept going all night. ᵃ___ The soft, bright green of grass, the dark green of the tall pine trees, the bright green of the nearby river, the light blue of the sky and the white of glaciers between mountain tops. While the breakfast water was boiling, I was given my camel ride – very short and not fun. One, the camel knelt down, two I sat on the saddle, three, the camel stood up, four the camel took one step, five I fell off. ᵇ___ . I'm sure there are ways of not falling off, but my Pushto* wasn't good enough to follow the owner's instructions.

After breakfast, two men were going on another cloth-selling expedition to three tiny mountain villages up in the mountains, and on invitation I accompanied them. We used mules for the steep rocky paths of the forest. ᶜ___ I tried to give them a present, but of course they refused.

There was an amusing incident today. I turned a corner and saw a group of four unmistakably English people walking towards me. I was surprised, but not as surprised as they were when they saw a European female coming towards them on a bicycle from the wild north. They stopped to solve the mystery. ᵈ___ Mrs Haddow invited me to stop off at their camp for some food and to stay with them in Delhi. The further I travel, the more I become aware of the extraordinary generosity and kindness that exists in the world.

*Pushto – a language in Afghanistan

KAGHAN VALLEY, 24 June

ᵉ___ It's wonderful how hospitable these people are – they saw me passing and waved to me to stop and have bread and tea with them. They make much nicer bread than the locals and drink their tea out of bowl, exactly as we have it in Ireland – strong and milky.

KAWAI, 25 June

The Afghans and I exchanged tips last night. I told them that thyme added to their goat or chicken stew would taste delicious and they told me that bark* of the walnut tree, slightly wet, was better than a toothbrush and toothpaste. They loved the wild thyme in last night's stew and I loved the walnut bark, it leaves your teeth brilliantly white.

ABBOTTABAD, 27 June

ᶠ___ It took nearly two hours in the bathroom to get looking like an ordinary citizen instead of a tribeswoman! I dressed in Pakistani costume after my bath and then went to the bazaar to get some clothes made.

The monsoon† seems to have arrived. I saw my first electric storm this evening and it was so beautiful I couldn't take my eyes off the sky for a moment. ᵍ___ Roz has gone for a brakes-check – the brakes were almost useless today after all the use they've had on the mountains in the past few weeks.

* bark – the outside part of a tree
† monsoon – the rainy season

something different

61

Dealing with unexpected problems

1 **Put the words in order to make sentences.**

Kate: I want to exchange this jumper, but I haven't got a receipt.

Assistant: anything/receipt./without a/can't/afraid/exchange/I

¹ I'm _afraid I can't exchange_
anything without a receipt.

Kate: I understand that but the receipt was in my bag which was stolen.

Assistant: very/but I'm/sorry,/there's/nothing/do./I can/afraid

² I'm _____
_____

Kate: a receipt./right?/exchange anything/without/Is that

³ So you won't _____
_____
_____

Assistant: Yes. That's right.

Kate: showed/it/if I/the/police report?/help/you

⁴ Would _____
_____

Assistant: I'm afraid not. The police report isn't proof of purchase.

Kate: but/sorry/that's/I/think/fair./don't

⁵ I'm _____
_____

Assistant: I realise you don't think it's fair but I'm afraid it's our company policy.

Kate: I/manager?/don't you/suggestion?/your/make/Why/ask/a

⁶ Can _____
_____

Assistant: I suppose I could ask her. Could you wait one moment, please.

A description of an event

2 **Match the questions 1–5 to the answers a–e.**

1 Why did you go to the event?
2 How was the event organised?
3 How did you spend your time at the event?
4 What was the best part of the event?
5 Would you recommend the event?

a I went to two talks, I spoke to a careers officer and I found out about different companies that want to employ young people.

b Because I wanted to find out more about different jobs.

c Yes. I thought it was well organised and it gave me plenty to think about.

d Being able to talk to careers advisers. They can give you lots of useful information.

e The event was divided into three areas: 1 talks and presentations, 2 careers officers, 3 company area.

3 **Write the second sentence so it means the same as the first using the correct word below. There are two extra words.**

[
eloquent   various   annual   burning
experienced ✓   recreational   fascinating
informative
]

1 The careers advisers have done it many times before.
   The careers advisers are very experienced.

2 We listened to a presenter who was very good at speaking.
   We listened to _____

3 The exhibition contained a lot of information.
   The exhibition was _____

4 The conference happens every year.
   It is _____

5 There were several different films you could watch.
   There were _____

6 I thought the talk about new jobs was very interesting.
   I thought the talk about new jobs was
   _____

Use of English

Synonyms and antonyms

1 Complete the sentences with the synonyms of the words in CAPITALS. Choose from the box below.

> soft   clever   spicy   elegant ✓
> affectionate   warm

1 You should wear _elegant_ clothes to that restaurant.   SMART
2 She made some _____ comments about the film.   SMART
3 We had ten days of very _____ weather last October.   HOT
4 The curry was incredibly _____ . They must have used some spices I don't know.   HOT
5 The steaks were excellent, _____ and juicy.   TENDER
6 She gave me a(n) _____ and loving smile. TENDER

2 Match the pairs of adjectives with the correct antonyms from the box.

> light ✓   delicate   stale   cool
> processed   poor ✓   weak   mild

1 **a** a *rich* man   a ___poor___ man
   b *rich* food   ___light___ food
2 **a** *warm* weather   _____ weather
   b a *hot* taste   a _____ taste
3 **a** *fresh* food   _____ food
   b *fresh* bread   _____ bread
4 **a** a *strong* man   a _____ man
   b a *strong* smell   a _____ smell

3 Complete the pairs of opposites with the correct antonyms below

> cold   easy   fatty   overweight
> soft ✓   tough

1 a *hard* bed   a ___soft___ bed
2 a *hard* task   a(n) _____ task
3 *lean* meat   _____ meat
4 a *lean* person   a(n) _____ person
5 *tender* meat   _____ meat
6 a *tender* smile   a _____ smile

Exam tasks

Multiple-choice cloze

4 Choose the best word a, b or c to complete the gaps in the text.

> **Cookery Blogs**
>
> **Simon's cooking**
> Posted Tue 27 Jan 14.50 GMT
>
> My friend Simon is learning to cook and he invited three of us to dinner. It was no [1] _easy_ task for him, because we all like different things. I like [2] _____ , creamy dishes. My girlfriend Emily prefers very [3] _____ food. Simon's girlfriend Katy only likes mild-tasting things. Well, the Indian dish Simon cooked for us was so [4] _____ and spicy that Katy couldn't finish it. It was also so [5] _____ and creamy that Emily later went on a diet for a week. I loved it! Anyway, we all think it's great Simon's learning to cook.

1 (a) easy   **b** soft   **c** hard
2 **a** rich   **b** wealthy   **c** expensive
3 **a** cheap   **b** poor   **c** light
4 **a** warm   **b** boiling   **c** hot
5 **a** rich   **b** lean   **c** overweight

Banked cloze

5 Complete the text with the words below. There is one extra word.

> lean   elegant ✓   processed   scruffy
> strong   tender   thin

> **47 Comments**
>
> Posted Thur 29 Jan 18.40 GMT
>
> **A restaurant to avoid!**
> My family decided to check out the new restaurant in Brampton Street, which is supposed to be French and very [1] _elegant_ . Mum told us to wear smart clothes. We all did, except Tim, who wore his [2] _____ old jeans and a T-shirt. I ordered a '[3] _____ steak with freshly grilled seasonal vegetables'. Well, the steak was so tough that it was difficult to bite into it and the vegetables were all [4] _____ . Mum asked specially for [5] _____ meat, and what she got was so fatty that she couldn't eat it. At the end we were served some cheese which had a very [6] _____ smell. The nicest part of the evening was going to our favourite small café afterwards for coffee and cake!

Reading

True/False

1 Read the pairs of sentences below. Write = if they mean the same and ≠ if they don't.

1 When I was staying in Budapest, my host let me use his bike.

   ☒ I wasn't allowed to make use of my host's bicycle in Budapest.

2 It's better not to travel in a large group if you want to get to know the local people.

   ☐ You're unlikely to meet the local people unless you travel alone or in a small group.

3 Every time I travel to another country, I try some new dish.

   ☐ I have experimented with new kinds of food only on a few of my trips.

4 They offered to pay us for giving them a lift.

   ☐ They wanted to give us money for the ride.

Exam TIP

In an extended level exam, the information in the text may be expressed in different words from those that are used in the exam questions. Look out for synonyms for key words and alternative structures that express the same thing.

2 Read the shorter extract. Tick (✓) true, cross (✗) false or write (?) if there is no information. For the true sentences, <u>underline</u> the synonyms or near synonyms in the text and the question that helped you to identify the answer.

1 ☒ Few capital cities in Africa have international-style hotels.

2 ☐ You won't be able to see much unless you're prepared to stay in simple conditions.

3 ☐ Hotels in the countryside are usually clean.

4 ☐ In rural hotels in Africa you may be allowed to bring your bike into your room.

3 Read a longer extract from the same book. Tick (✓) true, cross (✗) false or write (?) if there is no information in the text.

1 ☐ If you arrive in an African village in the evening, you may be invited to stay with the chief's wife and children.

2 ☐ You should offer money in exchange for accommodation.

3 ☐ The usual way to take a bath is using a bucket of water.

4 ☐ People in Africa bathe often.

5 ☐ In very dry areas of the country people wash once a week.

6 ☐ You should never use drinking water to wash your hands.

7 ☐ If you want a drink of water, always drink from a cup hanging near the water container.

8 ☐ Cultural sensitivity is shown by being careful not to waste water.

ACCOMMODATION IN AFRICA

If you choose to visit Africa by flying from capital to capital, you can stay in international-style, four- and five-star hotels every night. If you want to see rural areas, you will find that the choice of accommodation is much more limited and you will have to accept basic facilities. Most hotels in the countryside offer simple small rooms with one double bed. There may be no electricity, hot water or modern toilets. On the plus side, those hotels will often let you put your bicycle in the room for the night, where it will be a lot safer.

STAYING IN AN AFRICAN VILLAGE

If you are in a village at nightfall there may be no hotel available. To accommodate you the chief's wife and children may give up their beds for the night and stay with relatives. Compensating a village for its hospitality can be difficult and requires planning ahead. Generally people are uncomfortable if you offer them money and will refuse to take it. This is the ideal time to give gifts: pens, pins, postcards or stamps from home, T-shirts, maps, calendars, soap, batteries, books or whatever seems appropriate.

If you find accommodation in a rural area with a bath tub or shower you have found the exception, not the rule. If showers are not available, the bath will most likely come in the form of a bucket of water, a bar of soap and directions to the bath house. The water may be heated. In most areas, Africans take at least one bath, and often two baths a day and they offer the same opportunity to guests. The exception to the daily bath seems to be in the very driest regions. Remember that water is precious in the African countryside. If you want to wash your hands, DO NOT stick them in the first jug, pan or bucket of water you see. It may be drinking water. If you want to use it to wash, look for a glass or cup hanging nearby. Use this to dip water. Don't put the cup on the ground. And don't put your skin or the handle of the cup in the water. In short, it is a major mistake to pollute the drinking water supply.

Taking a bucket bath may also require some cultural sensitivity. The bucket of water which gives you a bath may have to be carried a quarter of a mile or more. You should be able to take a whole bath, including washing your hair, with one bucket of water – with practice this can be reduced to half a bucket.

If you get tired of the demands of country life, there are taxis and roads to the cities and the comfort and privacy of western-style hotels.

Listening

Multiple-choice

4 (10) **Listen to the beginning of an interview with an Italian chef. Choose the best answer.**

Why did Armando come to work on a Greek island?
a Because he won a competition.
b Because he likes kitesurfing.
c He wanted to be in a warmer climate.

5 **Match the explanations 1–2 below to the two *wrong* answers in exercise 4.**

1 He got interested in this *after* he had moved to Naxos.
2 This happened *earlier* and it had no connection with moving to the island.

6 (11) **Listen and choose the best answers.**

1 How is professional cooking different from cooking at home?
  a It's a more relaxing activity.
  b It requires you to work at a high speed.
  c If you ruin a customer's meal, it's dangerous.

2 What is the most dangerous thing in a professional kitchen?
  a the oven   **b** boiling water   **c** other people

3 Armando most enjoys the moments when
  a he stops noticing the passing of time.
  b the waiters take away the last dishes.
  c customers say how much they liked the food.

4 According to Armando, without which of the following would a chef's life be very hard?
  a the ability to multi-task
  b a clean kitchen
  c a love of cooking and working with people

5 On the whole, what is Armando's attitude to his job?
  a He finds it too exhausting.
  b He does it as it allows him to travel.
  c He really likes it.

self-assessment test 3

Vocabulary & Grammar

1 ~~Cross out~~ the word or phrase that you cannot use with the word in bold.

1. **strong** smell/~~course~~/flavour
2. **pick up** English/rubbish/nightlife
3. **release** an album/a hit single/a gig
4. **the audience** acts/claps/cheers
5. **send off** the application/the contest/the player
6. mashed/boiled/lean **potatoes**
7. beaten track/package/hiking **holiday**
8. **work out** the solution/suspense/at the gym
9. **the audience sits in** the dressing rooms/ the stalls/the circle

/8

2 Complete the sentences with one word in each gap.

1. Would you prefer a hotel with full b_oard_ or a self-catering apartment?
2. Our last stop was Pompeii, where we took a g_____ tour of the ruins.
3. Kylie Minogue is hoping to record and r'_____ her new album early next year.
4. An all-star c_____ is made up entirely of top performers.
5. The new director opted to shoot all the scenes on l_____ .
6. Many young artists try to s_____ up with a record label.

/5

3 Underline the correct words to complete the sentences.

1. It *believes/is believed* that the first mechanical calculating device was the abacus.
2. Do you know where *the post office is/ is the post office?*
3. She burst into tears, *which/what* upset me.
4. You need to add *a little/a few* more curry powder.
5. He is now *interviewed/being interviewed* by the police.
6. Diego Maradona, *who/that* used to play for Argentina, is widely regarded as one of the greatest footballers of all time.
7. You can see that there was *a great deal/ a large number* of care taken in these scenes.

/6

4 Correct the mistakes in the sentences.

1. Breakfast will serve from eight till ten.
   Breakfast _will be served_ from eight till ten.
2. With who did you go to the cinema?
   _____ you go the cinema _____ ?
3. It is says that we use only ten percent of our brain.
   _____ that we use only ten percent of our brain.
4. She bought only a little clothes.
   She bought _____ .
5. A screwdriver is a tool, who tightens or loosens screws.
   A screwdriver is a tool _____ .
6. Can you remind me how much did you pay for the ticket?
   Can you remind me _____ the ticket?
7. Two people have arrested in connection with the crime.
   Two people _____ in connection with the crime.

/6

5 Complete the email with the correct answer a, b, c or d.

☒

Hi Lizzy,

All the best from Paris! Yes, we are in France. Tom came ¹ _a_ with the idea of going back to the place ² ___ we met. Very romantic, don't you think? The journey was a bit of a nightmare though. We ³ ___ off quite early to make a seven a.m. flight from Gatwick. We thought we had ⁴ ___ of time. But there was an accident on the motorway and we ⁵ ___ onto a different route. We got to the airport two minutes before the check-in deadline only to learn that our flight ⁶ ___ due to a security alert! In the end, we managed to get seats on the plane the following day.

1 a up ✓	b for	c off	d into
2 a which	b where	c that	d when
3 a set	b got	c left	d made
4 a quite	b deal	c lot	d plenty
5 a diverted		c were diverting	
b were diverted		d have been diverted	
6 a cancelled		c had been cancelled	
b had cancelled		d has been cancelled	

/5

Listening

6 ⟨12⟩ **Listen to the conversation at the travel agency. Choose the correct answer a, b, c or d.**

1 Jack's father paid the travel agency for
   a a self-catering holiday.
   b a sightseeing tour.
   c a five-star city break.
   d a package holiday.

2 Jack's father complains that
   a he had to pay extra for a fly-ski shuttle.
   b transport was not included in the price.
   c he was forced to take a taxi to the hotel.
   d a travel rep didn't pick him up from the airport.

3 Jack thinks that
   a his father is exaggerating.
   b the mountain view was disappointing.
   c they could do with a bigger room.
   d the travel agency is at fault.

4 They were both disappointed in the food at the hotel because of
   a the high price.
   b the lack of variety.
   c the low nutritional value.
   d the overall quality.

5 During the conversation, Jack's father sounds
   a apologetic.   c understanding.
   b sarcastic.   d astonished.

/5

Communication

7 **Complete the sentences describing trends and statistics with one word in each gap.**

1 A t_iny_ minority of teenagers chose cucumbers as their favourite vegetable.

2 Ninety-five p _ _ _ _ _ _ of my school friends have a mobile phone.

3 There has been a s _ _ _ _ _ fall in mortality from cancer – about two–three percent per year.

4 The statistics p _ _ _ _ that women live longer than men.

5 About three-q _ _ _ _ _ _ _ of our listeners wanted more classical music.

6 The rules of the game have stayed pretty much the s _ _ _ throughout the years.

7 The vast m _ _ _ _ _ _ _ of voters are in favour of economic reforms.

8 More and m _ _ _ people use the internet for online dating.

9 Obesity rates have risen d _ _ _ _ _ _ _ _ _ _ in the US.

/8

8 **Complete the dialogue with the sentences a–i below.**

Jack: ¹ _e_

Bus driver: That's €2.50 please.

Jack: ² _____

Bus driver: I'm sorry but I can't accept a twenty-euro note.

Jack: ³ _____

Bus driver: That's right. You need to have change to buy a ticket on the bus.

Jack: ⁴ _____

Bus driver: I'm afraid the fare is €2.50, not two euros.

Jack: ⁵ _____

Bus driver: I'm afraid not. You'll need to change your money in a shop and catch the next bus.

Jack: ⁶ _____

Bus driver: What is it?

Jack: ⁷ _____

Bus driver: OK, that's €1.80 but you can only go to the central station not to the town centre.

Jack: ⁸ _____

a But I can't wait for the next bus – I'm in a hurry. Can I make a suggestion?

b Is there anything I can do to resolve this?

c So you don't want to sell me a ticket. Is that right?

d Here you are.

e Return to the town centre, please. ✓

g That's fine. I'll walk from there.

h I understand that but I only have a twenty-euro note and a two-euro coin.

i What if you sell me a cheaper ticket?

/7

Marks	
Vocabulary & Grammar	/30 marks
Listening	/5 marks
Communication	/15 marks
Total:	/50 marks

Vocabulary

Qualities of mind

1 Complete each sentence with three words or the phrases below.

> independent ✓   interpersonal skills
> quick-thinking   learning languages
> multi-tasking   spatial skills   verbal skills
> badly organised   processing information

1 She's ...   *independent*
_____   _____

2 He's good at ...   _____
_____   _____

3 They've got good ...   _____
_____   _____

2 Complete the tables with the adjectives.

Verb	Adjective
practise	1 *practical*
imagine	2 _____
analyse	3 _____

Noun	Adjective
art	4 _____
impulse	5 _____
empathy	6 _____

3 Complete the sentences with words and phrases from exercises 1 and 2.

1 Richard's very *impulsive* . He sometimes acts without thinking.

2 _____ is the ability to do several things at the same time.

3 Bill's excellent at Maths and Science. He's got an _____ mind and he's good at _____ .

4 This school is a good place for _____ students: there's a well-equipped art room.

5 In dangerous situations, it's good to be _____ , as you may need to react at once.

Grammar

Articles

4 (*) Match the pairs of sentences with the correct response a or b.

1 Can you give me an umbrella?   *b*

2 Can you give me the umbrella?   *a*

a But where is it?

b Do you want the red one or the grey one?

3 I'm looking for the yellow jumper.   ___

4 I'm looking for a yellow jumper.   ___

a All the jumpers are over here.

b We haven't got yellow. Orange, perhaps?

5 Andy's bought a black bike.   ___

6 Andy's bought the black bike.   ___

a He's been admiring it for a month.

b Tell me what make it is; that's more interesting than the colour.

5 (**) Underline the correct option *a*, *an*, *the* or no article (Ø).

1 I loved *a/the* Italian meal we had last Saturday.

2 I bought *a/the* skirt and *a/Ø* pair of shoes – *a/the* skirt is white and *the/Ø* shoes are red.

3 It's not easy to define *the/Ø* intelligence.

4 Our university has excellent facilities for *the/Ø* disabled.

5 There's *an/the* old castle on *a/the* left side of the river.

6 *An/The* elephant is *a/the* largest land animal in the world.

6 (**) Match the sentence beginnings 1–5 with the best endings a–e.

1 Our children go to school

2 Our children go to the school

3 I bought a camera

4 I bought the camera

5 I like strawberries

6 I like the strawberries

a at the end of our street.

b from my grandad's garden.

c four days a week instead of five.

d in order to photograph animals.

e more than any other kind of fruit.

f you recommended.

7 (✱✱✱) Complete the conversation with *a, an, the* or no article (Ø).

Oliver: I'd like to buy ¹ _Ø_ souvenir for Natalie.

Josh: I didn't know she liked ² ____ souvenirs.

Oliver: Normally she doesn't, but, you know, we've only just become engaged …

Josh: Right. ³ ____ love is a mysterious thing. And ⁴ ____ lovers can behave strangely. Anyway, there's ⁵ ____ souvenir shop on ⁶ ____ left side of the road as you walk to ⁷ ____ port.

(Later)

Oliver: I didn't really like any of ⁸ ____ things in that shop. Could you direct me to ⁹ ____ different one?

Josh: That is ¹⁰ ____ only souvenir shop in town. It's ¹¹ ____ small town, you know.

Grammar Plus

8 (✱✱✱) Complete the sentences with *the* or no article (Ø).

1 The highest peak in the Pyrenees is called _Ø_ Aneto.

2 September is a good time to visit ____ Majorca, the largest of ____ Balearic Islands.

3 Twelve European countries lie on ____ Mediterranean Sea.

4 ____ Ganges, the holy river of Hindus, flows into ____ Indian Ocean.

5 When John Speke reached ____ Lake Victoria in 1858, he was convinced he'd found the source of ____ Nile.

6 ____ Ben Nevis, the highest mountain in ____ British Isles, is located at the western end of ____ Grampian Mountains in Scotland.

Grammar reference

Articles

Indefinite article

We use *a/an* before singular countable nouns

- when we talk about a person or thing for the first time:

*I've got **a** dog and two cats. The dog's name is Basil.*

- when we talk about one of many things or people – it is not important which one exactly:

*Have you got **an** umbrella to lend me?* (any umbrella)
*I'd like **a** piece of cheesecake, please.* (It doesn't matter which piece.)

Definite article

We use *the* before singular and plural nouns

- when we mention somebody or something again:

*I've got a cat. **The** cat's name is Timmy.*

- when we talk about a concrete person or thing (in singular or plural), and the listener knows which person/thing we mean because it's described by the clause of phrase following it:

***The** boys in my youth group are very nice.*

- when there is only one of the things we talk about or it is unique in that context:

***the** sun, **the** Pope* (only one)
*Could you pass me **the** salt?* (the salt which is on the table)

- when the adjective used before the noun makes it unique:

*It was difficult to get used to driving on **the** left side of the road.* (There is only one left side.)

Other adjectives making nouns unique: *right, only, next, last, latest, first.*

- before a singular noun when we generalise:

***The** lion is a magnificent animal.*

- with certain adjectives to generalise about groups of people:

***the** poor = poor people generally, **the** disabled = disabled people generally*

- before the names of rivers (***the** Danube*), seas (***the** Black Sea*) and oceans (***the** Atlantic*), mountain ranges (***the** Alps*) and island groups (***the** Canary Islands*).

No article

We do not use articles

- before plural nouns when we talk about them in general or mention them for the first time:

(NOT ~~The~~) *Adolescents go through many physical and emotional changes.*
(NOT ~~The~~) *Rabbits make good family pets.*

- before uncountable nouns when we talk about something in general:

(NOT ~~The~~) *Love is one of the most important feelings.*

- with names of lakes (*Lake Erie, Lake Superior*), individual mountains (*Mount Everest, Mount Etna*) and individual islands (*Sicily, Bermuda*).

- with school/university unless we refer to a particular one:

She's going to (NOT ~~the~~) *university next year.*

Vocabulary

Describing people

1 Complete the information about the three 'Superheroes' with the words below.

> autistic backwards claims climb
> extraordinary ✓ gift incredible
> memorise ropes twist

Alain Robert, the man they call 'the real Spiderman', has an [1] _extraordinary_ ability to [2] _____ buildings without [3] _____ .

Daniel Browning Smith, the 'Rubber-boy', can bend and [4] _____ his body in [5] _____ ways. He can bend over [6] _____ and turn his head 180 degrees!

Daniel Tammet, who is [7] _____ , has an incredible [8] _____ for languages. He [9] _____ to be able to speak twelve. In 2004, he managed to [10] _____ a sequence of 22,500 numbers.

Grammar

Expressing ability: *can, could, be able to*

2 (✱) Read the pairs of sentences below. Write = if they mean the same and ≠ if they don't.

1 My brother Charlie can swim very well.
   - ☐= My brother Charlie is able to swim very well.

2 At the age of five he could swim to the other side of the lake.
   - ☐ At the age of five he managed to swim to the other side of the lake.

3 The rescue team succeeded in rescuing the climbers.
   - ☐ The rescue team were able to rescue the climbers.

4 The rescue team were unable to reach the climbers.
   - ☐ The rescue team managed to reach the climbers.

3 (✱) Underline the correct form.

1 Some day all people may *can/be able to* speak several languages.

2 Peggy *managed to/succeeded in* learning to use the new software in a week.

3 Frank *was unable to/didn't succeed in* complete his university course.

4 If we create a more equal society, more people *can/will be able to* develop their talents in the future.

5 Fortunately, we *could/were able to* find somewhere to stay and our problem was solved.

4 (✱✱) Complete the sentences with the correct form of *be able to*.

1 I'd like to _____ dance the salsa.

2 I hope more people _____ use the internet in the future.

3 She _____ ski since she was six years old.

4 If you turn into that street, you should _____ see the university.

5 If I knew how this machine works, I _____ repair it myself.

6 I _____ reach Paul on the phone since yesterday. (*negative*)

5 (✳✳) Complete the sentences with the best answer, a, b or c. Sometimes two options are possible.

1 Marta ___ write at the age of four.
   a ☑ could
   b ☑ was able to
   c ☐ managed to

2 I hope in the future people ___ travel to other planets.
   a ☐ could
   b ☐ will be able to
   c ☐ succeed in

3 We ___ get home by midnight.
   a ☐ were able to
   b ☐ managed to
   c ☐ succeeded in

4 Ellen ___ find the information she needed.
   a ☐ didn't succeed in
   b ☐ wasn't able to
   c ☐ was unable to

5 Chris ___ cycling 180 kilometres in one day.
   a ☐ succeeded in
   b ☐ managed to
   c ☐ was able to

6 Complete the second sentence so that it means the same as the first. Use the words in CAPITALS.

1 The children managed to find the hidden door.   ABLE
   The children _were able to find_ the hidden door.

2 Helen managed to climb the ten highest peaks in the Alps.   SUCCEED
   Helen _____ the ten highest peaks in the Alps.

3 After the accident the man couldn't speak for a year.   UNABLE
   After the accident the man _____ for a year.

4 Vera can dance for five hours non-stop.   ABLE
   Vera _____ for five hours non-stop.

5 We couldn't buy everything we needed.   MANAGE
   We _____ everything we needed.

6 The expedition failed to reach the South Pole.   SUCCEED
   The expedition _____ the South Pole.

Grammar reference

Expressing ability

Ability in the present

To talk about abilities in the present, we use

- *can, be able to*:

She **can/is able to** speak Japanese very well.
They **can't/aren't able to** use the new software yet.

Ability in the past

To talk about abilities in the past, we use

- *could, was/were able to* to express a general ability:

When I was six, I **could/was able to** dive very well. (This was possible for me at any time, whenever I wanted.)

- *was/were able to* to express a specific action:

They **were able to** finish their project before the deadline. (They actually did it.)

In negative sentences we use

- *couldn't* and *wasn't/weren't able to* for expressing a specific action. We can also use *be unable to*:

I came across her telephone number but I **couldn't/wasn't able to** find her email address.
Unfortunately, we **were unable to** process your order at this time.

- *managed to* + verb and *succeeded in* + *ing* to express a specific action, which was difficult to achieve:

I **managed to** learn all his poems by heart.
He **succeeded in** persuading his mum to let him go.

Can is used only in the present or in the past (*could*).

To express ability in all other forms and tenses, we use

- *be able to*:

Will you be able to help me tomorrow after dinner?
I'd love **to be able to** spend more time with my friends.
We **haven't been able to** get through to them yet.

Vocabulary

Health

1 Complete the table.

Verb	Noun	Adjective
donate	1 _donor_	
treat	2 _____	treatable
3 _____	suffering	
cure	4 _____	
5 _____	6 _____	caring/careful
	7 _____	ill
	8 _____ surgeon	surgical
	9 _____	obese
10 _____	damage	damaged/ damaging
	11 _____	therapeutic

2 Complete the sentences with the correct form of the word in brackets.

1 James is suffering from heart _failure_ (fail), he urgently needs a _____ (transplant). We have found an organ _____ (donate), now we just need a good _____ (surgery) to do the operation.

2 Many people damage their _____ (healthy) by eating too much. I'm a doctor and I have two patients at the moment who are both _____ (obesity).

3 He is seriously _____ (illness), but we can keep him _____ (life) until we can find a _____ (cure).

4 We have very good state-funded health _____ (careful) in this country. The _____ (treat) is very good.

5 People usually _____ (sufferer) from an _____ (ill) at some point in their lives but many diseases are _____ (cure) nowadays.

6 Would you consider using an alternative _____ (therapeutic), such as acupuncture, to _____ (treatable) your back pain?

Listening

3 ⟨13⟩ You will hear six interviews about organ donation. Match the speakers 1–6 with their opinions a–g. There is one extra opinion.

1 ☐ Justin   4 ☐ Mark
2 ☐ Connie   5 ☐ Beth
3 ☐ Sarah   6 ☐ Alex

a thinks it's awful that people who are sick have to wait a long time for a donor.

b believes that everyone should become a donor because it's the right thing to do.

c agrees that organ donation should be obligatory by law.

d says that organ transplantation is not a good idea.

e thinks organ donation should be a person's own choice.

f says there should be more campaigns to encourage people to become donors.

g thinks there would be more crime if organ donation was obligatory.

4 ⟨13⟩ Listen to the interviews again. Tick (✓) true, cross (✗) false or write (?) if there is no information.

1 ☐ Justin thinks the doctor's suggestion will encourage people to become donors.

2 ☐ Connie has never thought about organ donation being obligatory before.

3 ☐ Sarah thinks we'll need organ donors for a long time in the future.

4 ☐ Mark has donated one of his kidneys to his son.

5 ☐ Beth has already taken part in campaigns to get more people to become donors.

6 ☐ Alex has decided to become a donor.

Reading

5 Read the text on page 73 quickly and complete the table with the words below.

> Profession: doctor electrical engineer physicist
> Nationality: Canadian German Scottish
> Discovery: pacemaker penicillin X-rays

People	Professions	Nationalities	Discoveries
Wilhelm Roentgen	_____	_____	_____
Alexander Fleming	_____	_____	_____
John Hopps	_____	_____	_____

'Lucky accidents' in medicine

Around the world an astonishing £80 billion a year is spent annually researching and developing new medical treatments and cures for illnesses. Despite this, only about twenty new medicines are discovered each year. More surprising still is the fact that many of the most important scientific developments were made accidentally. Lucky accidents, it seems, play an unexpectedly important role in medical history.

One famous example of a lucky accident is the discovery of X-rays by the German physicist Wilhelm Roentgen in 1859. He discovered the technology by chance while he was experimenting with cathode ray tubes and a screen. He detected a new type of invisible rays which could pass through cardboard (which the cathode rays could not) to produce an image on a screen on the other side of the room. He realised these rays could be used to take pictures of the inside of the body. He called the new rays 'X-rays', 'X' meaning unknown. Two weeks after his discovery he managed to take his first picture – of the inside of his wife's hand. Now, there are X-ray machines in all hospitals and, of course, in airports, too.

Sixty years later, in 1928, Alexander Fleming, a Scottish doctor in the research department at St Mary's Hospital in London, had another lucky accident. Although he was a brilliant researcher, his lab was often untidy. One day he returned from holiday to discover that a mysterious mould had destroyed some bacteria samples he had accidentally left out on a bench. Fleming investigated the mould further and found it could destroy many types of bacteria. He called the mould 'penicillin' and continued to investigate it. This work later led to the development of the first antibiotics, drugs which destroy dangerous bacteria and save millions of lives every day.

The pacemaker, a device that keeps people with heart problems alive, is yet another example of an important medical discovery that was made accidentally. When the Canadian electrical engineer John Hopps was experimenting with ways to treat people who were suffering from hypothermia* he discovered that a heart that had stopped could be started again mechanically or electrically. From this discovery, Hopps developed and built the first pacemaker in 1950. The early models were too big to implant in the human body, but by 1958 scientists were able to make the device small enough. Nowadays, implanting a pacemaker is routine surgery. Hopps lived long enough to benefit from his invention and had his own pacemaker implant in 1984.

* hypothermia – a serious medical condition in which the body temperature is very low

6 Read the text and put the events for each discovery in the correct order.

1 Roentgen
a ☐ Roentgen took his first picture of the inside of a body.
b ☐ People started using the machines in hospitals.
c ☐ Roentgen started doing some experiments with different kinds of rays.
d ☐ Roentgen realised the rays could be used to create images of the inside of a body.
e ☐ Roentgen discovered some invisible rays.

2 Fleming
a ☐ Fleming went away on holiday.
b ☐ Fleming created some bacteria samples.
c ☐ Fleming investigated the mould.
d ☐ Fleming discovered the bacteria samples had been destroyed by a mould.
e ☐ Antibiotics were developed as a result of Fleming's work.

3 Hopps
a ☐ Hopps built the first pacemaker.
b ☐ Hopps had a pacemaker fitted in his own heart.
c ☐ It became possible to implant a pacemaker inside a human heart.
d ☐ Hopps started researching cures for hypothermia.
e ☐ Other scientists helped to develop the pacemaker.

7 Read the text again. Tick (✓) true, cross (✗) false or write (?) if there is no information in the text.

1 ☐ More money is spent on researching new medicines than on other scientific developments.
2 ☐ Roentgen was able to take a picture of the inside of the body immediately after discovering the invisible rays.
3 ☐ Fleming was working in a hospital when he discovered penicillin.
4 ☐ There are many different types of antibiotics.
5 ☐ During his experiments, Hopps discovered you could use electricity to start a heart.
6 ☐ Hopps decided to develop the pacemaker because he had heart problems.

Writing

A description of a person

1 In **paragraph 1**, say who the person is and why he/she is famous or how you know them.

2 Introduce the reason you admire him/her. Make sure it is clear how this person relates to the essay title.

3 In **paragraph 2**, describe his/her appearance. Try to use a variety of interesting adjectives to make your description livelier, for example use *slight* instead of *thin* or *intriguing* instead of *interesting*.

4 In **paragraph 3**, describe his/her character and main achievements using rich and varied language, for example use *huge/tremendous* instead of *big* or *renowned* instead of *famous*.

5 Include information about awards the person has won and what they have achieved in other areas of their life.

6 In **paragraph 4**, write your conclusion, saying what this person has taught you, how they make you feel and summarising why you admire them.

My hero

By Kate Mills

Bethany Hamilton is a surfer. She became world-famous six years ago when she lost her arm in a shark attack. However, she didn't give up surfing or her dreams of becoming a champion because of the attack and for this reason she is my personal hero.

The first thing you notice about Hamilton are her eyes and her determined expression. She is athletic-looking and very slight and has a mass of long blond hair. She's nineteen now. She looks lively and intriguing. She wears colourful, trendy clothes and she laughs a lot.

Although she nearly died in the shark attack, Hamilton got back on a surfboard again just one month later. She overcame tremendous obstacles and taught herself to surf with one arm. Not only that, she learned to surf in competitions again and she is now one of the ten best women surfers in the world. She won the 2004 ESPY sport award for Best Comeback Athlete and a special Teen Courage Award as a result. She is renowned for her courage, positive attitude and competitive spirit. Hamilton has also achieved a lot out of the water – she has her own successful business selling jewellery and environmentally-friendly shoes.

I admire Hamilton for her attitude to life. She makes me feel that it is possible to achieve anything even if you have to overcome severe problems. I think she is a terrific role model for young people and an inspiration for everyone.

Useful language

Saying why you admire someone

A person I really admire/who inspires me is …

I find his/her attitude to life inspiring because …

I think X is a fantastic/great role model because …

Describing appearance

The first thing you notice about him/her is …

He's/She's got a mass of blond hair.

He's/She's lively/slight/athletic-looking.

Describing character

One of the most interesting things about him/her is …

Talking about achievements

He/She has achieved a lot in his/her lifetime …

He/She is famous/renowned for …

1 Read the description essay. In which paragraph can you find the information a–e below? Write three details for each.

a the person's appearance

   para 2 very slight; long blonde hair, athletic

b the person's character

   _____

c a summary of her overall importance to the writer

   _____

d basic details about who the person is and why they are interesting

   _____

e more details about the person's activities and achievements

   _____

2 Find expressions in the text that have a similar meaning to the sentences below.

1 She's got fair hair.

   _____

2 She is famous for being brave.

   _____

3 She looks interesting.

   _____

4 She had big problems but she got through them.

   _____

3 Read the sentences from another essay about an inspiring person. Match the <u>underlined</u> errors in sentences a–h with the error descriptions 1–8.

1 Sp (spelling)
2 WO (word order)
3 Gr (grammar)
4 P (punctuation)
5 T (tense)
6 WW (wrong word)
7 / (word missing)
8 R (replace with more interesting word)

a She's got <u>green eyes sparkling</u>.

b Mrs Moore <u>is teacher</u> at my school.

c Although she had to start using a <u>wheelchair she</u> didn't stop teaching.

d Last year she <u>has won</u> an award for her services to the community.

e She has <u>inspried</u> me to do a sponsored run to raise money for disabled athletes.

f She is also <u>the</u> great photographer.

g She is a <u>small</u> woman.

h I admire her <u>due</u> of her positive attitude.

4 Correct the mistakes in the sentences a–h.

a *She's got sparkling green eyes.*

b _____

c _____

d _____

e _____

f _____

g _____

h _____

5 Rewrite these sentences from the notes. Replace the bold words and phrases with more interesting language.

1 I **remember** her on the dance floor at the school disco.

   I'll never forget the time when she went on the dance floor at the school disco.

2 She was really **good** at moving to the music in her wheelchair.

   _____
   _____

3 She **wears nice**, **modern clothes**.

   _____
   _____

4 I think she's a **good** role model for young people.

   _____
   _____

5 She is a **good** teacher.

   _____
   _____

6 The photos in the exhibition were **very interesting**.

   _____
   _____

6 Complete the strategies box with the words below.

[varied   first   mistakes   type ✓]

A description of a person

- Read the title and make sure you understand what [1] *type* of description you have to write.
- Make notes and organise your information into four paragraphs. Write your [2] _____ draft.
- Read your essay again. Can you improve it by using more [3] _____ language?
- Check your work carefully for different types of [4] _____ .
- Write your final draft.

7 Choose one of the tasks and write a description. Use the structure on the opposite page and the strategies in exercise 6 and ideas in the exercises to help you. Write 200–250 words.

1 Write a description of someone you know who has taught you something or inspired you to take action.

2 Write a description of a famous person who you think is a good role model for young people. In your essay say why he/she is a good role model.

Giving a speech (2)

1 Read this introduction to a talk about the teenage brain. Put the notes for the main part of the speech in the correct order 1–8.

The teen brain

Today, I'd like to talk about the teen brain. Some people say that by the time they are teenagers, young people should know what they want to do in life and they should start to specialise. In my opinion, this is not a good idea. Let me explain why …

a ☐ But, if not carry on with activities – connections disappear – lose your skills in these areas.

b ☑ Firstly – talk about what scientific research shows about teen brains.

c ☐ Means if you give up sport, music etc, – spend time lying on sofa/playing computer games – that is what brain will learn to do.

d ☐ Research shows – front part of the brain (part for organisation/planning) – not fully developed in teens.

e ☐ Sum up – teen years – time to try different things/learn new skills, not stop other things only do school work. More we use our brains – better they develop.

f ☐ Finally, – talk about time. People used to think – six years old the brain – developed. Now know brain continues to develop – teen years. The more skills we learn then, the more opportunity we give our brains to develop and grow connections that will help us during the rest of our lives.

g ☐ Secondly, abilities/skills many areas (music/dance/academic work) develop in teen years – connections grow in brain as does activities.

h ☐ However, do things often – connections become more permanent – So, what do in your teen years affects rest of your life. Meaning of this?

Answering challenging questions

2 Put the words in order to make questions and answers.

Q: [1] *What do you mean when you say* (what/mean/say) the brain continues to develop in teen years?

A: Well, [2] _____ (sound/odd), but if we do lots of different things when we're teenagers, the brain develops more.

Q: [3] _____ (surely/not believe/that/not a good idea) to specialise?

A: [4] _____ (understand/why/you/ask/that). I know many teens feel pressurised for time, so they give up hobbies. However, they shouldn't specialise. We have the rest of our lives to do that!

Q: [5] _____ (you/really/think) teens can develop their brains?

A: I know it sounds odd, but [6] _____ _____ (believe/It/true).

Q: But, [7] _____ (surely/not believe) if we stop doing sport as teenagers we can never do sport later in life?

A: [8] _____ (not exactly/I/mean). What I mean is that you should develop the ability now or it will be harder later.

Q: [9] _____ (what/mean/say) what you do in teen years affects you for the rest of your life?

A: [10] _____ (all/I/say) is that the skills we learn now will help us for the rest of our lives.

3 Use the ideas below to write three polite indirect questions and three answers about a speech.

1 Q: Why/teenagers/badly organised?
A: Part of brain/not developed

2 Q: If teenagers/spend/too much time/play computer games/what do to their brains?
A: Could limit/skills later life/computer games what brain knows/not other things

3 Q: Why so important/teenagers/do sport/if not interested?
A: General health/also set up/connections in brain/sports/for later in life

examtrainer 10

Use of English

Adjective suffixes

1 <u>Underline</u> the suffixes in the adjectives 1–6 below. Put the adjectives into the correct row of the table.

1 medic<u>al</u>   4 miserable
2 careful   5 talkative
3 careless   6 historic

suffix	
-al	*medical*
-ic	*energetic*
-ive	
-able	
-ful	
-less	

2 Form adjectives from the words below. Add them to correct row of the table above.

[energy ✓ success enthusiasm option
rely practice value use (2 adjectives)]

3 Complete the sentences with the correct form of the words in brackets.

1 Her *facial* (face) expression was difficult to interpret.
2 The final year of school can be very _____ (stress) because of exam pressure.
3 Modern medicine faces a number of _____ (ethics) problems.
4 Can you stop criticising me? I'd like some _____ (construct) comments, please.
5 The weather can be completely _____ (predict) at this time of year. Bring both light and warm clothes.
6 Amy is very _____ (art): she paints and sculpts and makes pottery, too.

4 Complete the pairs of sentences with the correct form of the words below. Use the suffixes -*ing* and -*ed*, -*ful* and -*less*.

[amaze exhaust ✓ help hope]

1 a Climbing the mountain was tiring but getting down was absolutely *exhausting* !
  b When we got home we were so *exhausted* that we went to sleep at once.
2 a The situation was _____ – there was nothing anyone could do.
  b I'm feeling quite _____ about the success of our plan; we've prepared it so well.
3 a I was lost in a foreign city with no map and no language skills, feeling completely _____ .
  b Thank you for your _____ advice.
4 a We were really _____ when we heard of the man who cycled around the world.
  b I've got some _____ news for you – you'll never guess what it is!

Exam task

Word building

5 Complete the text with the correct form of the words in brackets.

Many people believe women have weaker [1] *spatial* (space) skills than men. However, this is not true about my sister Maggie. Her sense of direction is really [2] _____ (amaze). When we were [3] _____ (enthusiasm) fourteen-year-old girl scouts, our instructor once led us into the forest and left us without a map to find our way back to the camp. Imagine how [4] _____ (surprise) he was to find us back in our tents when he returned to the camp himself. Maggie had led us back by a shorter route.

So it's not [5] _____ (surprise) that she has become a [6] _____ (success) architect. Her spatial sense is extremely [7] _____ (value) to her in her work. Her designs are original and [8] _____ (imagine) and they are also [9] _____ (practice).

8 consumer society

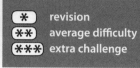
Vocabulary

Advertising

1 Label the picture with the words below.

> jingle target audience brand
> slogan logo

1 _____

2 _____

3 _____

4 _____

5 _____

2 Complete the sentences with the words below

> aimed brand campaign
> promote ✓ target

1 The company uses controversial methods to _promote_ its products.

2 They organised a huge advertising _____ in all the media, with ads on TV, on the radio and in magazines.

3 You can see men are the _____ audience of this ad. It's so focused on power and status.

4 The ad was clearly _____ at teenagers: it tried so desperately to look 'cool'.

5 I don't believe a product is necessarily better if it is a well-known _____ .

Grammar

Reported speech

3 ✱ Put the words in order to make indirect questions.

1 She asked ads/TV/whether/watched/on/I

She asked _whether I watched ads on TV_ .

2 He wanted to know seen/advertisement/had/I/latest/if/the/coffee

He wanted to know _____

_____ .

3 She asked wear/party/going/what/the/to/to/was/I

She asked _____

_____ .

4 She wanted to know my/boots/where/new/bought/had/I

She wanted to know _____

_____ .

5 He asked shopping/help/the/could/him/if/I/carry

He asked _____

_____ .

6 He wondered would/when/would/finish/ads/the/the/and/begin/film

He wondered _____

_____ .

4 ✱✱ Complete the report of the conversation with one word in each gap.

I had a strange conversation with my next door neighbour today. I was in my garden and she was in hers and suddenly she asked me [1] _if_ I'd ever tried a lipstick called *Enchantment*. I told [2] _____ that I didn't really use lipstick, but she said I'd change my mind if I tried this one. She said that she [3] _____ never used any either until she discovered this brand. She just went on talking about how wonderful it [4] _____ . I didn't really want to listen, so said I [5] _____ to go and do my homework, and she replied she [6] _____ drop in later and show it to me! I really don't want her to come at all.

5 (**) **Read the conversation. Complete the sentences with reported speech.**

Salesman: Do you like chocolate bars? But perhaps you worry that they are fattening. Well, have you ever tried *Chocosvelte*? It's the first chocolate bar that's got fewer calories than an apple. It was developed by American nutritionists specially for fashion models. And it's delicious. If you buy a pack of ten *Chocosvelte* bars now, you will get a free booklet with the *Chocosvelte* diet plan…

Lisa: Thank you, I think I'll buy one ordinary chocolate bar and some apples instead.

1 The salesman asked me *if I liked* chocolate bars.

2 He said perhaps _____ fattening.

3 He asked _____ *Chocosvelte*.

4 He told me _____ fewer calories than an apple.

5 He said _____ by American nutritionists specially for fashion models.

6 He also said _____ delicious.

7 Finally, he told me that _____ a free booklet with the *Chocosvelte* diet plan.

8 I thanked him and said _____ one ordinary chocolate bar and two apples instead.

6 (***) **Read the sentences in reported speech. Write what the people said in direct speech.**

1 The shopper said he'd left his wallet at home.
'*I've left my wallet at home*'

2 Ann told me she would have problems if I didn't help her.
'_____
_____'.

3 Peter and Alexandra said they had travelled all round South America in 2009.
'_____
_____'.

4 I asked the girl if she lived there.
'_____
_____'.

5 Ian asked what I was thinking about.
'_____
_____'.

6 Millie asked what we were going to do the following day.
'_____
_____'.

7 The teacher asked where I'd been on Monday.
'_____
_____'.

Grammar reference

Reported speech

tell and *say*

While reporting what somebody has said, we can *tell* someone *(that)* and *say (that)/say to* someone *(that)*:

He **told me** that he wanted to leave earlier.
Jane **said (that)** she didn't like the idea at all.

Tense shifts

In reported speech, we often move the original verb 'one tense back' (except for the past perfect tense and some modal verbs):

'They **haven't apologised** for their behaviour.'
He told me that they **hadn't apologised** for their behaviour.
'I **will pass** the message to Peter.'
She said she **would pass** the message to Peter.

It is not necessary to change the verb tenses in reported speech when

- we use a present simple or present perfect reporting verb:

She **says/has said** she **won't tell** you anything.

- the statement is reported soon after it was said so the situation is still relevant:

They said **it will** be sunny tomorrow. (reported on the same day)

- the reporter believes that the fact/opinion is still true:

She told me that London **is** bigger than Manchester. (still true)

Reported questions

When we report questions, we often use *ask, wonder, want to know* and change the same elements as in reported statements. We also use the same word order as in statements (the subject comes before the verb):

'**Why** did you tell John off?' → Robert wondered **why** I had told John off.

When we report *Wh-* questions, we use the same question word (*what, who, how, where, when*) as in the original question:

'**What time** are you leaving?' → He asked me **what time** I was leaving.

When we report *Yes/No* questions, we use *if* or *whether*:

'Do you fancy going shopping?' → She asked **if/whether** I fancied going shopping.
'Have you seen my new top?' → My sister wanted to know **if/whether** I had seen her new top.

Vocabulary

Shopping and money

1 Match the sentences a–f to the pictures 1–6.

a Here's your **change** and your **receipt**. ____

b And I bought a **fake** designer bag! ____

c I'll pay **in cash**. ____

d I'm afraid it's **faulty**. I'd like a **refund**, please. ____

e Shall I **wrap** them **up** for you? ____

f What a **bargain**! ____

2 Complete the conversation with the words below.

> charged   details   packaging
> receipts   secure   statement ✓

A: There's something wrong with my credit card
  ¹ _statement_ . It seems I've been ² _____ for several
  things I never bought.

B: Oh dear. Any idea how someone could have got hold of
  your credit card ³ _____ ?

A: Well, I bought some things online recently. Remember the
  glass figures that arrived in so much ⁴ _____ ?

B: I do. Was it a ⁵ _____ website?

A: Yes … At least I thought so. Well, I'll have to call the bank
  and discuss this. Now where have I put all the ⁶ _____ ?

Grammar

Reporting verbs

3 (✱) Complete the sentences with the verbs below.

> admitted   apologised ✓
> claimed   denied   offered
> persuaded   warned

1 Jane _apologised_ to everyone
  for being late.

2 Greg _____ Tom to lend him
  fifty euros.

3 My sister _____ to help me
  choose a new dress.

4 The cashier _____ stealing
  the money, but he _____
  leaving the safe open.

5 The policeman _____ us
  that it is illegal to own fake
  designer goods.

6 The saleswoman _____ that
  the shampoo would make my
  hair thicker.

4 (✱✱) Match the beginnings of
the sentences 1–6 with the
endings a–f.

1 John promised

2 Gail insisted on

3 Danny suggested

4 Bill begged

5 The salesman assured me

6 Rachel blamed

a Alice not to leave him.

b going to see the new Bond film
  that evening.

c her sister for the
  misunderstanding.

d paying for the coffee.

e that the watch was genuine.

f to love Sheila forever.

5 (✱✱✱) Complete the reported speech sentences with the correct form of the verbs below.

> accuse   advise ✓   explain
> urge   refuse   threaten

1 The doctor said to Mrs Leigh, 'You should get more sleep.'
  The doctor _advised Mrs Leigh to get more sleep_ .

2 'I'll take you to court!' the angry customer said to the shopkeeper.
  The angry customer _____
  _____ .

3 Alfie said, 'I can't do it because I don't speak French well enough.'
  Alfie _____

4 Bobby said to Mike: 'You stole my mobile phone.'
  Bobby _____ .

5 Katie said: 'No, I won't go to the show!'
  Katie _____ .

6 'You really must tell them the truth,' said my brother.
  My brother _____ .

Grammar Plus

6 (✱✱✱) Choose *two* correct answers to complete the sentences.

1 Luke denied ___ his father's credit card.
  a ☐ using   b ☐ to use
  c ☑ that he'd used

2 Claire warned me ___
  a ☐ not to buy the watch.
  b ☐ that the watch looked fake.
  c ☐ not buying the watch.

3 Zoe suggested ___ the problem with our parents.
  a ☐ to discuss   b ☐ discussing
  c ☐ that we should discuss

4 We agreed ___
  a ☐ to do the shopping.
  b ☐ Harry to do the shopping.
  c ☐ that Mike would do the shopping.

5 Julie reminded John ___ a birthday card to his aunt.
  a ☐ to send   b ☐ sending
  c ☐ that he should send

6 The company admitted ___ false claims in its ads.
  a ☐ to make   b ☐ making
  c ☐ that it had made

Grammar reference

Reporting verbs

We use reporting verbs other than *say*, *tell* and *ask* to report the speaker's main idea instead of reporting his/her every single word.

Common patterns of reporting verbs

Different reporting verbs follow different patterns

• verb + -ing – e.g. *admit, advise, deny, suggest*:

*He **admitted taking** the money from her purse.*

• verb + preposition + -ing – e.g. *apologise for, insist on*:

*Tom **insisted on buying** a new radio.*

• verb + object + preposition + -ing – e.g. *blame*:

*She **blamed me for losing** her bag.*

• verb + infinitive – e.g. *promise, refuse*:

*Mum **promised to let** me have a sleepover on Saturday.*

• verb + object + (*not*) + infinitive – e.g. *beg, offer, persuade, urge*:

*They **persuaded Rob not to leave** the party early.*

• verb + *that* + clause – e.g. *agree, claim, deny, explain*:

*The clerk **denied that he had received** my application.*

• verb + object + *that* + clause – e.g. *assure, persuade, remind, warn*:

*The doctor **warned me that I would feel** a bit dizzy for a while.*

Some reporting verbs follow more than one pattern:

• *admit* (verb + -ing/verb + *that* + clause)

*She **admitted breaking** the window.*
*She **admitted that she had broken** the window.*

• *suggest* (verb + -ing/verb + *that* + clause):

*She **suggested giving** it a try.*
*She **suggested that we gave** it a try.*
*She **suggested that we should give** it a try.*

• *offer* (verb + infinitive/verb + object):

*He **offered to help** me with the move.*
*He **offered his help** with the move.*

• *agree* (verb + infinitive/verb + *that* + clause):

*She **agreed to call** them again.*
*She **agreed that she would call** them again.*

• *remind* (verb + object + infinitive/verb + object + *that* + clause):

*She **reminded me to wash** the car.*
*She **reminded me that I should wash** the car.*

• *warn* (verb + object + (*not*) + infinitive/verb + object + *that* + clause):

*He **warned me not to go** there on my own.*
*He **warned me that it was dangerous to go** there on my own.*

Vocabulary

Money

1 Match the sentence beginnings 1–9 with the endings a–i.

1 Oh no! I'm nearly €300 overdrawn	a lot of money.
2 Can we really afford	b in debt!
3 It's time you opened	c for a loan.
4 I hate being	d on my account.
5 He's saving up	e over five years.
6 You should always try	f such an expensive computer?
7 I am repaying my debt	g to stay in credit on your account.
8 We owe the bank a	h for a new motorbike.
9 You'll have to ask the bank	i your own bank account.

2 Complete the text with words and expressions from exercise 1.

You and money

Do you want to open a bank [1] *account* ?
Look at the offers different banks have for young people. Choose the bank that is best for you!

Maybe you want to [2] _____ *your money rather than spend it?*
Banks love people like you! They always offer better interest rates on accounts that stay [3] _____ credit. Go in and talk to them about ways they can help you to make your money grow.

Are you [4] _____ *(you have spent more money than you have in your account) or do you* [5] _____ *money on your credit card?*
It's not a good idea to be in debt. Talk to your bank manager about how they can help you to [6] _____ the debt. Remember, if you can't [7] _____ something, don't buy it! Never ignore debt – it won't go away! Always take action.

Do you need a bank [8] _____ *?*
If you want to borrow money, look at the different options and choose the one that is best for you.

Reading

3 Quickly read the text on page 83 and choose the best summary.

The text is about:

1 ☐ the problems teenagers have learning to manage money.

2 ☐ why modern teenagers are obsessed with money.

3 ☐ the different ways modern teenagers manage and spend their money.

4 Read the text again and match the headings a–g with paragraphs 1–5. There are two extra headings.

a Taking control

b Parents teach their children about saving up

c Learning from their parents' mistakes

d Careful savers

e Hard-working and responsible

f Banks give teens more money nowadays

g Big spenders

5 Read the text again and choose the correct answers.

1 What does the research mentioned in the introduction show?

a That teenagers' attitudes to money have changed.

b That teenagers have more money now, but spend more.

c That teenagers are getting better at earning money.

d That teenagers know a lot about dealing with money.

2 Teenagers are more aware of money because

a they understand that possessing money is very important.

b their parents have taught them about dealing with money.

c their parents don't have any debts.

d their parents' lifestyles have improved.

Generation $

If 'spend, spend, spend' was your idea of a typical American teenager's attitude to money, the results of a recent survey among teens might surprise you. The research shows that as a group, teens today are money-savvy*. They're richer than ever before and might also be the best at earning, spending and saving money.

1 ___

So how did they get to be so savvy? Teenagers today have seen the problems their parents had during the financial crisis. Many parents got in debt or couldn't afford their previous lifestyles. Their children understand the importance of having money and keeping it.

2 ___

Today's hard-working teens often earn their own money – only 45 percent get pocket money from their parents and the rest make their own. Toni Calloway, 17, and Melissa Flowers, 13, are typical examples. Toni works after school in a supermarket and has a holiday job in a restaurant. 'My parents are sometimes overdrawn. Now I don't have to ask for money. I don't mind, it makes me feel more mature,' Toni says. Melissa earns $10 an hour keeping score for a softball team. With the money, she buys clothes and CDs, and she's saving up for a summer holiday. The teens who get money from their parents say they're expected to pay for their own clothes, music and entertainment.

3 ___

Over 75 percent of teens say that they are the ones are in charge of their cash, and most have their own bank accounts. They say it's a good way to learn to budget**. 'It's a useful life skill', says Matt Terrill, age 14, 'and it's good to learn before you go to college.'

4 ___

Typically, teens spend their money on shopping, going out with friends and buying music. For example, almost half the teens surveyed said they had spent at least $20 in shops in the last week, a third had gone to the cinema, a quarter had bought CDs and a fifth had bought a coffee drink. The way teens spend their money is no surprise, but the amount they spend is astonishing – teens spent a record $141 billion last year, an average of $4,548 each!

5 ___

However, an astonishing 90 percent of teens regularly save money: two-thirds say they have saved money in the past week and only 8 percent don't save at all. Girls tend to save for university and boys for cars – but both have goals for saving up. 'You have to think long-term,' explains 17-year-old Brook Richey. 'I know how expensive college is, and you have to go if you want to get a good job. That's why, instead of going shopping every weekend, I save my money.'

---

* money-savvy – know a lot about money
** budget – to plan the way you spend your money, especially so you don't spend too much

3 What does the text say about Toni Calloway?
   a She only works during term-time, not in the holidays.
   b She is saving money to go on holiday this summer.
   c She feels more adult because she earns her own money.
   d She gets money from her parents and from working.

4 Three-quarters of teens
   a don't know how to plan their spending.
   b have at least one bank account.
   c have never controlled their own money.
   d are responsible for their own money.

5 Last year, teens spent
   a at least $20 a week.
   b less on going out than on shopping.
   c an incredibly large amount.
   d most money on buying music.

6 … save money.
   a Almost all teens
   b Very few teens
   c More boys than girls
   d More girls than boys

6 **Answer the questions using from one to five words.**

1 What percentage of teens earn their own money?

_____

2 What does Melissa buy with the money she earns?

_____

3 What do teenagers who get pocket money have to pay for?

_____

4 What percentage of teens had been shopping in the previous week?

_____

5 How much did teenagers in America spend in total last year?

_____

6 Do both girls and boys have a reason for saving money?

_____

realtime 8

Vox pop interviews

1 Put the expressions a–h into the correct category.

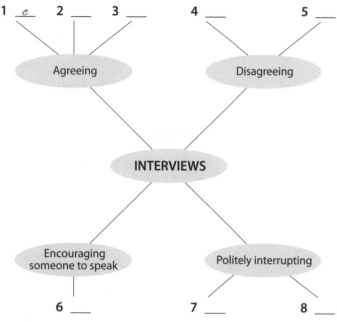

1 _e_ 2 ___ 3 ___ 4 ___ 5 ___

Agreeing

Disagreeing

INTERVIEWS

Encouraging someone to speak

Politely interrupting

6 ___ 7 ___ 8 ___

a I don't think that's true.

b Why do you say that?

c Yes, but just a minute …

d I don't know about that.

e I think that's true.

f Sorry to interrupt, but …

g I totally agree.

h Absolutely.

2 Complete the responses using the prompts in brackets.

A: I think teenagers spend too much money.

B: (you agree) [1] _I totally agree. /_
Absolutely! / I think modern
teenagers spend far too much. .

A: I think teenagers spend too much money. They …

B: (you interrupt) [2] _____
_____ .

A: I think teenagers spend too much money.

B: (you disagree) [3] _____
_____ .

A: I think teenagers spend too much money.

B: (you want the person to say more) [4] _____
_____ .

An anecdote

3 Complete Kate's plan for an anecdote about a party with the notes a–h below.

<u>Paragraph 1:</u> Introduction (background to story – time, place and setting)

1 _b Just moved schools / Jack,_
classmate / invited me party .

2 _____ .

3 _____ .

<u>Paragraph 2:</u> Main event (what happened and how)

4 _____ .

5 _____ .

6 _____ .

<u>Paragraph 3:</u> Consequences (people's reactions, consequences)

7 _____ .

8 _____ .

<u>Notes</u>

a People all laughed/when realised mistake./ Then went up road to Jack's party.

b Just moved schools/Jack, classmate/ invited me to party/very happy

c 9 p.m. last Saturday/Arrived party/ got some food and a drink.

d As standing alone at party with plate and glass/ realised/didn't recognise anyone!

e Also realised people/looking at me strangely/ someone asked who was/why there.

f Not know Jack well/but party/great way/ meet some new friends.

g Result/made lots of new friends/both parties!

h That's how discovered at wrong party/ 29 Hill Street/Jack's house 39 Hill Street!

4 Now write Kate's anecdote in full sentences. In the anecdote, try to:

use interesting time expressions.
repeat key phrases.
use direct speech.
talk directly to the reader.
comment on your own actions and feelings.
exaggerate some details.

examtrainer 11

Use of English

Preposition + noun

1 Complete the sentences with the correct preposition *in* or *on*.

1 I've stayed ___ touch with the people from the sailing camp.

2 The mp3 player seemed ___ good condition when I bought it, but it's stopped working.

3 The whole film was shot ___ location in India and London.

4 The shop didn't accept my credit card and I had to pay ___ cash.

5 I don't believe it was an accident. She did it ___ purpose!

6 Sarah is ___ charge of the preparations for the end-of-year party.

7 ___ average, UK students can expect to graduate with debts of £25,000.

2 Complete the sentences with the prepositions below.

> at   as   by   in   off   on

1 I found this café ___ accident while I was looking for a friend's house.

2 When the great actress appeared ___ stage, the audience started clapping and cheering.

3 My parents met while they were both ___ university.

4 Last summer in Macedonia we saw some interesting places that were ___ the beaten track.

5 If you write your essay ___ a rush, you'll make more mistakes.

6 Claire got into debt ___ a result of spending too much using her credit card.

Noun + preposition

3 <u>Underline</u> the correct word.

1 I'm taking a course *in/about* commercial photography.

2 The secret *of/for* my success is a lot of work and a bit of luck.

3 Are you paying attention *on/to* the speaker?

4 The trouble *in/with* this exercise is that it's too easy.

5 He's doing research *into/about* the behaviour of dolphins.

6 I've had no influence *for/on* his decision to leave.

Exam tasks

Multiple-choice cloze

4 Choose the correct answer a, b or c to complete the text.

Citizens Advice is a UK charity that helps people ¹ _b_ trouble. If you are ² ___ debt, you can go to a Citizens Advice Bureau for free advice. Volunteers will help you find a solution ³ ___ your problem. With the recent economic crisis, there has been a rise ⁴ ___ the number of people in need of advice. Because of its knowledge of social problems, Citizens Advice also has an influence ⁵ ___ government policy.

1 a on	**b** in ✓	**c** into	**d** with
2 a in	**b** into	**c** with	**d** on
3 a for	**b** of	**c** to	**d** on
4 a of	**b** on	**c** in	**d** to
5 a to	**b** for	**c** in	**d** on

Exam **TIP**

In a gap-fill task, look at the structure of the whole sentence. See if you can identify structures, such as noun + preposition phrases of which the missing word could be a part.

Open cloze

5 Complete the text with one word in each gap.

Last August I went to Turkey with my sister Eva. We were travelling ¹ _on_ a budget. We agreed to spend no more than £20 per person per day ² _____ average. I was ³ _____ charge of our finances. The problem ⁴ _____ Eva is that she likes food too much! One day she kept moaning that she wanted ice cream; I paid no attention ⁵ _____ her. But then we met a man selling fresh fruit juice. (Look – I've still got a photo ⁶ _____ my phone.) Even I couldn't resist it. We spent more ⁷ _____ our limit, but it was worth it!

exam trainer 12

Reading

Gapped text

1 For each pair of sentences 1–4, <u>underline</u> the person or thing which the highlighted word(s) refers to.

1 The results are surprising, says <u>Anne Hammond</u>, head of the team that conducted the study. In her opinion, both the good and bad effects of video games seem to be different from what was expected.

2 A new TV commercial for the fast food chain StarBurgers has provoked controversy. It shows an overweight child eating a super-size burger.

3 Patrick owed his bank £10,000. It took him five years to repay the debt.

4 Because of university fees, students graduate with an average debt of £25,000. Many young people end up discouraged and depressed as a result of this situation.

Exam TIP

In a gapped text, a sentence is always linked to the place from which it was removed by meaning, and often also by structure. Read carefully the removed sentences as well as the sentence *before* and *after* each gap. Typical structural links include:
– references – referring to things or persons mentioned earlier in the text by pronouns (*he, she, it, they, this, that*) or by other words (e.g. *£10,000 – the debt*);
– linking words – e.g. but or however to show contrast between the sentences, or time expressions (*before, after*) to show the sequence of events;
– a question followed by an answer.

2 Complete the gaps in the text 1–2 with the sentences a–c. There is one extra sentence. <u>Underline</u> the words or phrases which show the connection between each sentence and the text.

Video games have their enemies. Some people see them as stupid, childish and a waste of time. ¹___ After all, its aim is to entertain. Shigeru Miyamoto, who created the *Super Mario* family of video games, specialises in games which are funny and a bit silly. ² ___ And he has certainly succeeded in doing just that.

a The famous designer has said he likes the idea of creating games a grandchild and a grandparent can play together.

b There is no certain evidence that video games cause violent behaviour in children or teenagers.

c But why should a game be serious?

3 Complete the gaps in the text 1–4 with the sentences a–f on page 87. There are two extra sentences.

Improving your brain with video games

Instant messaging, cell phones, e-mail, TV, video games, animated billboards – the modern world is full of nonstop action, and it all seems to be happening at once. ¹___
The reason is that their brains are trained to handle it. Practice at multi-tasking increases one's ability to pay attention to many things at the same time. A major source of this kind of practice is playing action video games – you know, the kind that parents hate, where the aim is to shoot as many enemies as possible before they shoot you. ² ___ Unfortunately, playing puzzle games such as *Tetris* doesn't have the same effect on the brain, perhaps because they require players to concentrate on only one object at a time, rather than multi-tasking.

In one study, college students who played action games regularly could count fifty percent more items which they'd seen for a very short time than students who didn't play. The game-players also processed information more quickly, could track more objects at once, and had a better ability to switch from one task to another. ³ ___ But a group of non-players was able to improve their attention after training one hour per day for ten days on an action game, suggesting that these skills develop as a direct result of practice.

Does this mean that parents should encourage their children to play shoot-'em-up action games? ⁴ ___ In the long run, we'd love to see somebody make a lot of money by designing action-based video games that motivate children to practise multi-tasking and improve their attention without using violence as the motivator. Kind of like *SimCity* . . . on a runaway bus!

a He found that the students' attention had improved as a result of playing the games.

b We don't especially recommend exposing kids to violent images, but at least parents may be pleased to hear that video game playing has positive effects.

c You might imagine that people with naturally strong abilities were better at the games and so chose to play more often.

d How do we know learning actually takes place?

e If you're over thirty, you've probably wondered why younger people aren't overwhelmed by this situation.

f These games require players to pay attention to the whole screen, notice events quickly and react to them.

Listening

Choose one or two correct answers

4 ⒁ **Listen to the introduction to a radio discussion about advertising. Circle the correct answers. Both answers to a question may be correct.**

1 In the UK, advertising of foods that are high in fat, salt and sugar is not allowed
   a on TV channels for children.
   b during programmes for children.

2 Trevor Bolton is
   a from the Advertising Federation.
   b from the National Parenting Institute.

Exam TIP

In this kind of task, one or two answers may be correct. This may seem difficult, as choosing one answer does not eliminate the other. However, if you look at each answer separately and decide whether it is true or false, it is no more difficult than a series of true/false statements.

5 ⒂ **Listen to the rest of the discussion. Circle the correct answers. Both answers to a question may be correct.**

1 Amanda says that young children
   a believe what they hear from grown-ups.
   b don't understand what advertising is.

2 In Sweden and Norway
   a advertising which targets children is banned.
   b it is illegal to advertise some products to children.

3 Trevor thinks parents should
   a decide what their children watch on TV.
   b discuss ads with their children.

4 Amanda believes parents
   a don't pay enough attention to what their children watch.
   b may find their influence is weaker than that of a commercial.

5 Trevor thinks education
   a allows people to make their own decisions.
   b helps solve only some of the problems connected with advertising.

6 Amanda says
   a education is not effective in protecting very young children from the effects of advertising.
   b advertising agencies have more money than the Department of Education.

self-assessment test 4

Vocabulary & Grammar

1 Match the verbs 1–7 with the phrases a–g.

1 have
2 repay
3 promote
4 suffer
5 wrap
6 damage
7 get

a beauty products
b from an illness
c a refund
d a debt
e your health
f good spatial skills
g a present up

/6

2 Correct the underlined mistake in each sentence.

1 It's not only big, it's <u>petite</u>! *huge*

2 We can't <u>save</u> a new car at the moment, maybe next year if I get a pay rise.

3 My mother can do several things at the same time – she's very good at <u>processing information</u>.

4 Somebody who shows his/her understanding of other people's feelings and problems is very <u>analytical</u>.

5 Their <u>logo</u> was so popular that it was recorded as a full-length song.

6 I decided to order a CD and gave them my credit card <u>statement.</u>

7 Repeated surgery managed to <u>cure</u> my grandmother alive for many years.

/6

3 <u>Underline</u> the correct words to complete the sentences.

1 Is it true that *a/the/–* cheetah is the world's fastest land animal?

2 I believe our government should do more for *a/the/–* poor.

3 Fortunately he *could/succeeded/managed* to get to the airport before the flight closed.

4 I quickly got used to driving on *a/the/–* left side of the road.

5 Has anybody got *a/the/–* pen? Mine has just run out of ink.

6 I'd love to *be able to/manage/can* help you with this but I'm really pressed for time now.

7 It's obvious that *a/the/–* teenagers are very conscious about their looks.

8 He *was able to/could/succeeded in* reach the nearest hospital three hours after the accident.

/7

4 Rewrite the sentences as reported speech using the reporting verbs below.

> ask   congratulate ✓   apologise
> refuse   remind   deny   suggest

1 My best friend: 'You've passed your driving test. Well done!'

My best friend congratulated me on passing my driving test.

2 Robert: 'Why don't we go out on Sunday night?'

_____

3 My sister: 'I didn't take your money!'

_____

4 The airline representative to my boyfriend and me: 'How many pieces of luggage do you have?'

_____

_____

5 The teacher: 'Don't forget to hand in your history assignment on time, Carla.'

_____

_____

6 Jessica's father: 'I won't let you go to New York on your own, Jessica.'

_____

_____

7 Ian: 'I'm really sorry I didn't come to the meeting.'

_____

/6

5 Complete the email with one word in each gap.

Hi Tim,

I'm really sorry I'm late with the money I [1] *owe* you. I was supposed to give it to you by [2] _____ end of the month. I'm sorry I [3] _____ unable to do it. I've been busy helping my aunt. She has recently had [4] _____ on her hip (the operation was two weeks ago) and can't really move yet. I know it sounds like an excuse – I'm so [5] _____ organised. Sorry!

I've got money in my bank [6] _____ and will transfer it to you online tonight. Is that OK?

My apologies again,
Paul

/5

Reading

6 Complete the gaps in the text 1–6 with the sentences a–g. There is one extra sentence.

TV adverts blamed for children's gift greed

Children under seven who watch a lot of television adverts ask Father Christmas for five times as many presents as those who watch less.

A study into the deliberate marketing of toys and games at children found that prolonged exposure to adverts in November and December dramatically increased children's demands. [1]___ They studied letters written to Father Christmas by eighty-three four-, five- and six-year-olds and interviewed the parents of sixteen three-year-olds about their expectations for Christmas. [2]___ Children who watched more commercial television, requested far more toys and presents, with the heaviest viewers typically asking for five or six presents, while those who watched the least asked for just one. [3]___ Top of the lists were Barbie dolls, Furby toys and Action Man figures – three of the most advertised products. However, recognition of other brands was low. [4]___

Researchers found that, during three hours on one Saturday morning, ITV showed 127 adverts for children's toys or food. Children in Britain watch television for an average of two and a half hours a day and sixty-three percent have their own set. [5]___ It found that children there wanted significantly fewer toys than British youngsters.

Dr Karen Pine, who presented the findings to the conference in Glasgow, said: 'What this study shows is that increased exposure to commercials has the effect of making children want more toys in general, rather than specific named products.' [6]___ Dr Pine added, 'A society which exposes young children to many thousands of adverts every year also has a duty to educate those children in consumer literacy and critical viewing.'

a Heavy viewers also asked for far more branded toys.

b The research is the most comprehensive analysis to date of the increasing impact of advertising on children.

c However, those who watched television with a parent were far less susceptible to advertisers, researchers at the University of Hertfordshire in Hatfield found.

d Almost 90 percent of the toys advertised did not appear on the Christmas lists.

e She pointed out that watching with parents seemed to make children less vulnerable because an adult could help teach the difference between adverts and programmes.

f A similar study was conducted in Sweden, where advertisements can't be aimed at children under twelve.

g They compared this data with the children's viewing habits and the content of 1,300 adverts shown in the five weeks before Christmas.

/6

Communication

7 Complete the sentences from a speech and question-and-answer session with one word in each gap.

1 What do you _mean_ when you say 'health risk'?

2 The important _____ is most people are now aware that not all food is healthy.

3 _____ me give you one more example.

4 _____ is really interesting is that more and more young people take up a sport to keep fit.

5 All I'm saying is _____ awareness is the first step to change.

6 Do you _____ think that it is healthy?

7 I know it _____ odd but I believe it's true.

8 That's not _____ what I mean. What I mean is there have been many changes.

9 I understand _____ you're asking that.

/8

8 **Underline** the correct word to complete the dialogues.

1
A: In my opinion this article is silly.
B: *Just/only* a minute, not everything in it is silly.

2
A: Avocado contains a lot of fat.
B: I think that's *truth/true*.

3
A: We should get more pocket money.
B: Absolutely! I totally *know/agree*.

4
A: This is the worst thing that can happen.
B: Why do you *say/talk* that?

5
A: They did it on purpose.
B: *Exactly/Surely* you don't believe that they wanted to do it?

6
A: Life expectancy is lower for men than for women.
B: Are you sure? I don't *know/think* about that.

7
A: This increase is due to increased marketing efforts and …
B: *Excuse/Sorry* to interrupt you but this is only part of the picture.

/6

Marks	
Vocabulary & Grammar	/30 marks
Reading	/6 marks
Communication	/14 marks
Total:	/50 marks

Vocabulary

Crime and justice

1 Match the people 1–5 to the statements about what they did in court a–e.

1 the accused
2 the defence lawyer
3 the judge
4 the prosecution lawyer
5 a witness

a She told the court that she'd seen the crime committed.
b He presented evidence to show the man was guilty.
c She tried to prove the man was innocent.
d He confessed in the end.
e She sentenced the criminal to two years in prison.

2 Number the events in the order in which they happened. The first and last one have been done for you.

a ☐ Her guilt was proven.
b ☐1 Jennifer committed a crime: she stole fifty pairs of designer shoes.
c ☐ She pleaded not guilty.
d ☐ She was arrested.
e ☐ She was sentenced to six months in prison.
f ☐ She went on trial.
g ☐8 The court case was described in the papers.
h ☐ She was charged with theft.

3 Complete the sentences with the verbs below.

> accuse ✓   arrest   charge   commit   go
> plead ✓   prove   sentence

1 The woman was _accused_ of murder, but she _pleaded_ not guilty.
2 The bank robber was finally _____ last night at his girlfriend's house. He will be _____ with five different crimes.
3 The Mafia boss _____ on trial next week. It may be difficult to _____ anything against him, as the witnesses are afraid to speak.
4 The man was _____ to ten years in prison for a crime he hadn't _____ .

Grammar

Gerunds and infinitives

4 (*) Match the sentence beginnings 1–6 with the endings a–f.

1 I switched on the TV
2 The gang spent a lot of time
3 The police found the crime difficult
4 The witness chose
5 The thieves ran away after
6 The boy's mates forced

a discussing their strategy.
b hearing the police car.
c him to take part in the robbery.
d to hear the details of the crime.
e not to tell anyone what she'd seen.
f to solve.

5 (**) Cross out the verb or phrase which does *not* fit the sentence.

1 I can't ___ cooking for twenty people.
   a imagine   b stand   c promise   d avoid
2 The teacher ___ to discuss the problem with the whole class.
   a planned   b expected   c agreed
   d considered
3 We don't ___ talking about politics.
   a enjoy   b plan   c spend much time
   d like
4 My cousin ___ me to take up dancing.
   a encouraged   b suggested   c inspired
   d persuaded
5 Pat ___ going shopping.
   a is keen on   b can't stand   c enjoys
   d plans
6 The criminals ___ to enter the house from the lake.
   a admitted   b attempted   c chose
   d found it easy

6 (✱✱) <u>Underline</u> the correct form (gerund or infinitive).

1 Jessica's parents allow her *to go*/*going* out late at night.

2 The manager considered *to contact*/*contacting* the police immediately.

3 If you are a witness, it is important *to tell*/*telling* only the truth.

4 I called my best friend *to ask*/*asking* her opinion.

5 The criminals hid in the bushes *to avoid*/*avoiding to* getting caught.

6 *To read*/*Reading* crime novels is the favourite pastime of many people.

7 (✱✱✱) Complete the text with the verbs in the correct form (gerund or infinitive).

The criminals who succeeded in ¹ *stealing* (steal) £1m worth of art from the National Gallery last September go on trial today. The thieves avoided ² _____ (catch – passive) for several months as they attempted ³ _____ (sell) the paintings. However, they found it difficult ⁴ _____ (attract) a buyer, as the works are very famous and easy ⁵ _____ (identify). They became increasingly afraid of ⁶ _____ (arrest) and even considered ⁷ _____ (destroy) the paintings.

In the meantime, the police started an undercover operation ⁸ _____ (recover) the stolen works of art. In March, an 'anonymous collector from New York' contacted the gang and offered ⁹ _____ (buy) all the pictures. During a meeting in a hotel room the thieves were arrested. They agreed ¹⁰ _____ (cooperate) with the police in the hope of ¹¹ _____ (receive) shorter prison sentences.

Grammar reference

Infinitives and gerunds

Infinitives

We use an infinitive with *to*

* after some verbs (for example: *agree, attempt, choose, expect, offer, plan, promise, refuse, wait*):

*They agreed **to cooperate** very closely.*
*I'm planning **to study** medicine.*

* after some verbs followed by an object (for example: *allow, encourage, force, inspire, persuade*):

*I don't think my parents will allow me **to stay** longer.*
*They persuaded us **to accept** a lift to the station.*

* after some adjectives (for example: *able/ unable, dangerous, difficult, easy, helpful*):

*Mount Everest is very dangerous **to climb**.*
*It was quite easy **to follow** his directions.*

* to explain the purpose of an action:

*I waited for her **to apologise** for my behaviour.*
*Honey has been used **to treat** a variety of ailments.*

In negative sentences *not* comes before the infinitive:

*She promised **not to speak** Spanish during our English classes.*
*It was difficult **not to burst out** laughing when he slipped on the banana skin.*

Gerunds

We use a gerund (*-ing* form):

* after some verbs (for example: *admit, avoid, can't stand, consider, enjoy, fancy, imagine, spend time, suggest*):

*I don't fancy **going** out on Sunday night.*
*My boyfriend doesn't enjoy **dancing**.*

* after prepositions:

*I'm not very keen on **going** to the cinema tonight.*
*You shouldn't swim immediately after **eating** lunch.*

* as the subject of the sentence:

***Skipping** school is against the law in most countries.*
***Drinking** water makes the body more relaxed.*

In passive sentences we use *being*:

*I can't stand **being** talked about behind my back.*
***Being** an only child is not as easy as people think.*

9

Vocabulary

Truth and lies

1 Match the nouns 1–5 with the verbs a–e to make collocations.

1 forge	**a** out of some money
2 con	**b** the truth
3 cheat someone	**c** people
4 lie	**d** documents
5 admit	**e** to someone

2 Complete the text with the words in the box. Change the form of the word if necessary.

admit   deception   forge ✓   fraud
genuine   pretend   take in   trick

Britain's most famous art forger

Tom Keating, who was an art restorer by profession, ¹ _forged_ about 2000 paintings as a form of protest against the huge profits made by art galleries. He used to ² _____ that he'd discovered lost masterpieces by famous artists. His copies were so good that collectors and art historians were ³ _____ .

Keating ⁴ _____ everyone for many years. The ⁵ _____ was finally revealed in the 1970s. When thirteen similar pictures by the same artist, Samuel Palmer, were offered for sale at the same time, gallery owners began suspecting they might not be ⁶ _____ . It was then that Keating ⁷ _____ the truth and explained why he'd done it.

In 1977 Keating was accused of ⁸ _____ , but the trial was stopped because of his poor health. However, he became so famous that his copies are now considered quite valuable.

Grammar

Modals of deduction

3 (✱) Complete the answers with *must, might* or *can't* and the verbs below.

be ✓   be   have   remember
know   miss

1 A: Whose car is that outside the school?
   B: It _must be_ Michelle's father's. She said he'd bought a green Saab.

2 A: Lily looks a bit depressed.
   B: She _____ her boyfriend, who's gone to Spain for a year. Or perhaps she's just tired!

3 A: Is Mike still in bed?
   B: Surely he _____ asleep at this time? It's noon!

4 A: Why are all those people waiting here?
   B: They _____ something we don't know, I'm sure.

5 A: Grace never goes out with us these days.
   B: She _____ a lot of work before the exams. Or perhaps she just spends all her time with Sean.

6 A: Your brother told me how you tried to teach your cat to swim when you were four.
   B: But he _____ that! He was too young.

4 (✱✱) Complete the sentences with the verbs in brackets in the correct form to make deductions about the past.

1 A: Lucy's wearing a diamond ring.
   B: Ryan _____ (must/buy) it for her.

2 A: How did the burglars get in?
   B: They _____ (may/climb) up the drainpipe or they _____ (could/use) the basement window.

3 A: Where do you think Charlie is now?
   B: His plane _____ (must/land) in Tokyo about half an hour ago.

4 A: Have you heard that Chloe has left town?
   B: What? She _____ (can't/do) that. I've just seen her.

5 A: Bill didn't come round last night.
   B: His car _____ (may/break down).

6 A: Do you think anyone saw the thieves?
   B: They _____ (can't/see them). They would have told us.

5 (✱✱✱) **Complete the dialogue between with modal verbs and the correct forms of the verbs in brackets.**

A: I had a date with John and he hasn't come and he hasn't called. Something terrible ¹ _must have happened_ (happen)!

B: He ² _____ (forget)!

A: Forgotten about our date? Impossible! He ³ _____ (do) that!

B: Well, then the bus ⁴ _____ (be) stuck in a traffic jam.

A: Why doesn't he call? I'm telling you, he ⁵ _____ (have) an accident!

B: Angie, relax. His mobile ⁶ _____ (stop) working. The battery ⁷ _____ (be) flat. Or he may still be at school. The football coach ⁸ _____ (ask) the whole team to stay behind and discuss the match.

A: Do you think he ⁹ _____ (decide) to finish with me? Do you think he ¹⁰ _____ (meet) another girl since our last date on Saturday?

B: Oh, you're just impossible! No, he ¹¹ _____ (finish) with you, because you're far too beautiful. Now calm down.

Grammar Plus: continuous forms

6 (✱✱✱) **Complete the sentences with the verbs in brackets using past or present continuous forms.**

1 Dave says he's not interested in motorbikes any longer. He _must be joking_ (must/joke)!

2 The neighbour didn't hear the burglars. She _____ (may/sleep).

3 The fridge is making a lot of noise. It _____ (can't/work) properly.

4 Mike doesn't remember anything from the previous lesson. He _____ (can't/pay attention).

5 Nobody's answering the door. They _____ (may/watch) TV upstairs.

6 The children have just run away giggling. They _____ (must/do) something naughty.

Grammar reference

Modals of deduction

Deduction in the present

To speculate or make deductions about the present we use *must/might/may/could/can't* + infinitive. Different modal verbs express different degrees of certainty.

We use *must* when we are almost sure/certain that something is true:

*They **must be** very rich. (I'm sure that they are rich.)*
*They **must be** on their way to Spain now*

We use *might, may* and *could* when we think that things/events are possible:

*She **might/may/could** need your help.*
*He **could/might/may** be the man the police are looking for.*

We use *can't* when we are almost sure/certain that things/events are not true:

*He **can't be** more intelligent than John.*
*They **can't be** on their way to Spain now.*

To make deductions about the actions which are happening at present we can use *must/might/may/could/can't* + be + *-ing* form:

*This is not true! You **must be** joking!*
*Tom is not answering his phone. He **might be** driving now.*
*Surely you **can't be** considering his offer!*

Deduction in the past

To speculate or make deductions about the past we use *must/might/may/could/can't* + have + past participle.

We use *must* + have + past participle when we are almost sure/certain that something was true:

*She **must have been** very angry with you.*

We use *might, may* and *could* + have + past participle when we think that things/events were possible:

*They **might/may/could have** missed the meeting.*
*She **may/might/could have** told him about the accident.*

We use *can't* + have + past participle when we are almost sure/certain that things/events were not true:

*He **can't have** done it on its own. (I'm sure that he didn't do it on his own.)*

To make deductions about the actions which were happening in the past we can use *must/might/may/could/can't* + have + been + *-ing* form:

*Ian didn't want to leave the party. He **must have been** enjoying himself.*
*He left in the middle of the match? His favourite team **might have been losing**.*
*You **can't have been** listening carefully if you don't know what to do.*

Vocabulary

Crime and justice

1 Complete the texts with the correct form of the words in the box.

> death   fine ✓   prison
> parole   sentence   serve
> suspend

Have your say blogs

How should we punish crime?

Samantha, Bristol
Posted Tue 30 Jan 14.50 GMT

I was attacked and robbed at knifepoint. I still have nightmares. I don't think people who commit these kinds of crimes should be [1] _fined_ or given community [2] _____ . They should be given a harsh prison [3] _____ . Violent crime is increasing and if these types of offenders aren't punished, our country will become a dangerous place to live.

Ali, South Wales
Posted Tue 30 Jan 17.30 GMT

There are too many people in our prisons! I think people who commit minor offences such as shoplifting should be given [4] _____ sentences. Prisoners who have committed non-violent crimes and behave well in prison could get [5] _____ early.

Kali, London
Posted Tue 30 Jan 19.37 GMT

Nobody should ever be sentenced to [6] _____ , no matter what crime they have committed. We don't have the right to take a life. For serious crimes, like murder, I think life [7] _____ is the only possible punishment. This is still a terrible thing. Imagine what it feels like to know that you're going to die in prison.

Listening

2 You are going to hear a news broadcast about crime. Before you listen, match the words below 1–8 with the definitions a–h.

1 gang *n*

2 goods *n*

3 vandal *n*

4 self-defence *n*

5 the High Court

6 death penalty *n*

7 minor offences *n*

8 criminal record *n*

a a court that has more power than other courts, and which can change previous court decisions

b crimes that are 'minor' or not serious

c an official list of crimes that a criminal has committed

d punishment of a crime by death

e someone who deliberately damages property (vandalism)

f a group of people who often cause trouble or commit crimes

g protecting or defending yourself from dangers

h objects that you can buy in shops

3 ⏺16 Listen to the news broadcast and choose the correct answers.

1 The students
  a have been stealing technology goods.
  b have been stealing things for two years.
  c will all be fined for their crimes.
  d had not committed any crimes before this.

2 Jason Williams
  a has just killed a man outside a nightclub in Glasgow.
  b says he committed the crime in order to defend himself.
  c has apologised to the victim's family.
  d plans to take his case to the High Court.

3 The newsreader says that in the US
  a only four states still have the death penalty.
  b hundreds of people have been arrested at a demonstration.
  c fifty-two people were executed last year.
  d thirty-four people were sentenced to death last year.

4 British government officials want
  a to reduce the number of people who commit minor offences.
  b people who commit minor offences to stay in prison for longer.
  c to reduce the number of people who get parole.
  d more people who are in prison for minor offences to get parole.

5 The vandal
  a sprayed graffiti over the walls of several primary schools.
  b is going to get a suspended prison sentence.
  c will have to pay a fine to the local community.
  d is going to paint the walls of local primary school playgrounds.

4 (**16**) Listen again and match the numbers below with things a–h that they refer to. There are three extra numbers.

> 2   2.3   3   3.4   6   8   10 ✓
> 23   34   10,000   25,000

a the number of shoplifters ___10___

b the value (in pounds) of the goods the police found _____

c the number of years the shoplifters could go to prison for _____

d the number of years Jason Williams has spent in prison _____

e how many million people are in prison in America _____

f the number of months the vandal will do community service _____

g the age of the vandal _____

h the number of primary schools he will decorate _____

Reading

5 Look at the article and choose the best summary a, b or c.

a It is an article about a man who suffered a crime, but who doesn't believe in prison.

b It is an article about a man who helped someone who committed a crime against him.

c It is an article about a man who helps criminals and who gives them money.

6 Read the text and tick (✓) true, cross (✗) or write (?) if there is no information about this in the text.

1 ☐ When the crime happened, Diaz panicked.

2 ☐ Diaz gave the boy his money and something to wear.

3 ☐ The boy was surprised at the way Diaz behaved.

4 ☐ The boy had been living on the streets and was cold and hungry.

5 ☐ It was not the first time that Diaz had been to the diner.

6 ☐ The boy had to pay for dinner because he had Diaz's money.

7 ☐ Diaz forced the boy to give him the knife.

DAILY NEWS   15 MARCH

Victim helps mugger   by Michael Garafalo

It's a situation when most people panic, but when thirty-one-year-old Julio Diaz was mugged last night on his way home from work, he decided to try to help his attacker. Diaz, a social worker in New York, had just got off the subway train at his usual station in the Bronx to go to his favourite diner, where he eats every night on his way home from work. As he was walking towards the stairs, a teenage boy pulled out a knife and demanded his money.

Diaz not only gave the boy his wallet, but then went on to offer him his coat. 'I said, *Hey, wait a minute. You forgot something. If you're going to be robbing people for the rest of the night, you might as well take my coat to keep you warm,*' Diaz told reporters. The boy was so surprised he stopped and asked why. He was even more surprised when Diaz then invited him to dinner. 'I felt he needed some help … If he was willing to risk prison to steal a few dollars then he must have really needed the money.'

Diaz took his would-be mugger to his favourite diner. At the diner, Diaz, as he usually does, said hello to everyone. The teen was surprised Diaz was so nice to everyone – 'I didn't think people actually behaved that way,' he said.

After the meal, Diaz told the teen he would have to pay, since he had Diaz's wallet. But he also offered to treat the boy to dinner if he returned the wallet – which the boy did straightaway. Diaz paid for dinner and also gave the boy an extra $20 to help him. However, this time he asked for something in return – the teen's knife – which he also handed over without protest.

Asked why he had helped someone who had tried to rob him, Diaz explained, 'I think if you treat people right, you can only hope that they treat you right. It's as simple as it gets in this complicated world.'

right & wrong

95

Writing

An opinion essay

9

Teen courts are the best way of dealing with young offenders. Do you agree or disagree? Why?

1 In **paragraph 1**, explain the question and introduce some of the important issues.

2 Give your own opinion about the question.

3 In **paragraph 2**, explain and develop the issues related to the question introduced in paragraph 1. Give evidence to support the opinion you put forward.

4 Use linking words of addition to introduce each new point, e.g. *furthermore*, *in addition* and linking words for explaining consequences to give reasons, e.g. *as a result*, *due to this*, etc.

5 In **paragraph 3**, give other arguments to support your opinion.

6 In **paragraph 4**, describe the arguments on the opposite side.

7 In **paragraph 5**, sum up by (briefly) countering the arguments in paragraph 4, but do not give any new arguments.

8 Restate your opinion to conclude.

Teen courts are special courts to deal with young offenders who have committed minor offences such as vandalism or shoplifting. Some people argue that they do not punish teenagers seriously enough. However, I strongly disagree and firmly believe that they can stop teenagers from committing further crimes.

Firstly, young people are sent to teen courts for a first offence. One advantage of this is that they avoid getting a criminal record. **Furthermore**, in teen courts, offenders are treated fairly by people their own age and given a chance to speak. **Due to this**, they are more likely to follow their punishment and less likely to re-offend.

It is important to remember that the sentences tend to be harder than ordinary courts. Offenders usually have to do community service and pay for any damage they caused. What is more, they often have to write letters of apology to their parents and any victims. **In addition**, offenders often have to take part in other trials as jury members. As a result, they become involved in making decisions for the good of society.

However, there are some arguments against teen courts. It has not been proved that they are more effective than ordinary courts in deterring criminal behaviour. **Even though** they give strict punishments, some young offenders do not take teen courts seriously and think they have got away with committing offences.

Having said that, those offenders who re-offend after being tried by a teen court might have done exactly the same thing if they had gone through the adult system. Teen courts support vulnerable young people and I believe the advantages are far greater than any possible disadvantages. To sum up therefore, teen courts are the best way of dealing with young offenders.

Useful language

Giving an opinion

I strongly/firmly think/believe that …

I agree/disagree that …

Emphasising your arguments

It is important to remember that …

Concluding the essay

To sum up, …

1 Read the essay quickly and <u>underline</u> the correct answers.

1 The writer *agrees/disagrees* with the statement.

2 Teen courts are usually used *any time/the first time* a teenager commits an offence.

3 The writer thinks it's *more/less* probable that teens will commit another offence.

4 Sentences in teen courts are usually *stronger/lighter* than in other courts.

5 It *has/hasn't* been proved that teen courts work better than other courts.

6 The writer thinks teen courts have more *advantages/disadvantages* than other courts.

96

2 Complete the table with the words and expressions below.

> although for this reason   because of this
> moreover ✓   as a result   what is more
> despite this

Adding information	Contrasting information	Explaining consequence
besides	nevertheless	therefore
moreover	_____	_____
_____	_____	_____
_____	_____	_____
	_____	_____

3 Put the expressions in bold in the essay in the correct column in the table.

4 Read the sentences and decide what type of linker – addition (A), contrast (C) or explaining consequences (EC) – you need to complete the sentences. Complete the sentences with one suitable word/expression.

1 [EC] People who do community service spend many hours doing tasks to help the community. _As a result_ , they become more involved in the community.

2 [   ] _____ some people have done community service, they continue to commit crimes and it would be better to send them to prison.

3 [   ] There are many arguments in favour. _____ , there are also arguments against.

4 [   ] Offenders often learn new skills when they do community service. _____ they may find it easier to get a job if they are unemployed.

5 [   ] Doing community service means offenders often learn useful skills. _____ the community gets necessary tasks done for free.

6 [   ] Learning new skills can help offenders to find employment. _____ they are less likely to re-offend.

5 Underline the correct answers in the sentences below.

1 _Even though/Nevertheless_ some people benefit from doing community service, there are many hardened criminals who do not.

2 Community service is useful for people who commit minor offences. _However/Although_ it is not suitable for dangerous criminals.

3 Community service benefits the whole community. _Even though,/Having said that,_ I think prison is the only solution for dangerous criminals.

4 Young people often commit minor offences, such as shoplifting, without thinking about the consequences. Community service gives them an opportunity to do something positive. _Although,/Nevertheless,_ serious offences should be tried in a normal court in my opinion.

5 Community service is a good idea. _Having said that,/Although_ it can be hard to organise, both offender and other people in the community can benefit.

6 Complete the strategies box with the words below.

> support   agree ✓   grammar   linking

An opinion essay

- Read the title carefully and decide if you [1] _agree_ or disagree. Then make notes following the paragraph plan for an opinion essay.

- Add ideas or explanations to [2] _____ your arguments.

- Decide which [3] _____ words/expressions to use to present your ideas and write your first draft.

- Check your work for mistakes of [4] _____ , spelling or punctuation and check you have used the linking words correctly. Then write your final draft.

7 Read the task and write an opinion essay. Use the structure on the opposite page and the strategies in exercise 6 and ideas in the exercises to help you. Write 200–250 words.

> Community service is good for the community and for criminals. Do you agree?

Understanding headlines and summarising articles

1 Look at the newspaper headlines. What do all three stories have in common?

1 **Museum learns of theft from police**

2 **Wedding dress search helps solves burglaries**

3 **Dog catches would-be thief**

2 Match the headlines 1–3 above with the stories a–c below.

a ___

Police say a 25-year-old woman's search for her stolen wedding dress led them to solve several burglaries. After her dress was stolen, Alena Gadke tracked it down on Craigslist. She contacted the seller and arranged to meet. Gadke alerted police who arrested the seller when she arrived. This first arrest led police to two accomplices who confessed to multiple burglaries.

b ___

POLICE who were investigating a break-in at a museum last night were able to arrest the suspect thanks to their dog. The man was wearing a special disguise made of leaves and detectives had not seen him in the dark. Luckily the dog bit the man and police heard him.

c ___

A Swedish museum only discovered that three of its works of art, including a valuable Edvard Munch painting, had been stolen when police contacted them to say that the paintings had been recovered in a raid. The theft of the works – which were not on display, but in storage – is thought to have taken place two weeks ago. The museum director said he was shocked that the museum hadn't realised that the paintings were missing.

3 Complete the summaries of the three stories.

1 Article **a** talks about _____
_____ .

2 Article **b** explains how _____
_____ .

3 According to article **c**, _____
_____ .

4 All three articles are related to the topic of
_____ .

Talking about photos, statistics and headlines

4 Look at the results of a UK survey on crime. Complete the description with the words below.

> half   three-quarters   stayed   third
> fallen   bar chart ✓   tiny minority

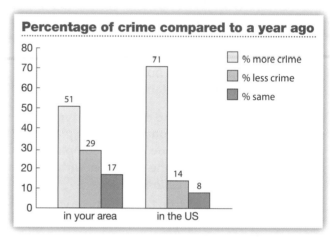

Percentage of crime compared to a year ago

- ☐ % more crime
- ☐ % less crime
- ■ % same

The ¹ _bar chart_ shows how people in the UK perceive crime now compared to a year ago in their area and in the US. It shows that around a ² _____ think that there's more crime in their area and around a ³ _____ believe crime has ⁴ _____ . Only seventeen percent believe the level of crime has ⁵ _____ the same. Nearly ⁶ _____ of people think that crime in the US has increased. Only a ⁸ _____ of people – eight percent – think crime rates have stayed the same.

5 Write a description of the pie chart below. Use the language and ideas in exercise 4 to help you.

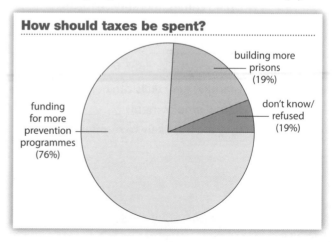

How should taxes be spent?

- building more prisons (19%)
- don't know/refused (19%)
- funding for more prevention programmes (76%)

examtrainer13

English in Use

Verb + preposition

1 Complete the sentences with the prepositions below.

> for   at   in   on ✓   to

1 The jury's decision will largely depend _on_ what this witness says.
2 I'd never want to be in a relationship with someone who lied _____ me.
3 The burglar said he wanted to apologise _____ the distress he'd caused his victims.
4 The burglars succeeded _____ escaping with the stolen paintings.
5 The film is aimed _____ a teenage audience.

Verb + object + preposition

2 Underline the correct answer.

1 The criminals cheated the old lady *out of/from* her savings.
2 The Chief of Police congratulated the old lady *on/for* her role in helping to catch the thieves.
3 The security system prevented the thieves *to/from* stealing the painting.
4 She provided the burglar *with/for* an alibi.
5 The crime reported in today's news reminds me *of/to* something I saw in a film.

3 Complete the sentences with the prepositions below.

> for   of ✓   of   to   with

1 Fred's neighbour accused him _of_ stealing things from her garden.
2 The man was charged _____ armed robbery.
3 He was convicted _____ a crime he hadn't committed.
4 My wife blamed me _____ leaving the car unlocked.
5 The judge sentenced the vandals _____ 200 hours' community service.

Adjective + preposition

4 Complete the sentences with prepositions.

1 Watching too much TV is bad _for_ your eyes.
2 This meat is high _____ protein.
3 They are responsible _____ our security.
4 I'm very grateful _____ your help.
5 This house is famous _____ a murder that was committed here 100 years ago.

Exam tasks

Sentence transformations

5 Complete the second sentence so that it means the same as the first.

1 Mo's employer said she'd stolen the money.
Mo's employer accused
_____ money.
2 Because of the boy's clever action, the thieves couldn't escape.
The boy's clever action prevented
_____ .
3 This witness will give us the evidence we need.
This witness will provide _____ we need.
4 The police managed to catch the robbers.
The police succeeded _____ the robbers.

Open cloze

6 Complete the text with one word in each gap.

The internet criminals who cheated 500 people [1] _out_ of more than a million pounds over the past six months have finally been captured. They are responsible for obtaining the banking details of thousands of individual customers and stealing a total of about £1.1m from their accounts. The men will be charged [2] _____ fraud and deception. The consumer organisation SafeOnLine is planning a public information campaign to prevent more people [3] _____ being cheated in the future. The campaign will be aimed especially [4] _____ elderly internet users.

Vocabulary

Home and environment

1 Match the beginnings 1–6 with the endings a–f to make collocations.

1	a lively	**a**	links
2	a sense	**b**	diverse
3	green	**c**	friendly
4	culturally	**d**	spaces
5	transport	**e**	of community
6	family-	**f**	atmosphere

2 Complete the conversation about country life versus city life with the words below.

> community cramped diverse facilities litter lively
> nightlife traffic scenery ✓ spaces transport views

Sarah: So what's it like in the village where you live?

Alice: It's so beautiful! I just love the ¹ _scenery_ . The ² _____ from some of the hills are breathtaking.

Jack: It's boring. There's absolutely nothing to do in the evening.

Alice: Some of the local ³ _____ are really good.

Jack: Which ones? And you can't even go to a larger town for the day because the ⁴ _____ links are so bad. I wish I lived in a city! So what's it like where you come from?

Bob: Well, we live in a busy part of town, so there's a ⁵ _____ atmosphere … I really enjoy the entertainment and the ⁶ _____ .

Sarah: But the ⁷ _____ is awful – there are far too many cars and you can never park anywhere. The air pollution is really bad as well and people throw ⁸ _____ in the street.

Bob: But we do have some green ⁹ _____ . There's a big park around where we live.

Sarah: Big? You can walk all around it in fifteen minutes. That's another problem, it's all so ¹⁰ _____ . Too many people, too little space.

Bob: But you have to admit the city is culturally ¹¹ _____ . We've got about twenty nationalities living there.

Sarah: I'd much rather live somewhere that's small and family-friendly, with a strong sense of ¹² _____ .

Jack: You mean somewhere where everyone knows everything about you, like our village? No thanks!

Grammar

I wish and If only

3 (*) Put the words in the correct order to make sentences. Write (PR) if the sentence refers to the present or (PA) to the past.

1 camera/only/left/If/hadn't/my/home!/at/I

   If only I hadn't left my
   camera at home!   PA

2 my boyfriend/wish/much/do./I/as/liked/ dancing/I/as

   _____
   _____

3 work/parents/only/didn't/much./If/so/my

   _____
   _____

4 money/wish/quickly!/I/spent/my/hadn't/all/I/so

   _____
   _____

5 could/well/Mark./as/guitar/only/play/If/I/the/as

   _____
   _____

4 (**) Complete the wishes with the correct form of the verb in brackets.

1 I wish we _lived_ (live) in a warmer climate. The winters are so long and cold here.

2 If only the teachers _____ (not give) us so much homework every weekend!

3 I wish I _____ (can) do all the tricks on my bike that Simon can do.

4 If only I _____ (start) studying Spanish earlier. I might be fluent by now.

5 I wish I _____ (be born) in the 1960s. There was a lot of good pop music in those days.

6 If only the TV _____ (broken down) yesterday! I wanted to watch the World Cup tonight.

5 (✷✷) **Complete the wishes with the correct form of the verbs below.**

[buy   can   have   be ✓   know   say]

1 I crashed my dad's car! If only I _had been_ more careful!
2 Sue wishes she _____ a bike. She's fed up with taking the bus to school.
3 There's something wrong with my computer. If only I _____ what.
4 Millie has told Mike about the surprise party we're preparing! I wish I _____ anything to her!
5 I have to study all Saturday. If only I _____ go out!
6 There's so much food left over from the party. I wish I _____ so much.

6 (✷✷) **Complete the pairs of sentences with one wish that relates to the present situation and one wish that relates to the past.**

1 Patricia is unfit because she didn't do any exercise last winter.
  a She wishes she _was_ fit.
  b She wishes she _had done_ some exercise last winter.
2 My best friend is angry with me because I shouted at her.
  a I wish she _____ angry with me.
  b I wish I _____ at her.
3 Greg feels sick because he's eaten too many chips.
  a He wishes he _____ sick.
  b He wishes he _____ so many chips.
4 Jane can't concentrate because she went to bed very late last night.
  a She wishes she _____ concentrate.
  b She wishes she _____ to bed earlier last night.
5 Jeremy's in jail because he stole a car.
  a He wishes he _____ in jail.
  b He wishes he _____ the car.

Grammar Plus: *It's time/I'd rather*

7 (✷✷✷) **Complete the second sentence so that it means the same as the first.**

1 You really should start thinking about your future now.
  It's time _you started thinking_ about your future.
2 I'd prefer the children to sit by the window.
  I'd rather _____ by the window.
3 Julie should get dressed for the party now.
  It's time _____ for the party.
4 I'd like you not to tell anyone about this conversation.
  I'd rather _____ anyone about this conversation.
5 We should discuss buying a new house now.
  It's time _____ buying a new house.
6 I'd prefer John not to come to the party.
  I'd rather _____ to the party.

Grammar reference

wish/if only

Wishes about the present

To talk about present wishes and regrets we use

- *wish/if only* + past simple to express a wish for things/situations to be different. These things/situations are usually impossible or unlikely:

*I **wish** I **was** slimmer.* (but I'm not)
***If only** my sister **didn't talk** so much.* (but she does)

- *wish/if only* + *could* to express a wish for things that are impossible or which we are unable to do:

*I **wish** I **could** fly.* (but I can't)
***If only** I **could** speak Chinese.* (but I can't)

If only is stronger and more emphatic than *wish*.

We also use

- *it's time* + person + past simple to say what we think should happen now:

*It's almost 8 p.m. **It's time the children started** tidying up their rooms.*
*Stop messing about! **It's time you got round** to some serious work.*

- *would rather* + person + past simple to say that the subject of the first clause wants someone else to do/not to do something:

*Don't call me tonight. **I'd rather you called** tomorrow morning.*
*Peter doesn't like dancing. **He'd rather we didn't go** to the disco.*

Wishes about the past

To talk about past wishes and regrets we use

- *wish/if only* + past perfect to express a regret that something happened or didn't happen:

*I **wish** I **hadn't hurt** her feelings yesterday at the party.* (but I did)
***If only** my girlfriend **had accepted** the job she was offered.* (but she didn't)

Vocabulary

Buying and selling houses

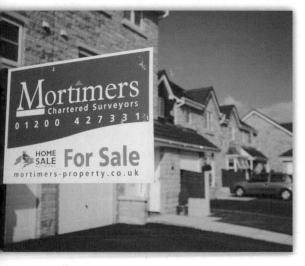

1 Complete the phrasal verbs in the sentences with the words below.

> in out round
> through up

1 I've put my house _____ for sale.

2 I arranged to look _____ the house I'm interested in.

3 I have to move _____ by the end of this month.

4 I can move _____ to the new flat next month.

5 Now that sale has gone _____, I've got a lot of money.

2 Read the sentences from exercise 1 again and decide who said them:

The buyer: ___ ___

The seller: _1_ ___ ___

3 Match each of the sentences below to the house buyer (B) or the seller (S).

1 The estate agent took photos of my house. ___

2 I made the homeowner an offer. ___

3 I rejected the offer because I wanted more money. ___

4 The owner and I negotiated for a week and we agreed a price. ___

5 I went to the bank to get a mortgage. ___

Grammar

The third conditional and mixed conditionals

4 (*) **Match the sentence beginnings 1–6 with the endings a–f.**

1 I would have come sooner

2 If we'd left the house five minutes later,

3 They could have had a good time

4 I could have helped her

5 If Chris had played,

6 If the driver hadn't stopped immediately,

a if she'd told me she had a problem.

b if they hadn't started arguing.

c we would have missed the flight.

d she might have hit the motorcyclist.

e we might have won the match.

f if I had known you were here.

5 (**) **Read the story of Andrew and Zoe's engagement. Complete the third conditional sentences below.**

Andrew wanted to ask Zoe to marry him, and he wanted to make it really special. He planned to buy a beautiful ring in Venice and propose to Zoe on a bridge above a canal. But everything went wrong. They were robbed on the first day, so Andrew didn't have the money to buy a ring. Because he didn't have a ring, he couldn't propose. They were both so upset by the incident that they had an argument and returned home in a bad mood. Eventually, Andrew proposed to Zoe on a rainy November day in London, when she had a cold and her nose was red. Zoe says because she looked so awful on that day, she was sure he really loved her! She wrote a story about her engagement for a women's magazine and won the first prize. With the prize money they were able to afford a wedding reception for a hundred guests.

1 If they _hadn't been robbed_ (not/be robbed) on the first day, Andrew _would have bought_ (buy) a ring.

2 If he _____ (buy) a ring, he _____ (propose) to Zoe in Venice.

3 If they _____ (not/be) upset by the incident, they _____ (not/have) an argument.

4 If Zoe _____ (not/have) a cold in November, her nose _____ (not/be) red.

5 If Zoe _____ (not/look) so awful, she _____ (not/be) sure Andrew really loved her.

6 If all this _____ (not/happen), Zoe _____ (not/write) a story about her engagement.

7 If she _____ (not/write) the story, she _____ (not/win) the first prize.

8 If she _____ (not/win), they _____ (not/be able) to afford a wedding reception.

9 If Andrew and Zoe _____ (not/be robbed), they _____ (not/have) such a great wedding!

6 (✱✱) Complete the second sentence so that it means the same as the first.

1 I didn't buy you a present because I didn't know it was your birthday.

If I _had known it was your birthday, I would have bought_ you a present.

2 I didn't write to you because I was busy.

If I _____ to you.

3 I ordered this dish but I didn't realise how expensive it was.

If I _____
_____ it.

4 I didn't phone you earlier because I didn't notice your text message.

If I_____
_____ you earlier.

5 I didn't lend him any money because he didn't ask.

If he _____ some money.

7 (✱✱✱) Complete the mixed conditional sentences using the verb in CAPITALS.

1 Ian loved swimming as a child. He's a champion swimmer now.   WOULD

If Ian _hadn't loved swimming as a child, he wouldn't be_ a champion swimmer now.

2 I didn't do my piano practice every day. I didn't become a pianist.   MIGHT

If I _____
a pianist now.

3 We moved to the countryside ten years ago, so I don't have any stress-related health problems now.   WOULD

If we _____
_____ stress-related health problems now.

4 Claire met Philippe at university in France. They got married and she doesn't live in Manchester any more.   MIGHT

If Claire _____
_____ in Manchester.

5 Daniel trained to be a chef, so he doesn't have to work in the coal mine, like his father.   MIGHT

If Daniel _____
_____ work in the mine, like his father.

6 I lived in this city for five years. I know it well.   WOULD

If I _____ it so well.

Grammar reference

Third and mixed conditionals

The third conditional

We use the third conditional (*If* + past perfect, *would* + *have* + past participle) to talk about an imaginary situation in the past and its effects/consequences in the past.

PAST SITUATION → EFFECT IN THE **PAST**
*If he **hadn't lost** his job, he **wouldn't have moved** to a different city.*
(He lost his job and that's why he moved to a different city.)
*If you **had asked** me, I **would have picked** you **up** from the airport.*
(You didn't ask me and that's why I didn't pick you up from the airport.)
If the effect is not certain, we can use *might* in the main clause.

PAST SITUATION → EFFECT IN THE **PAST**
*If Tom **hadn't taken** the risk, he **might never have won** the talent competition.*
*If you **had asked** her out the other day, she **might have agreed** to go out with you.*

Mixed conditional

We use a mixed conditional (*If* + past perfect, *would* + infinitive) to talk about an imaginary situation in the past and its effects/consequences in the present.

PAST SITUATION → EFFECT IN THE **PRESENT**
*If you **hadn't used** an online dating site, you **wouldn't be** happily married now.*
(You used an online dating site and that's why you are happily married now.)
*If I **had revised** before the exam, I **wouldn't have** to retake it now.*
(I didn't revise before the exam and that's why I have to retake it now.)
If the effect is not certain, we can use *might* in the main clause.

PAST SITUATION → EFFECT IN THE **PRESENT**
*If you **had paid off** some of your other debts, I **might lend** you some money.*
*If Ian **hadn't criticised** his sister's cooking yesterday, she **might cook** lunch for him today.*
*If they **had apologised** for their rude behaviour, the teacher **might not be** so angry.*

Reading

1 Look at the picture on page 105 and read the title and introduction. Choose the best answers to the questions.

1 It is an article about
   a a city that has already been built.
   b a city that could possibly be built in the future.

2 The text will probably contain information about
   a solutions for the problems cities have.
   b the biggest cities in the world.

2 Find these words in bold in the text and choose the best meaning.

1 *overcrowding*
   a encouraging more people to move to cities
   b unpleasant conditions caused by too many people in one place
   c people gathering together for a particular reason

2 *cope with*
   a deal successfully with something
   b understand why something happens
   c experiment with something

3 *unsustainable*
   a unhealthy
   b not able to continue at the same rate
   c impossible to stop

4 *platform*
   a a kind of plate
   b an area that you can walk around
   c a structure for people to walk on that is built higher than the ground

5 *consumption*
   a eating, drinking or buying something
   b selling something on the street
   c discussing a problem with a group of people

3 Read the text. Tick (✓) true, cross (✗) false, or write (?) if there is no information in the text.

1 ☐ Although most cities are bigger nowadays, they don't have as many problems as before.

2 ☐ The exhibition organisers asked architects to create a design for a city in ten years' time.

3 ☐ The Multiplicity design means it is not necessary to prevent the city population from increasing.

4 ☐ The idea of making cities 'greener' is not new in the US.

5 ☐ The Multiplicity architects believe that high temperatures due to climate change will cause problems for cities in the future.

6 ☐ Tony Downs doesn't think the design will help the environment much.

4 Look at the picture on page 105 and read the title and introduction. Choose the best answers to the questions.

1 Cities
   a are slowly becoming better places to live.
   b account for a very small area of the world's land.
   c cover large areas of land all over the world.
   d don't have such a large population as the countryside.

2 According to the text, the exhibition
   a contains plans for many of Australia's cities.
   b is all about the problems of cities in Australia.
   c has a new and very different design for Melbourne.
   d is all about Australia's biggest city.

3 The Multiplicity design
   a looks very much like an ordinary city today.
   b was inspired by a science fiction story.
   c doesn't reflect city planners' worries.
   d is intended to give solutions for problems that cities have.

4 Which would the platform above the city NOT be used for?
   a As farmland to grow produce.
   b Giving more space to build houses.
   c Providing areas such as parks for people.
   d Providing shade for the city.

5 Architects had the idea for the platform because
   a they had heard about the idea of rooftop gardens.
   b all Australian cities already have green rooftops.
   c rooftops are a good way of building up in cities.
   d in some cities in the US small ones already exist.

6 The Multiplicity design
   a means that nobody will have to travel to work.
   b will solve the problem of global warming.
   c offers protection from the effects of global warming.
   d is not really very eco-friendly.

COULD WE BE LIVING HERE SOON?

We are an urban planet. Today, the majority of the world's population lives in cities, yet cities and urban areas make up only 2 percent of the world's land. *FutureLife* talks to architect Tony Downs about the problems this creates and what solutions we might find for the future.

FutureLife: What are the biggest problems our cities face?

Tony Downs: Well, as our cities become bigger, problems such as traffic jams, pollution and **overcrowding** are getting steadily worse.

FL: So, what is being done about it?

TD: Well, the people responsible for planning the cities of the future are working hard to find possible solutions for these increasingly urgent problems – with some surprising results. In one attempt to see how cities could be transformed in the future, architects in Melbourne, Australia have come up with a revolutionary plan for the nation's second biggest city. It's called 'Multiplicity', and it's part of an exhibition called *Now + When: Australian Urbanism*.

FL: What can you tell us about Multiplicity?

TD: For the exhibition, architects were asked to imagine what cities might be like in a hundred years. The result might look like something from a science fiction film, but it was inspired by real problems faced by city planners, especially the problem of how to **cope with** population growth. That was their biggest dilemma.

FL: And why is that such a big problem?

TD: Well, usually, the bigger the population, the bigger the city. However, when cities become too big they become **unsustainable**.

FL: So what was their solution?

TD: The architects decided that instead of trying to limit the population their design would reflect what would happen if there was a much higher population in the same space. For this reason, in Multiplicity, the idea is to build up, not out. In addition, the plan is to create a giant **platform** which would be suspended over the city. The platform would be used to grow food, give green spaces for people to enjoy and to give shade from the sun to the city below.

FL: Where did they get the idea?

TD: The idea for the platform grew out of the concept of rooftop gardens. In cities such as Chicago and New York in the US urban planners have been talking about 'greening' cities by creating gardens on all rooftops. However, the architects took the idea much further. They designed it on a grand scale and in a way that meant the area could even produce food for local **consumption**.

FL: So, would you say the design is environmentally-friendly?

TD: Definitely. The architects' design also makes sense in terms of solving environmental problems. There would be a local supply of food, so energy wouldn't be wasted on transport – and because the city grows up rather than out, people won't have to travel so far, again saving fuel and energy. Finally, if temperatures do rise due to global warming, then the overhead platform will help keep the city cool.

Inviting and persuading

1 Complete the dialogues with one word in each space.

A: ¹ _Would_ you like to come for dinner?

B: ² _____ you, I'd ³ _____ to come.

A: Do you ⁴ _____ going for a coffee?

B: Not ⁵ _____ now, thanks.

A: Can I ⁶ _____ you to come to the restaurant with us?

B: I'd ⁷ _____ to, but I'm not sure if I can. I need to finish my work.

A: It would ⁸ _____ a lot to me if you came.

B: OK, ⁹ _____ not?

2 Put the sentences in the correct order 1–12 to form a dialogue.

a [1] Chris: Hi, Lisa. Sam, Kate and I are going to Marco's restaurant. Would you like come with us?

b [ ] Chris: Sure, how about at 9 p.m?

c [ ] Chris: Don't worry about money! It's my birthday, so it's my treat.

d [ ] Chris: On Saturday night at 7.30 p.m.

e [ ] Chris: Your grandparents? Would they mind if you came out? It would mean a lot to me if you came.

f [ ] Chris: Please come. I don't see you very often either!

g [ ] Lisa: That's very kind of you. In that case, I'd love to come. When are you going?

h [ ] Lisa: I know … could we eat a little later? That way I can see my grandparents and come out with you.

i [ ] Lisa: That sounds very nice, but I'm afraid I can't really afford it.

j [ ] Lisa: I'd love to, but we don't see other very often and …

k [12] Lisa: OK, why not? See you at 9 p.m. on Saturday.

l [ ] Lisa: Saturday? Oh, no! My grandparents are coming on Saturday.

A description of a place

3 Look at the photos and complete the sentences about Cuenca with the words below.

> located struck ✓ crowded unlike
> distinctive worth cliff landscape
> realise highlights world

1 When you arrive in Cuenca, you are immediately _struck_ by the dramatic _____ .

2 It's a _____ away from the noisy _____ streets of London.

3 Cuenca is _____ in central Spain, about an hour from the capital city, Madrid.

4 One of the _____ of Cuenca is the old town. The _____ buildings hang over the cliff and the views are spectacular.

5 You quickly _____ that the people are friendly and the buildings are beautiful.

6 It's _____ any other place I've visited.

7 In my opinion, Cuenca is a uniquely beautiful place that is well _____ a visit.

8 It is a small town and it sits at the top of a huge _____ .

4 Look at the sentences in exercise 3 again. Write the expressions that mean

1 you notice straightaway.

2 it's a good idea to go there.

3 the most important or exciting things to see.

4 it's very different from …

Use of English

Linking

1 Complete the sentences with the linking words below.

a Time

[as soon as   before   since ✓   until   while]

1 I haven't seen Laura _since_ we were at school together.
2 We negotiated with the seller _____ we agreed a price that we can afford.
3 We'd like to move in _____ the sale goes through.
4 I hope they finish renovating the house _____ we have to move in!
5 _____ we were talking to the estate agent, the children played outside.

b Cause and effect

[as a result   because ✓   due to   since   so]

1 I like this neighbourhood _because_ it's so culturally diverse.
2 They decided to move _____ problems with traffic.
3 Ted had to sell his house _____ of family problems.
4 _____ we were already in the area, we decided to visit Chris.
5 There was no work in my town, _____ I moved to the capital.

c Condition

[in case   if ✓   provided that   unless]

1 _If_ I hadn't left England, I wouldn't have my own lemon tree.
2 You can stay in my flat _____ you keep it clean.
3 We'll never have the life we want _____ we are prepared to take a risk.
4 Close the windows _____ it rains at night.

d Contrast

[although   but ✓   despite   however]

1 I was born in the city, _but_ I'd prefer to live in the countryside.
2 _____ his age, Mr Jones still spends several hours a day gardening.
3 _____ I like my flat, I wish I had house with a garden.
4 The house is attractive. _____ , the price is too high.

Exam tasks

Open cloze

2 Complete the text with one word in each gap.

How to stay sane while your flat is being done up

[1] _If_ you're having any building or redecoration work done in your flat, the first thing to do is to arrange to live with a friend [2] _____ it's being done. [3] _____ you move out, you'll be living on a building site, with dust, noise and no privacy. You may be tempted stay in spite [4] _____ these disadvantages, thinking you'll be able to keep an eye on the work. [5] _____ , that just means you'll be constantly upset by the delays. You'd better accept from the start that building work always lasts longer than planned, due [6] _____ problems an ordinary person cannot possibly understand. One way of preventing extreme delays is to agree with the builders you'll pay them as soon [7] _____ the work is finished, but not before that. And then, just be patient, and think how lovely your flat will be [8] _____ it's all over!

Reading

Multiple-choice

1 Read the introduction to an article about living abroad. Choose the best answer.

A lifetime of changes

Supposing you were offered a job in a far-off country. It would mean leaving behind everything you're used to: the people, the language, the scenery, the food. How would you react? Some of us would be excited, others might feel afraid.

For Simon Grant, that sort of change has been a way of life for the last forty years. He has lived and worked in eight countries, learning the language and exploring the culture of every one of them.

Going to live in a different country

a is always exciting.

b frightens everyone at first.

c requires you to learn the language before you go.

d is something Simon has done many times.

2 How did you know which answers were incorrect in exercise 1? <u>Underline</u> the words that give this information.

Exam TIP

To eliminate the wrong answers, you have to identify the difference in meaning which makes them wrong. One reason why an answer may be incorrect is that it is too general, for example, it says that something happens 'always' or to 'everyone', while the text says it happens 'sometimes' or to 'some people'.

3 Read the rest of the article. Choose the best answers.

'I've never wanted to be a tourist,' says Simon. 'I don't think you can learn anything significant about a country by staying in a hotel and walking around with a guidebook. Living the everyday life of a place, working, shopping for food, reading the newspapers, talking to people in their own language, has given me what I hope is real insight into each country's culture. It's been wonderfully enriching.'

It all started when he was 25. He was offered a teaching job at the University of West Indies in Barbados. 'We packed everything we had, which wasn't much in those days – mostly books – and we set off with our baby daughter, who was less than a year old. Until that time, we'd lived in Lancaster, renting a small, cramped and uncomfortable flat with the cheapest furniture. Then we arrived in Barbados, and there waiting for us was this terrific bungalow with palm trees around and a sea view from the patio. We simply couldn't believe it.'

Since then, Simon has lived in Nigeria, the Netherlands, Italy, Belgium, Poland and Spain, changing countries every few years. His three children grew up speaking not only English, but Dutch, French and Italian fluently. And as they went to international schools, they made friends of many different nationalities. The family returned to England briefly when the children went to university there.

What are some of Simon's most striking memories? 'There have been so many things: the climate and exotic fruit in Barbados, completely new to me then; living in the very democratic, tolerant and well-educated society of the Netherlands; the relaxed lifestyle of the Italian countryside; the incredibly rich cultural life of Brussels, with its museums and theatres; and I'll never forget the huge lemon tree outside my house in Ibiza … And, of course, the food in all these different places!'

Simon is now 65 and has just retired from teaching mathematics in Spain. His latest plan is to go back to university – this time as a student. He's starting a history degree at Liverpool University this October. And then, who knows? 'I've never lived in the Far East,' reflects Simon.

1 In Simon's opinion, other countries can best be explored by
   a leaving behind everything you're used to.
   b using a good guidebook.
   c adopting the local lifestyle.
   d reading about them in the papers.

2 The most memorable thing about moving to Barbados was that
   a there was so much packing to do.
   b travelling with a baby was difficult.
   c it was a very long journey.
   d the new home was impressive.

3 Simon's children
   a were educated outside England.
   b went to Dutch, French and Italian schools.
   c are fluent in several languages.
   d made friends for life.

4 In all the countries he's lived in, Simon has enjoyed
   a the climate.
   b the food.
   c the lifestyle.
   d the society.

5 In the future Simon
   a might travel again.
   b is going to teach at a British university.
   c does not intend to move again.
   d is going to settle down in Liverpool.

Listening

Matching

4 ⟨17⟩ **Listen to the beginning of a classroom discussion about lying. Choose the best summary of Natalie's opinion.** *Don't check the answer before doing exercise 5.*
   a It's not OK to lie to your parents.
   b Some lies are harmless and practical.
   c Lies are never serious.

5 ⟨17⟩ **Listen again and complete the sentences below. Check your answer to exercise 4.**
   1 I'm not talking about really _____ , _____ _____ .
   2 You know, everyday stuff, like at school when you haven't done your homework or when you don't want to tell _____ _____ where you're going.
   3 It makes everything _____ _____ _____ .
   And it doesn't _____ _____ .

Exam TIP

When matching statements to speakers, you should think about the general or overall meaning of what each speaker says. Listen to everything a speaker says before you decide on an answer.

6 ⟨18⟩ **Listen to the rest of the discussion about lying. Match the speakers 1–4 with the statements a–e. There is one extra statement.**
   a ☐ It is not necessary to lie in order to be kind to people.
   b ☐ I have never told a lie in my life.
   c ☐ Lies can have dangerous results and can destroy trust.
   d ☐ Situations in which lying is justified do not happen in everyday life.
   e ☐ Sometimes you may have to lie to be nice to someone.

self-assessment test 5

Vocabulary & Grammar

1 ~~Cross out~~ the word(s) that can't be used with the words in bold.

1 she's decided to **move** *in/~~at~~/out*
2 *do/reject/make* an **offer**
3 **he** was *fined/forged/tricked*
4 *cheat/con/pretend* **people**
5 they were **charged with** *shoplifting/parole/fraud*
6 *prosecution/accused/defence* **lawyer**
7 the man was **sentenced to** *death/community service/trial*

/6

2 Complete the sentences with one word in each gap.

1 Good *transport* links are important for anyone commuting to work.
2 There's a strong _____ of community among the people who live in my area.
3 The man is expected to _____ not guilty to new charges.
4 There should be fines for people who don't tidy up after themselves and leave _____ on the beach.
5 Life in my village is terribly boring. There are no _____ of any kind, not even a football pitch or a café, and there's nothing to do.
6 First-time home buyers find it difficult to get a _____ from a bank.
7 At what age did he _____ his first crime?

/6

3 Complete the sentences with the correct present or past form of the verbs in brackets.

1 She would be very unhappy now if she *had married* (marry) him.
2 I wish I _____ (be) faster – I could play football much better.
3 If we had saved more money last year, we _____ (go) on a long holiday now.
4 If only he _____ (not lose) his wallet the other day.
5 If you had told me you were not coming, I _____ (not make) a cake yesterday.
6 They can't _____ (see) Ian at the weekend – he was in Paris!
7 You'd have succeeded if you _____ (do) your best.
8 If only I _____ (know) his email address. I could contact him right now.

/7

4 Correct the mistakes in the sentences.

1 He didn't like rich food and avoided (to eat) out.
   He didn't like rich food and *avoided eating out* .
2 They asked me to leave, but I refused doing it.
   They asked me to leave, but I _____ .
3 You must be very tired yesterday if you fell asleep in front of the TV.
   You _____ yesterday if you fell asleep in front of the TV.
4 Ron suggested to go to the cinema but my parents didn't allow me to go.
   Ron _____ to the cinema, but my parents didn't allow me to go.
5 My parents encouraged to work in the summer, but I chose to go on holiday instead.
   My parents _____ in the summer, but I chose to go on holiday instead.
6 For me learn English is easy because I'm good at languages.
   For me _____ because I'm good at languages.
7 They're such a happy couple. It mustn't be true that they're getting divorced.
   They are such a happy couple. It _____ that they're getting divorced.

/6

5 Complete the text with the correct form of the words in CAPITALS.

Newspaper Blogs

We need tougher punishment!
Posted Mon 18 Jun 19.50 GMT

I've read today's papers and I'm appalled. A <u>murderer</u> ¹ (MURDER) gets away with a fifteen-year sentence. Only fifteen years! Where is the logic in it? He should be sentenced to life ² _____ (PRISON). And then we wonder why we have so many ³ _____ (ROB) and ⁴ _____ (THEFT) out there waiting to steal our property or burgle our houses. ⁵ _____ (BURGLE) and similar crimes should be punished very severely. Punishment is supposed to deter ⁶ _____ (CRIME) from illegal actions, not encourage them!

Well, that's my opinion. What's yours?

David

/5

Listening

6 (19) Listen to the news on the radio. Tick (✓) true, cross (✗) false or write (?) if there is no information.

1 The crime happened in the early evening. ☐

2 The robber must have watched all six films of the *Star Wars* series. ☐

3 At first the staff and customers thought it might not have been a serious attempt at a robbery. ☐

4 One customer forced the robber to leave the bank without money. ☐

5 So far the criminal has avoided being arrested. ☐

6 All three strange bank robberies have been found to be connected to each other. ☐

/6

Communication

7 Complete the summaries of headlines and newspaper articles with one word in each gap. The first letter of each word is given.

1 The article t<u>alks</u> about current issues in advertising.

2 A_____ to this article, teenagers need more sleep than adults.

3 The article s_____ that plants and animals can adapt in response to climate change.

4 It's also related to the t_____ of globalisation.

5 The article e_____ why online games have become so popular in recent years.

6 I think this headline m_____ that a lot of people are going to lose their jobs.

7 The article i_____ that downloading films is legal, but in fact, it's not.

/6

8 Complete the dialogues with the words below.

> can   fancy   invite ✓   know
> kind   love   mean   treat
> would

Dialogue 1

A: Mrs Jenkins, I'd like to ¹ <u>invite</u> you to my grandmother's 80th birthday.

B: Thank you very much but I'm afraid I have other plans.

A: It would ² _____ a lot to her if you came.

B: Well, OK. I promise I'll try.

Dialogue 2

A: We have a break now.
³ _____ you like to come for a cup of coffee with me?

B: Oh … that's very ⁴ _____ of you but I wanted to go through my notes.

A: Oh, go on. It's my ⁵ _____ . I've got some money on me and it won't take us long.

B: All right then.

Dialogue 3

A: ⁶ _____ I invite you to the hotel restaurant with us, Mr Jones?

B: Oh, yes. Thank you. I'd ⁷ _____ to come.

Dialogue 4

A: Do you ⁸ _____ going to the club with the three of us?

B: No, not this evening, thanks.

A: Oh … come on! You ⁹ _____ you'll enjoy it.

B: OK then.

/8

Marks

Vocabulary & Grammar	/30 marks
Listening	/6 marks
Communication	/14 marks
Total:	/50 marks

Reading

SUNDAY COMMENT   24 March

Sharing a house

John and Hannah met Peter and Laura when they came to teach English in Spain three years ago. After a year of living in uncomfortable flats, the two couples decided to rent a large farmhouse in the countryside together. Today they tell us about their experience.

A John, 60

Living with those two young people is sometimes a bit tiring. They're forever leaving dirty dishes in the sink. They leave things lying around in the shared living room, and if you speak to them about it, they'll say something like, 'But it's only a few dishes!' But apart from that they're very nice people, friendly and interested in the world. Laura grows wonderful vegetables in the garden, which we all benefit from. And the place itself here is just so beautiful that sharing with them was definitely a good move. At night, you can see lots of stars.

B Hannah, 48

I really love the house and the garden – the flowers (from February to November!) are beautiful and the orange trees are absolutely wonderful. At night, it's wonderfully quiet, with just the sounds of birds, frogs and insects. The fields around are full of peppers and watermelon and strawberries too. Our housemates get on my nerves sometimes, especially if they spoil the quiet by having the stereo on at full blast, but then I just go to my study and read. And they're nice kids. Peter makes terrific coffee, and he'll just knock on your door and bring you a cup when you're working.

C Peter, 28

Having John and Hannah around is a bit like living with your parents again – they tell you to tidy up or to turn the stereo down. But there are good sides too. John is extremely knowledgeable; he knows so much about books, films and history that sometimes it feels like having an interactive encyclopaedia at home. And I can always talk to Hannah about my work, or about anything for that matter. They both cook very well, so when one of them cooks and I make the coffee, that makes it a perfect meal.

D Laura, 27

John and Hannah can be a bit tiresome. They're always nagging us about keeping things tidy. And they don't like loud music, or what they call loud anyway, so we can only have it on properly when they're out. But the house is great. I spend a few hours every day working in the garden, and the way the vegetables grow is just incredible – everything is twice as big and twice as colourful as back home. I've learned a few new recipes from Hannah and John as well.

---

1 Read the paragraphs about sharing a house in Spain. Match ONE of the people A–D to the statements 1–10.

Which person mentions:

1 finding a way of being alone? _____
2 someone being a good listener? _____
3 cultural interests? _____
4 someone not treating complaints seriously? _____
5 wildlife? _____
6 a difference between Spain and his/her own country? _____
7 gardening? D and _____
8 the opportunity to learn from another person? C and _____
9 food preparation? B and _____
10 the volume at which music is played? C, D and _____

/10

Listening

2 (20) Listen to a radio discussion about a book on poverty. Tick (✓) true, cross (✗) false or write (?) if there is no information.

1 ☐ The author, Barbara Ehrenreich, had no qualifications.
2 ☐ She worked in a restaurant.
3 ☐ The author of the book believes that if you work hard, you will succeed.
4 ☐ Barbara Ehrenreich lived in a trailer.
5 ☐ Some poor people eat junk food because they have nowhere to cook.
6 ☐ The author of the book discovered she couldn't live on the money she was earning.

/6

Use of English

3 Complete the text with the correct form of the words in brackets.

Alice's diary

Saturday morning

I've been a bit depressed lately. I feel tired, physically and ¹_____ (mental). My ²_____ (motivate) is really low. Mum keeps lecturing me. She says I should be ³_____ (thank) for what I've got and so on. Well, I try to, but I'm just so ⁴_____ (exhaust)! Maybe I just need a holiday.

Saturday evening

Peggy's just phoned. She wants us to go to sailing next weekend! She sounded really ⁵_____ (enthusiasm). In fact, she's already made all the ⁶_____ (arrange)! The more I think about it, the more I like the idea. Peggy's a bit crazy, but as a source of ⁷_____ (inspire), she's brilliant! She is so ⁸_____ (energy)! I feel better already.

/8

4 Choose the correct answer a, b, c or d to complete the text.

Blogs

Commitment phobic
Posted Mon 8 Feb 17.36 GMT

My older brother Charlie is getting married tomorrow. So why is this interesting? Because until recently he was 'commitment phobic', that is, he was afraid to settle ¹___ with one person. Charlie used to say, 'If you look at the divorce ²___ in this country, it doesn't make any sense to get married.' He also said he didn't want to give ³___ his freedom. Then he met Natalie. Even though she's a really impressive girl, Charlie ⁴___ ages to make up his mind and propose to her. But finally they've ⁵___ the decision and now he seems really happy. I'm looking forward ⁶___ seeing the ex-commitment phobic have a family to look after!

	a	b	c	d
1	down	up	in	on
2	size	rate	number	amount
3	in	away	up	off
4	got	made	lasted	took
5	done	had	made	got
6	to	at	for	on

/6

Marks	
Reading	/10 marks
Listening	/6 marks
Use of English	/14 marks
Total:	/30 marks

Reading

1 Read the text about the effect of music on brain development. Match the sentences a–g to the gaps 1–6. There is one extra sentence.

a A few journalists noticed this interesting science story but it wasn't widely reported in the media.

b So the story became familiar to people in dozens of countries.

c It hardly matters that such a failure calls into question the reliability of the original results with the college students.

d In this second study, the results were even more impressive.

e Down in Florida, state-funded day care centres for children were obliged to play classical music every day.

f Children who learn to play a musical instrument have better spatial reasoning skills than those who don't take music lessons, maybe because music and spatial reasoning are processed by similar brain systems.

g For obvious reasons, sellers of classical music for children also encouraged the belief every chance they got.

/6

The Mozart Effect

One of the most persistent mistaken beliefs about brain development is that playing classical music to babies increases their intelligence. Despite the lack of evidence to support it, the theory has become widespread, probably because it seems to provide parents with an easy way to assist their children's intellectual development. [1]___ So what are the origins of this idea and is there any truth in it?

It all started in 1993, when a report in the scientific journal *Nature* claimed that listening to a Mozart sonata improved the performance of college students on a complex spatial reasoning task. [2]___ However, when popular science writer, Don Campbell, published a book called *The Mozart Effect* in 1997, it became a bestseller and the idea took off. Over the next few years, the theory that classical music makes babies smarter was repeated countless times in newspapers, magazines, and books. [3]___ In the US, the state government of Georgia sent classical music CDs to all parents of newborns in the state. [4]___ Interestingly, what all these authorities failed to notice was a basic fault in logic. How could they claim that listening to music would lead to lifelong intelligence improvement in babies based on an effect that (in the original experiment) lasted less than fifteen minutes in adults?

In 1999, another group of scientists repeated the original experiment on college students and found that they could not get the same results. [5]___ What is most significant here is that all these experiments were with college students. In the retelling, the stories about the Mozart effect had gradually replaced the college students of the original experiment with children or babies. In actual fact, no one had tested the idea on babies, ever. Other, more reliable research suggests you can use classical music to help your child's brain development, but only if you buy them a musical instrument and pay for some lessons. [6]___ Music may indeed improve children's intelligence – but only if they become active producers of music and not just passive consumers.

Listening

2 (21) Listen to an interview with a woman who runs a market research company. Choose the correct answer.

1 The main point of a market researcher's work is to
   a improve products.
   b design new packaging.
   c recommend marketing strategies.
   d investigate the buying decisions people make.

2 An example of a small-scale research method is
   a using questionnaires.
   b studying sales figures.
   c following a shopper.
   d contributing to internet forums.

3 The most important reason why the work is interesting is
   a it involves computer games.
   b each day is different.
   c there are no rules.
   d you learn about changes in society.

4 In the project Katherine describes, people
   a liked one kind of drink more because the packaging was nicer.
   b objected to the same drink having a higher price.
   c believed two samples of the same drink tasted different.
   d liked a drink more after their brains had been scanned.

5 Market researchers
   a must know advanced mathematics.
   b don't need to be precise.
   c have to be able to chat to clients.
   d must be prepared to learn.

/5

Use of English

3 Complete the text with the correct form of the words in brackets.

A cure for stress

I had a very ¹_____ (stress) week last week. On Friday I was feeling quite ²_____ (misery) and I guess I complained a bit. My boyfriend Bill said, 'You know, this moaning isn't especially ³_____ (construct). Let's do something to chill out. How about going to the Lake District?' And we did – it took us thirty minutes to make the decision and buy the tickets – I didn't realise I was so ⁴_____ (impulse)! The weather in the Lakes can be very ⁵_____ (predict), but we got lucky: it was sunny most of the time and it didn't rain at all. On the first day we walked along the shore of Ullswater, just to relax and admire the views, which were really ⁶_____ (amaze). On the second day we decided to climb Helvellyn. It was more ⁷_____ (exhaust) than I expected, and the walk took seven hours, so we were really ⁸_____ (starve) when we came back. We still had Monday off, so we used that to visit a few ⁹_____ (history) places connected with the Lake Poets. It was a really ¹⁰_____ (memory) trip.

/10

4 Choose the correct answer a, b, c or d to complete the text.

A false bargain

I bought a laptop last week. I'd been saving forever and I finally had enough money. I looked at a large ¹___ of offers, trying to choose the best one. Finally, almost ²___ accident I found a laptop I liked in a second-hand shop. It seemed to be ³___ good condition, and it was a great bargain. I worked ⁴___ if I bought it instead of a new one I'd still have enough money left for a few small gadgets. I had to ⁵___ a decision quickly – the salesman insisted other people were interested in the laptop. He also said I could have ten percent off if I paid ⁶___ cash. So I did, and after two days the laptop started malfunctioning. I took it back to the shop, but they ⁷___ me they didn't give refunds or exchange goods. My friend Sasha says it's obvious, that's the difference ⁸___ buying new and second-hand things. But I'm still disappointed! Fortunately, I still have some money left. Perhaps my parents will give me some more, they are very sorry ⁹___ me.

1 a amount   c number
  b deal   d lot

2 a by   c through
  b in   d on

3 a on   b in   c at   d the

4 a on   b up   c out   d for

5 a do   c make
  b have   d get

6 a by   b in   c for   d on

7 a said   c talked
  b spoke   d told

8 a in   c from
  b between   d of

9 a at   c for
  b about   d to

/9

Marks

Reading	/6 marks
Listening	/5 marks
Use of English	/19 marks
Total:	**/30 marks**

exam test 2

115

exam test 3

Reading

1 **Read the book review. Choose the correct answer.**

1 Caspar Walsh
   a spent most of his life in prison.
   b was arrested for theft.
   c had a father who was a criminal.
   d first entered a prison at the age of twenty.

2 Caspar returned to prison
   a to visit his father.
   b because he was dealing drugs again.
   c after his rehab programme ended.
   d to help other prisoners.

3 The book *Criminal* is
   a a novel.
   b not very attractively written.
   c a true story.
   d the story of Caspar's childhood.

4 One of the things that make the book special is that
   a Walsh is not sorry for himself.
   b it is written brutally and bitterly.
   c Walsh describes his own father as a bad man.
   d there are many fascinating characters.

5 The reviewer thinks the book
   a is for teenagers.
   b can interest people for several reasons.
   c may affect children negatively.
   d is only for adults.

/5

Listening

2 (22) **Listen to four recordings about famous art thefts. Match the recordings 1–4 to the sentences a–e. There is one extra sentence.**

1 ☐   2 ☐   3 ☐   4 ☐

a This robbery is compared to an action movie.

b The thieves claimed they wanted to teach the museum a lesson.

c This theft increased the popularity of the painting.

d This robbery was extremely brutal.

e The thief wanted money, but not for himself.

/4

BOOK REVIEW

Criminal by Caspar Walsh

In the foreword to *Criminal*, Caspar Walsh says: 'In one way or another, I've been involved with the British prison system for most of my life.' He was twelve years old when he started visiting his father, who was a thief and a drug dealer. At the age of twenty, already addicted to drugs and alcohol himself, Caspar was arrested for drug dealing. Whilst in prison, he eventually entered a rehab programme and took stock of his life for the first time. He made the decision to break away from his past life and on leaving prison, he promised himself he'd never return. He ended up by breaking that promise, but in a way he could never have imagined: for the past twelve years he's been running creative writing workshops for prisoners, based on his own experience of using writing as a tool for self-development and renewal.

Written as a novel, *Criminal* tells the vivid, shocking story of Walsh's life. He recounts his wild, confused childhood in the hands of a mother who was unable to look after him and a father who, despite his irresponsible, criminal lifestyle, loved his son and cared about him. He tells of his unhappy adolescence, increasingly dominated by drugs and crime, and of the arrest, which gave him the shock he needed to make him want to turn his life around. In the final chapters he describes some of the workshops he's been running, including one in which male prisoners wrote stories for their children. In Walsh's own words, it is a book about the decision he made to stop being the victim of his upbringing.

The book is brutally honest, often painful, but written without bitterness or self-pity. There are no good or bad guys. Caspar's father in particular comes across as a fascinating, complex character; and the complicated, loving yet disastrous relationship between father and son is difficult to condemn, despite its terrible consequences.

If you want to understand what draws teenagers into the world of drugs and crime, and how difficult it is for them to get out of it again, read *Criminal*. You should also read it if you're interested in children and the way they are affected by the actions of the adults around them; in fact, if you're interested in people at all, this book is for you. You won't be able to put it down!

Use of English

3 Complete the second sentence so that it means the same as the first.

1 Because the traffic was so bad, we couldn't get to the centre.

The traffic prevented _____ to the centre.

2 I'm in trouble because I borrowed so much money.

If _____ , I wouldn't be in trouble.

3 Despite being warned, the lady believed the conman.

Although _____ the lady believed the conman.

4 Bob and Alice managed to find a house they both love.

Bob and Alice succeeded _____ a house they both love.

5 If his lawyer doesn't come up with something brilliant, the man will be convicted.

Unless _____ something brilliant, the man will be convicted.

6 I'm sure this house was built in the nineteenth century.

This house must _____ in the nineteenth century.

7 It was such a daring robbery that a film was made about it.

The robbery was _____ a film was made about it.

8 The number of houses for sale has increased this year.

The number of houses for sale _____ up this year.

9 Frank regrets choosing a life of crime when he was young.

Frank wishes _____ a life of crime when he was young.

10 Our neighbours said we'd damaged their rose bushes.

Our neighbours accused _____ their rose bushes.

/10

4 Complete the text with one word in each gap.

House of dreams

My parents are thinking [1]_____ buying a holiday home. In fact, they've been trying to choose one for the last three years, [2]_____ they cannot agree on what they want. Dad would like a place in Scotland, [3]_____ spite of the cold weather. Mum insists [4]_____ being not too far from London. She says she can't go on holiday [5]_____ she can drive to her office and back when necessary. She also insists [6]_____ having a house with proper heating; Dad thinks that's too expensive. Today they asked my opinion: I said I don't mind where the place is, provided [7]_____ it has a fast internet connection! They didn't like that very much; they both object [8]_____ the amount of time I spend online. [9]_____ , they did ask me to look for interesting offers on the internet! I hope they make up their minds [10]_____ the next holidays; I'm looking [11]_____ to having somewhere to relax after the exams.

/11

Marks

Reading	/5 marks
Listening	/4 marks
Use of English	/21 marks
Total:	/30 marks

writing reference

Notes

1 Changing arrangements/asking to do something

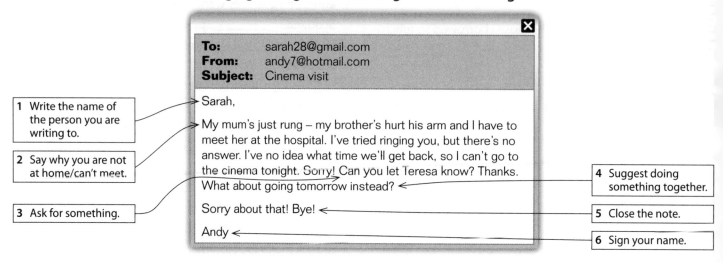

1 Write the name of the person you are writing to.

2 Say why you are not at home/can't meet.

3 Ask for something.

To: sarah28@gmail.com
From: andy7@hotmail.com
Subject: Cinema visit

Sarah,

My mum's just rung – my brother's hurt his arm and I have to meet her at the hospital. I've tried ringing you, but there's no answer. I've no idea what time we'll get back, so I can't go to the cinema tonight. Sorry! Can you let Teresa know? Thanks. What about going tomorrow instead?

Sorry about that! Bye!

Andy

4 Suggest doing something together.

5 Close the note.

6 Sign your name.

2 Making suggestions

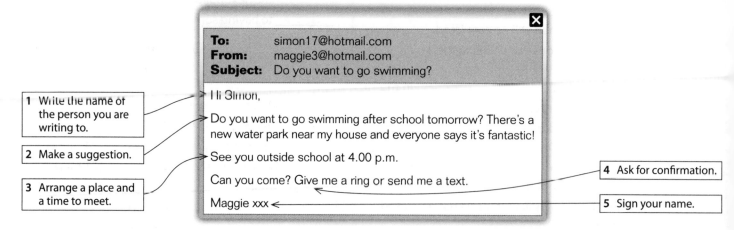

1 Write the name of the person you are writing to.

2 Make a suggestion.

3 Arrange a place and a time to meet.

To: simon17@hotmail.com
From: maggie3@hotmail.com
Subject: Do you want to go swimming?

Hi Simon,

Do you want to go swimming after school tomorrow? There's a new water park near my house and everyone says it's fantastic!

See you outside school at 4.00 p.m.

Can you come? Give me a ring or send me a text.

Maggie xxx

4 Ask for confirmation.

5 Sign your name.

Useful language

Making suggestions

Let's go to the cinema/ watch a DVD/go to the park.

Do you want to come/meet me?

Come to the park/for a coffee!

What about tomorrow/next week?

What about meeting later/ having pizza?

Are you free at the weekend/ on Friday?

Arranging a place

See you at/outside …

The/My address is …

Here's a map.

Let's meet at my house/at the café.

Arranging a time

Let's meet at 2 p.m./after school.

See you at 5 p.m.

Asking for confirmation

Can you come?

Send me a text.

Give me a call.

Saying why you are not at home/ can't meet

I'm going out because …

I'm going to … so I can't meet.

I can't go out tonight because … Sorry!

I've just received a call that …/ My dad's just rung to say that …

Asking for something

Can you bring a DVD/ buy some bread?

Do you mind ringing Kate to let her know?

Closing

See you soon/later/ in the afternoon/in the evening.

I hope to see you at/in …

Have a good/great day.

Bye!

Sorry!/Sorry about that!

Love/Lots of love,

Postcards

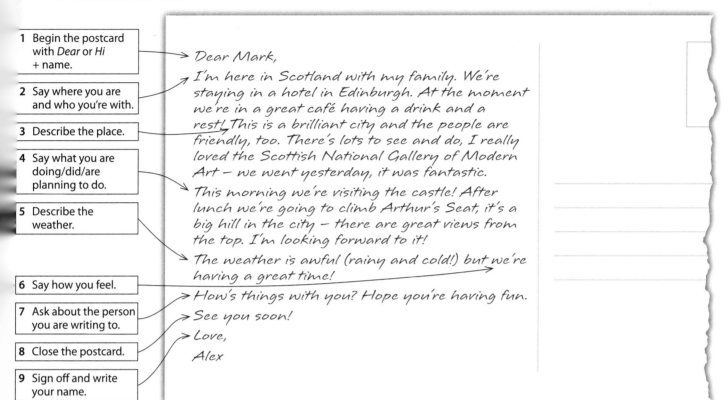

1 Begin the postcard with *Dear* or *Hi* + name.

2 Say where you are and who you're with.

3 Describe the place.

4 Say what you are doing/did/are planning to do.

5 Describe the weather.

6 Say how you feel.

7 Ask about the person you are writing to.

8 Close the postcard.

9 Sign off and write your name.

Dear Mark,

I'm here in Scotland with my family. We're staying in a hotel in Edinburgh. At the moment we're in a great café having a drink and a rest! This is a brilliant city and the people are friendly, too. There's lots to see and do, I really loved the Scottish National Gallery of Modern Art – we went yesterday, it was fantastic.

This morning we're visiting the castle! After lunch we're going to climb Arthur's Seat, it's a big hill in the city – there are great views from the top. I'm looking forward to it!

The weather is awful (rainy and cold!) but we're having a great time!

How's things with you? Hope you're having fun.

See you soon!

Love,
Alex

Useful language

Beginning a postcard

Hi,/Dear Anna,

I hope you're okay./I hope you're well.

How's things?

Information about the place where you are/who you're with

I'm in Prague.

I've just arrived at/in …

I'm spending my holiday/weekend in/at …

I'm on a school trip in …

I'm with my friends/family/classmates.

Describing a town

There is/are …

My favourite shop/place is …

The shops/restaurants/cafes/museums are interesting/expensive/great/fantastic.

The city is exciting/fantastic/brilliant/boring/polluted/crowded.

There's lots to see and do.

Places

galleries, museums, beach, forest, amusement park, old town, park, castle, shops

Accommodation

We're staying in a hotel/guest house/campsite.

I'm staying with friends.

Information about what you are doing/did/going to do

I've been really busy!

I'm here on a language course. We have five classes every day, but there's evening activities, too.

At the moment, I'm sitting in a café.

Today we're visiting museums/relaxing/sitting on the beach.

Yesterday we visited a museum/went to the beach/did some sightseeing.

Tomorrow we're going to go on a coach trip/relax/explore the city centre.

This evening I'm going to a restaurant/concert.

Later I'm meeting friends/going to a nightclub.

Activities

sightseeing, walking, sailing, windsurfing, snorkelling, climbing, skiing, sunbathing, shopping, studying

Talking about the weather

It's sunny/rainy/windy/snowy.

It's raining/snowing/sunny/hot/cold all the time.

The weather is great/terrible/OK/pretty good/awful.

Saying how you feel

We're having a great/terrible time.

I'm having lots of fun/enjoying myself a lot.

This is my best/worst/favourite holiday.

I'm enjoying/hating every minute!

Asking about the person you are writing to

How about you? What are you up to?

Hope you're fine and enjoying your holiday.

How's your summer/holiday?

Closing a postcard

See you soon.

Bye for now!

Signing off

Love/Lots of love,

Take care.

Best wishes/All the best.

Notices

1 Offers

1 Write a heading.	→	**FOR SALE**

Looking for a new guitar?

Classical guitar in great condition. Only £75.

Contact Terry on
0171 35787624
(mob 07856 3345321).

Pls call eves after 8 p.m.

1 Write a heading.

2 Give details of what you are offering.

3 Give your name and contact details.

2 Organising something

TRIP TO THEATRE

I'm organising a trip to the Manchester Royal Exchange Theatre to see 'Macbeth' on Sat 27 May.

Cost: £5 transport (coach)

Tickets for play £30.

Phone Dave on
01204 576231

1 Write a heading.

2 Give details of what you are organising (what is it, where, when, how much does it cost, etc).

3 Give your name and contact details.

3 Lost or found objects

1 Write a heading.

2 Describe the animal/object.

LOST!!

Small black dog with brown collar, called Blackie.
Lost in Queen's Park Tues 23 April about 5 p.m.
If you've found Blackie, please contact me ASAP!
£45 reward!
Contact Kathy on 03827 718926

3 Give details of when/where lost or found.

4 Give your name and contact details.

Useful language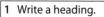

Headings

Lost!/Found!

Wanted!

Guitar/Snowboarding/
French lessons available.

Trip to Paris/London

Room for rent

For sale

A competition

Giving details of offers

Skis for sale, in great condition/
nearly new/never used.

2 tickets for Muse concert, only
£15 each.

Experienced teacher – classes for
all ages.

Individual or small groups – eves
and wknds only.

Room for rent – £23 p.w.

£10 reward!

Organising things

Trip to London on 24 August.

Cost of trip £40 (including ticket
and transport).

I'm organising a talent
competition …

The prizes include …

Anyone can take part!

Giving contact details

Phone/Call/
Contact Nick on 346 7789.

Please contact/call/
phone Jackie on …

Send me an email to (Kate) at …

Text me on …

If you've found it, please call (Sally).
My mobile is …

Describing something

It's a brown dog with a red collar/
small black and white cat.

It's a camera/mobile phone.

It's got stickers on/a black case.

Saying where/when lost or found

I left it at the gym/café.

I lost/found it at the sports centre.

I lost/found it on Sat a.m./around
3 p.m./on 5 May.

Last seen in the park/at the
shopping centre.

Abbreviations

Mon (Monday), Tues (Tuesday),
Weds (Wednesday),
Thurs (Thursday), Fri (Friday),
Sat (Saturday), Sun (Sunday)

a.s.a.p./ASAP (as soon as possible)

pls (please)

N/S (non-smoker)

mins (minutes)

mob (mobile)

yr old (year-old)

p.w. (per week)

p.h. (per hour)

wknds (weekends)

eves (evenings)

a.m. (morning)

p.m. (afternoon/evening)

Invitations

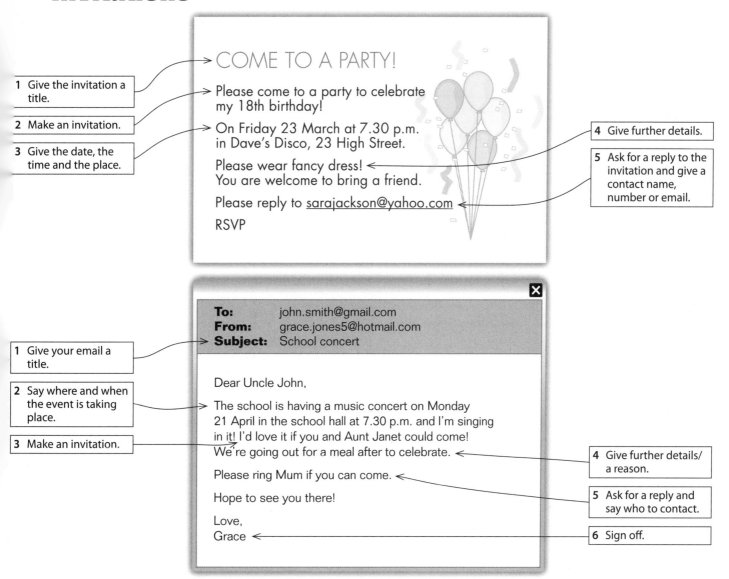

1 Give the invitation a title.

2 Make an invitation.

3 Give the date, the time and the place.

COME TO A PARTY!

Please come to a party to celebrate my 18th birthday!

On Friday 23 March at 7.30 p.m. in Dave's Disco, 23 High Street.

Please wear fancy dress!
You are welcome to bring a friend.

Please reply to sarajackson@yahoo.com

RSVP

4 Give further details.

5 Ask for a reply to the invitation and give a contact name, number or email.

To: john.smith@gmail.com
From: grace.jones5@hotmail.com
Subject: School concert

1 Give your email a title.

2 Say where and when the event is taking place.

3 Make an invitation.

Dear Uncle John,

The school is having a music concert on Monday 21 April in the school hall at 7.30 p.m. and I'm singing in it! I'd love it if you and Aunt Janet could come! We're going out for a meal after to celebrate.

Please ring Mum if you can come.

Hope to see you there!

Love,
Grace

4 Give further details/ a reason.

5 Ask for a reply and say who to contact.

6 Sign off.

Useful language

Giving a title

Fancy dress/Halloween party!

Come to a party!

Farewell Mrs Smith

Celebrate the end of the exams!

Happy Birthday!

School concert

Inviting people

Please come to …

We'd like to invite you to …

I'm having a birthday party …

We request the pleasure of your company (= we'd like to invite you).

I'd really love it if you could come.

Giving a reason

A party to celebrate …

An evening to learn about …

A party to say farewell to …

A welcome party for …

Giving further details

Live music and dancing.

Please bring drinks.

Bring your family and friends!

With drinks, food and dancing!

Casual dress/Fancy dress

We're going out for a meal after (the concert).

I'm singing in the concert/performing/in the play.

Asking for confirmation

If you want to come/are interested, contact/call …

RSVP (RSVP = French for 'Please reply')

Please call me if you can come/make it.

Please reply to john999@hotmail.com

Personal letters

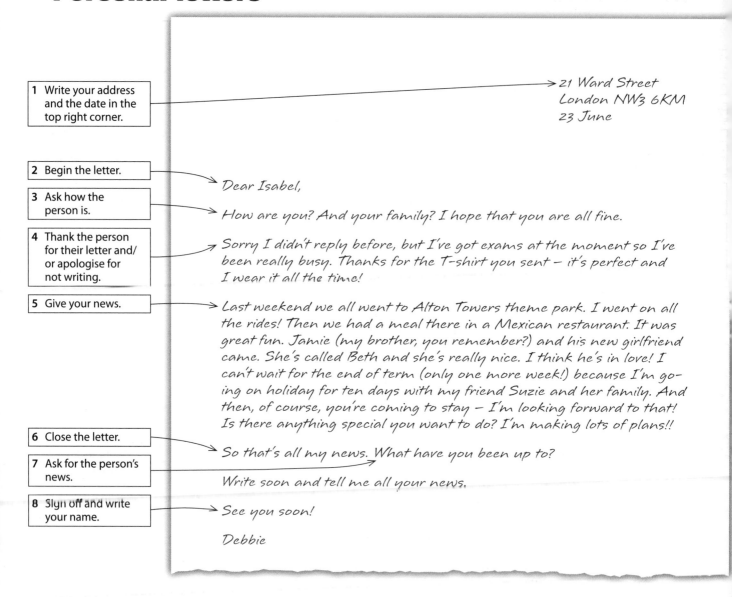

1 Write your address and the date in the top right corner.

> 21 Ward Street
> London NW3 6KM
> 23 June

2 Begin the letter.

Dear Isabel,

3 Ask how the person is.

How are you? And your family? I hope that you are all fine.

4 Thank the person for their letter and/or apologise for not writing.

Sorry I didn't reply before, but I've got exams at the moment so I've been really busy. Thanks for the T-shirt you sent – it's perfect and I wear it all the time!

5 Give your news.

Last weekend we all went to Alton Towers theme park. I went on all the rides! Then we had a meal there in a Mexican restaurant. It was great fun. Jamie (my brother, you remember?) and his new girlfriend came. She's called Beth and she's really nice. I think he's in love! I can't wait for the end of term (only one more week!) because I'm going on holiday for ten days with my friend Suzie and her family. And then, of course, you're coming to stay – I'm looking forward to that! Is there anything special you want to do? I'm making lots of plans!!

6 Close the letter.

7 Ask for the person's news.

So that's all my news. What have you been up to?

Write soon and tell me all your news.

8 Sign off and write your name.

See you soon!

Debbie

Useful language

Opening

Dear/Hi Sue,

Dear Granddad/Uncle Ben,

Asking how someone is

How are you?/How are you doing?

I hope you are well/fine.

How are things?

Thanking and apologising

Thanks for your letter/card …

It was good to hear from you.

Thank you for your letter/ the cheque/the book/ the present you sent …

I'm writing to thank you for …

It was really kind of you to …

Thank you so much!/Thank you very much!

Sorry I didn't write/reply before, but …

I'm really sorry that …

Sorry for not replying/writing …

Apologies for not writing sooner/ forgetting your birthday …

It won't happen again!

Giving your news

I'm writing to tell you …

My latest news is …

Last weekend I …

Finishing the letter

Well, I think that's all my news …

So that's my news.

Well, I think that's everything.

I've got to go now (because …)

Say hello to …

Asking for news

I'd love to hear all your news.

What's your news?

So that's my news. What about you?

Write soon and tell me your news.

Signing off

Lots of love,/Love,/All my love,

All the best,/Best wishes,

Take care,

See you soon!

Give my love to …

Bye for now.

Write soon.

That's all for now.

Letters from a reader

1 Write your address and the date in the top right corner.

2 Begin the letter.

3 Explain which article you are writing about.

4 Give the date when the article appeared.

5 Lead in to the topic.

6 Say what you agree with.

7 Contrast information.

8 Say what/who you disagree with.

9 Give your general opinion.

10 Sign off and write your name.

73 Albert Road
Manchester MC2 5GD
11 March

Dear Editor,

I have just read your article *Helping young people find employment* which appeared on 10 March.

I could not agree more with the opinion that young people really do want to work and that their biggest problem is getting experience. I found this article very interesting because I did not realise there were so many local companies that offer work experience programmes for teenagers. However, I am not sure that doing unpaid work experience is what all teenagers want to do.

I must strongly disagree with Mr Robbins when he says that being forced to do unpaid work should be obligatory. I think many teenagers do not know what job they want to do. Also, teenagers often do part-time jobs to earn money, so being forced to do unpaid work would mean they cannot do this.

In my opinion, work experience programmes are a great thing for young people who know what job they want to do. They are a great opportunity to learn new skills as well as getting experience.

Yours faithfully,

Jack Robertson

Useful language

Opening
Dear Sir,/Dear Sir or Madam,
Dear Editor,

Explaining your reason for writing
I am writing in connection with (+ title) …
I have just read your article (+ title) …
I am writing about the article/report/editorial …

Saying where/when you saw the article
… which appeared in the paper on (6 January).
… which was in last Saturday's paper/last month's magazine.

Leading into the topic
As a (teenager/writer/student) myself, I …
I would like to thank you for/congratulate you on the article.
The article was very interesting because …
I found the article very interesting/informative …
I was surprised/shocked to read that …
I completely/totally agree with the opinion that …

Saying you agree
I agree with (Mr Robbins)/that …
I completely agree …
I could not agree more with the writer/that …
I agree that it is true that …

Contrasting an opinion
However,/Having said that,/Nevertheless, …
Although/Even though …
On the other hand, …

Saying you disagree
I do not agree that …
I disagree with (Mr Robbins)/that …
I strongly disagree …

Giving your opinion
In my opinion, …
I think that …
I believe that …
It seems to me that …
From my point of view, …

Closing
Yours faithfully,

Letters of complaint

1 Write your address and the date in the top right corner.

2 Write the name and address of the company you are writing to on the left.

3 Begin the letter.

4 Paragraph 1: Give your reason(s) for writing.

5 Paragraph 2: Explain the problem in detail.

6 Paragraph 3: Say what you want to happen as a result of your letter.

29 Mill Lane
Brighton BR2 3RF
16 January

Customer Services
Diamond Hotel,
34 Holborn Road,
London NW3 2JM

Dear Mr Hobbs,

I am writing to make a complaint about our stay in the hotel on 14 January.

We chose your hotel to celebrate our wedding anniversary and our night was completely ruined. Firstly, we asked for a quiet room when we made the reservation. However, there was a problem with overbooking and when we arrived we had to take the only room available. It was extremely noisy and small. Secondly, the heating was not working properly and the room was very cold. Finally, room service was very slow and the food was cold when it arrived. I complained when we left the hotel, but the manager told me I had to contact you directly.

I enclose a copy of the receipt. In view of the fact that the overbooking, heating problem and terrible room service were the hotel's fault I do not think we should have to pay the full cost of the room. Could you please give me a refund as soon as possible?

I look forward to hearing from you in the near future.

Yours sincerely,

Charles Anderson

CHARLES ANDERSON

7 Say that you expect a reply.

8 Sign off and write your name.

9 Print your name underneath or write it in CAPITAL LETTERS.

Useful language

Beginning a formal letter
Dear Sir or Madam,
Dear Mr White,/Ms Reid,

Saying why you are writing
I am writing to complain about …
I am writing to make a complaint about …
I am writing about a fault in a TV/camera/phone.
I am writing about a problem with my course/hotel reservation/holiday.

Giving details
I bought it/them from Super Stores on (5 May).
I bought a watch/mobile phone/dress at your store yesterday.

I visited your restaurant/hotel last week.
I started a course at your language school (ten days ago).

Describing problems
We had a terrible meal because …
The room was very noisy/dirty and the service was slow/terrible.
The (battery) does not work.
There is a problem with (the remote control).
It is impossible to (use the phone camera).
There is a fault in the (controls).
It broke two days after I bought it.
The (remote control) was missing.
The (TV) suddenly stopped working.
The course is very disorganised.

Saying what you expect
Could you please send me …
I would like a refund/replacement.
I enclose a copy of the receipt.
I would be grateful if you could repair/replace the camera/phone/watch.

Showing you expect a reply
I look forward to hearing from you in the near future.
I look forward to hearing from you as soon as possible.
I look forward to your prompt response.

Signing off a formal letter
Yours sincerely, (with *Dear* + name)
Yours faithfully, (with *Dear Sir or Madam*)

Letters of application

1 Write your address and the date in the top right corner.

235 Ryedale Road,
Bristol BR3 5BB
15 May

2 Write the address of the organisation or person you are writing to on the left. Include the person's job title if you know it.

The Manager
Office Creations
23–25 Park Street
Bristol BR7 4ED

3 Begin the letter.

Dear Sir or Madam,

4 Say why you are writing. If appropriate say where and when you saw the advertisement/ information about a course etc.

I am writing in response to your job advertisement in the Bristol Times on 14 May for summer jobs. I would like to apply for the post of Office Assistant.

5 Say which job or course you would like to apply for.

I am in my last year of school and I am planning to go to university to study Business Management so I am very interested in working for a successful company such as Office Creations. Although I do not have any experience, I am a very organised person, I can type and I am very hard-working. I am sociable and I enjoy working with other people.

6 Give relevant information about your studies, qualifications, personal qualities and interests. If appropriate describe your future plans and ambitions.

I am enclosing my C.V. If you require any further information, please do not hesitate to get in touch. You can contact me by email (annab63@yahoo.com) or by phone (07796 654379). I would be very happy to come for an interview any day next week after school.

I look forward to hearing from you.

Yours faithfully,
Anna Bland
ANNA BLAND

7 Say what you are enclosing with the letter, e.g. a CV, photograph or application form.

8 Say that the person can contact you for further information and give your contact details.

9 Offer to give references and/or say when you are available for interview.

10 Close the letter by saying you expect a reply.

11 Sign off and write your name.

12 Print your name underneath or write it in CAPITAL LETTERS.

Useful language

Beginning a formal letter
Dear Sir or Madam,
Dear Mr White,/Ms Reid,

Explaining your reason for writing
I am writing with regard to/ in reply to/ in response to/ in connection with …

I have just seen your advertisement for a job/course.

I am writing to apply for …

Describing your qualification and experience
I have worked for (two months) as (a shop assistant).

My experience includes …

Although I do not have any direct experience, …

I have three A-levels in English, History and French.

I have completed my first year of a university course in …

Describing your personal qualities and interests
I am hard-working/organised/ practical/sociable.

I can type/speak French/drive.

I enjoy working with people/ helping others/ visiting other countries.

Talking about your ambitions
In the future I hope to …

My ambition is to …

I am planning to …

My dream is to …

I have always wanted to …

Giving other details
I enclose my CV/application form/ personal letter/photograph/ references.

You can contact me by email/ by phone/in the evenings.

Please do not hesitate to contact me if you require any further information/other details/ a reference.

I would be happy to answer any further questions/come for an interview.

I am available for interviews any afternoon/at any time that is convenient for you.

Showing you expect a reply
I look forward to hearing from you in the near future.

I look forward to hearing from you as soon as possible.

I look forward to your prompt response.

Signing off a formal letter
Yours sincerely, (with *Dear* + name)

Yours faithfully, (with *Dear Sir* or *Madam*)

exam topic wordlist

country and society

crime and law

abolish (v)
accuse (v)
arrest (v)
attack (v)
break the law (v)
burglary (n)
burgle (v)
case (n)
charge sb with (phr v)
cheat sb out of sth (phr v)
claim (v)
commit (v)
community service (n)
confess (v)
convict (n)
convict (v)
conviction (n)
copyright (n)
court (n)
crime (n)
criminal (n)
death penalty (n)
deception (n)
defence (n)
defend (v)
deterrent (n)
escape (v)
evidence (n)
execute (v)
execution (n)
fine (v)
fine (n)
forged (adj)
fraud (n)
fraudster (n)
gang (n)
guilty (adj)
hoax (n)
illegally (adv)

in prison (prep phr)
innocent (adj)
jail (v)
judge (n)
judge (v)
judgement (n)
judgemental (adj)
jury (n)
kidnap (v)
lawyer (n)
life imprisonment (n)
murder (v)
parole (n)
plead (v)
police (n)
possession of drugs (n)
prosecute (v)
prosecution (n)
prove (v)
punishment (n)
reform (v)
release (v)
rob (v)
robber (n)
robbery (n)
sentence (n)
sentence (v)
shoot (v)
shoplift (v)
shoplifter (n)
shoplifting (n)
steal (v)
suspect (v)
terrorism (n)
theft (n)
thief (n)
trial (n)
victim (n)
witness (n)
wound (v)

truth and lies

admit (v)
con (v)

deceive (v)
fool (v)
genuine (adj)
lie to sb (v)
pretend (v)

culture

art

art collector (n)
artist (n)
auction house (n)
exhibition (n)
museum (n)
painting (n)
restore (v)

film

angle (n)
blockbuster (n)
budget (n)
camcorder (n)
centre on (v)
cinema (n)
climax (n)
come up with (phr v)
direct (v)
do research (v)
DVD (n)
end up (phr v)
extra (n)
fail (v)
fan (n)
fantasy (adj)
fault (n)
festival (n)
film (n)
film studio (n)
filmmaker (n)
good point (n)
movie (n)
on location (prep phr)
original (adj)

pick up (phr v)
play (v)
plot (n)
point of view (n)
recommend (v)
release (v)
review (n)
romance (n)
rope sb in (phr v)
script (n)
set (v)
shoot a scene (v)
special effect (n)
special feature (n)
storyline (n)
succeed (v)
suspense (n)
take place (v)
talent (n)
talk sb into (phr v)
tell the story (v)
turning point (n)
twist (n)
walk around (phr v)
well-rounded (adj)
worldwide (adj)

literature
come out (v)
criticism (n)
constructive (adj)
edit (v)
feedback (n)
literary agent (n)
publish (v)
publisher (n)
publishing deal (n)
reader (n)
review (v)
thriller (n)
writer (n)

music
album (n)
band (n)
base on (v)
baton (n)
club (n)

concert (n)
conduct (v)
conductor (n)
get hits (v)
gig (n)
music (n)
number one single (n)
orchestra (n)
overnight sensation (n)
pop star (n)
post (v)
record label (n)
recording deal (n)
release (v)
sign (v)
singer (n)
talent contest (n)
venue (n)
world tour (n)

theatre
acting (n)
audience (n)
backstage (n)
bow (v)
cast (n)
cheer (v)
circle (n)
clap (v)
costume (n)
curtain (n)
dressing room (n)
first act (n)
go up (phr v)
interval (n)
make-up (n)
musical (n)
on stage (prep phr)
opening night (n)
performance (n)
producer (n)
production (n)
put on (v)
refreshment (n)
refund (v)
set (n)
show appreciation (v)
stalls (n)

take a seat (v)
theatre (n)
ticket (n)

family and social life

family and life stages
breadwinner (n)
bring up (phr v)
child (n)
dad (n)
family (n)
full-time (adj)
generation (n)
give up (phr v)
go up (v)
head of the household (n)
household (n)
househusband (n)
housewife (n)
housework (n)
husband (n)
in charge of (v)
inherit (v)
kid (n)
leave home (v)
marry (v)
matriarchal (n)
mother (n)
move back (v)
mum (n)
nest (n)
one-parent family (n)
parent (v)
stay-at-home-dad (n)
wife (n)

relationships
[live] happily ever after (v)
arranged marriage (n)
ask sb out (phr v)
avoid (v)
behave (v)
boyfriend (n)
chore (n)
communicate (v)

company (n)
conflict (n)
crazy (adj)
custom (n)
date (v)
divorce rate (n)
drive sb mad (phr v)
dump (v)
enjoy sb's company (v)
finances (n)
forget (v)
get married (v)
get on sb's nerves (phr v)
give back (phr v)
go off with (v)
go out with (phr v)
gossip (v)
hand over (phr v)
have a chat (v)
have a laugh (v)
interrupt (v)
issue (n)
leave a mess (v)
live with sb (n)
habit (n)
look after (phr v)
make a drama out of sth (v)
mislay (v)
nag (v)
partner (n)
pay for (phr v)
reasonably (adv)
relationship (n)
responsibility (n)
row (n)
rule (n)
settle down (phr v)
share (v)
show off (v)
take ages (v)
tie the knot (v)
treat with respect (v)
trust (v)
upset (adj)
wind someone up (phr v)
work out (phr v)

food

describing food and drink
boiled (adj)
delicious (adj)
disgusting (adj)
fizzy (adj)
fried (adj)
grilled (adj)
lean (adj)
mashed (adj)
nutritious (adj)
pickled (adj)
processed (adj)
raw (adj)
rich (adj)
roast (adj)
runny (adj)
soft (adj)
spicy (adj)
strong (adj)
sweet (adj)
tender (adj)

food items
aubergine (n)
bean (n)
bread (n)
cabbage (n)
cheese (n)
chicken drumstick (n)
chilli (n)
curry powder (n)
drink (n)
fish (n)
flavouring (n)
fruit (n)
fruit salad (n)
garlic (n)
haggis (n)
herb (n)
kangaroo (n)
kiwi (n)
lamb (n)
liver (n)
mango (n)
meat (n)
muffin (n)

nut (n)
oatmeal (n)
pigeon (n)
pizza (n)
potato (n)
prawn (n)
protein (n)
rice (n)
salad (n)
sauce (n)
sausage (n)
seafood (n)
soup (n)
steak (n)
spice (n)
tuna (n)
turnip (n)
vegetable (n)
watermelon (n)
wine (n)

meals
barbecue (v)
chef (n)
cuisine (n)
dessert (n)
dinner (n)
dish (n)
feed (v)
kitchen (n)
main course (n)
meal (n)
menu (n)
packaged food (n)
ready meal (n)
recipe (n)
restaurant (n)
special offer (n)
speciality (n)
starter (n)
three-course meal (n)
toast (v)
vegetarian (n)

health

body and illness
body (n)

good for you (adj)
ill (adj)
illness (n)
infection (n)
liver failure (n)
lung cancer (n)
motor-neuron disease (n)
nose (n)
obsess (v)
paralysed (adj)
physical (adj)
virus (n)

healthcare and treatment
antibiotic (n)
bacteria (n)
chemotherapy (n)
cure someone (v)
damage your health (v)
dialysis (n)
ethical (adj)
have surgery (v)
healthcare (n)
hospital (n)
keep sb alive (v)
medical (adj)
medicine (n)
obese (adj)
operation (n)
organ donor (n)
risk your health (v)
sick (adj)
suffer from an illness (v)
take care of (v)
therapy (n)
transplant (n)
treatment (n)
wheelchair (n)

house

building
apartment (n)
architect (n)
build (v)
building (n)
conventional (adj)

demolish (v)
make room for (phr v)
roof (n)
skyscraper (n)
structure (n)
tree house (n)

buying a house
accommodation (n)
agree a price (v)
buyer (n)
cramped (adj)
estate agent (n)
go through (phr v)
homeowner (n)
look round (phr v)
make an offer (v)
mortgage (v)
move (house) (v)
move in (phr v)
move out (n)
negotiate (v)
property (n)
reject an offer (v)
rent (n)
up for sale (prep phr)

location
atmosphere (n)
cave (n)
city centre (n)
colonise (v)
colony (n)
crowded (adj)
culturally diverse (adj)
family-friendly (adj)
floating city (n)
green space (n)
litter (n)
local facilities (n)
locate (v)
nothing to do (phr)
pollution (n)
sense of community (phr)
town (n)
traffic (n)
transport links (n)
village (n)

natural environment

environmental issues
climate (n)
energy (n)
environment (n)
global warming (n)
grow crops (v)
habitable (adj)
melt (v)
mine (v)
mineral (n)
natural resource (n)
oil (n)
population (n)
purify (v)
rainwater (n)
raise animals (v)
renewable (adj)
rise (v)
sea level (n)
uninhabitable (adj)

landscape
cliff face (n)
countryside (n)
desert (n)
glacier (n)
ice cap (n)
island (n)
landscape (n)
scenery (n)
waterfall (n)

people

appearance
colourful (adj)
description (n)
huge (adj)
petite (adj)
slender (adj)
unusual (adj)
wild (adj)

emotions and feelings

amazed (adj)
boiling (adj)
brilliant (adj)
desperate (adj)
exhausted (adj)
freezing (adj)
furious (adj)
hilarious (adj)
outstanding (adj)
soaked (adj)
starving (adj)
terrible (adj)
terrifying (adj)

personal qualities

achieve (v)
achievement (n)
admire (v)
analytical (adj)
artistic (adj)
attitude (n)
badly organised (adj)
behave (v)
challenge (n)
competition (n)
confidence (n)
dedication (n)
depressed (adj)
determination (n)
discipline (n)
empathetic (adj)
energetic (adj)
famous (adj)
hard work (n)
imaginative (adj)
impulsive (adj)
independent (adj)
inspiration (n)
inspire (v)
luck (n)
make an impression (v)
memorable (adj)
motivation (n)
multi-tasking (n)
natural talent (n)
personality (n)
possible (adv)

practical (adj)
pressure (n)
process information (v)
quick-thinking (adj)
reasonable (adj)
respect (n)
role model (n)
sacrifice (n)
satisfaction (n)
self-confidence (n)
skill (n)
spatial skills (n)
support (n)
unpredictable (adj)
verbal skills (n)

social interaction

accuse (v)
advise (v)
agree (v)
apologise (v)
deny (v)
dunno (contraction)
explain (v)
Globish (n)
innit (contraction)
insist (v)
lol (contraction)
non-native (adj)
promise (v)
refuse (v)
sick (adj)
slang (n)
social network (n)
warn (v)
wassup (contraction)

school

education

A-levels (n)
course (n)
curriculum (n)
education (n)
learn (v)
lesson (n)
life skill (n)
literacy (n)

numeracy (n)
pupil (n)
schoolboy (n)
study (v)
teach (v)
teacher (n)

subjects and curriculum

basic (n)
chemistry (n)
happiness (n)
History (n)
ICT (n)
music (n)
politics (n)
subject (n)
well-being (n)

science and technology

technology

3D (adj)
app (n)
battery life (n)
character (n)
communication technology (n)
digital (adj)
figure (n)
gadget (n)
games console (n)
hand-held (adj)
handset (n)
hands-free (adj)
high-definition (adj)
landline (adj)
media player (n)
mini projector (n)
mobile phone network (n)
refusnik (n)
smartphone (n)
state-of-the-art (adj)
techie (adj)
technology (n)
technophobe (n)
text message (n)
texting (n)

touch-screen (adj)
transfer (v)
video (n)
wireless (adj)

computers and internet
blog (n)
blogger (n)
computer virus (n)
desktop (n)
download (v)
email (n)
hard drive (n)
high-speed (adj)
internet connection (n)
internet-enabled (adj)
laptop (n)
online (adj)
operating system (n)
phishing (n)
profile (n)
search engine (n)
social networking site (n)
update (v)
upload (v)
web browser (n)
web page (n)
wind-up (adj)
World Wide Web (n)
YouTube (n)

shopping and services

advertising
advert (n)
advertising agency (n)
advertising campaign (n)
aim at (v)
billboard (n)
brand (n)
fly poster (n)
jingle (n)
leaflet (n)
logo (n)
pop-up (adj)
product (n)

promote (v)
promotional (adj)
slogan (n)
stealth marketing (n)
word-of-mouth (n)
target audience (n)

money
afford (v)
bank (n)
bank account (n)
bank loan (n)
bill (n)
borrow (v)
cash (n)
change (n)
charge (v)
cheap (adj)
cough up (phr v)
credit card (n)
debt (n)
details (n)
expensive (adj)
free (adj)
ignore (v)
in credit (prep phr)
in debt (prep phr)
in the red (prep phr)
live the high life (v)
loan (n)
overdraft (n)
overdrawn (adj)
owe (v)
pay (v)
pay sth back (phr v)
payment (n)
price (n)
receipt (n)
refund (n)
repay (v)
save up (phr v)
spend (v)
statement (n)

selling/buying
bargain (n)
buy (v)
chain store (n)
consumer (adj)

consumer (n)
department store (n)
designer (adj)
fake (adj)
faulty (adj)
in stock (prep phr)
market (n)
on special offer (prep phr)
order (v)
packaging (n)
retailer (n)
second-hand (adj)
secure (adj)
shop assistant (n)
shopper (n)
steal (v)
stock (v)
supermarket (n)
wrap sth up (v)

sport

competition
compete (v)
competition (n)
event (n)
finishing line (n)
match (n)
play (v)
race (n)
team (n)
train (v)
training (n)
win (v)

sports and sports people
boxer (n)
coach (n)
competitor (n)
goalkeeper (n)
hike (v)
hiking (n)
hockey (n)
sportsman (n)
surfing (n)
swimmer (n)

travelling and tourism

describing a trip
all of a sudden (adv)
amazingly (adv)
eventually (adv)
fortunately (adv)
gradually (adv)
sadly (adv)
strangely (adv)
suddenly (adv)
surprisingly (adv)
thankfully (adv)
to my horror (adv)
unfortunately (adv)

holidays
backpack (n)
beach resort (n)
chilling out (n)
eating out (n)
full board (n)
guided tour (n)
hiking holiday (n)
hire (v)
nightlife (n)
off the beaten track (prep phr)
room service (n)
package holiday (n)
self-catering (adj)
sunbathing (n)
the locals (n)
tourist (n)

travel
abroad (n)
couch surfing (n)
country (n)
culture (n)
hitch-hike (v)
host (n)
landmark (n)
travel (v)
traveller (n)

work

career and employment
achieve (v)
assess (v)
career (n)
degree (n)
develop (v)
employer (n)
experience (n)
job (n)
job offer (n)
journalism (n)
work in a team (v)

describing jobs and skills
ability (n)
confident (adj)
enthusiastic (adj)
highly-motivated (adj)
interpersonal (adj)
lifestyle (n)
low-paid (adj)
positive attitude (n)
proven (adj)
report (v)
senior (adj)
sound IT skills (adj)
well-paid (adj)
well-qualified (adj)
willing (adj)

jobs
correspondent (n)
hospital porter (n)
journalist (n)
kitchen porter (n)
manager (n)
miner (n)
nurse (n)
telesales worker (n)
tour guide (n)
travel rep (n)

irregular verbs

Infinitive	2nd Form (Past Simple)	3rd Form (Past Participle)
be	was/were	been
become	became	become
begin	began	begun
break	broke	broken
bring	brought	brought
build	built	built
burn	burned/burnt	burned/burnt
buy	bought	bought
catch	caught	caught
choose	chose	chosen
come	came	come
cost	cost	cost
cut	cut	cut
dig	dug	dug
do	did	done
draw	drew	drawn
dream	dreamed/dreamt	dreamed/dreamt
drink	drank	drunk
drive	drove	driven
eat	ate	eaten
fall	fell	fallen
feed	fed	fed
feel	felt	felt
fight	fought	fought
find	found	found
fly	flew	flown
forget	forgot	forgotten
forgive	forgave	forgiven
get	got	got
give	gave	given
go	went	gone
grow	grew	grown
have	had	had
hear	heard	heard
hide	hid	hidden
hit	hit	hit
hold	held	held
hurt	hurt	hurt
keep	kept	kept
know	knew	known
lead	led	led
learn	learned/learnt	learned/learnt
leave	left	left

Infinitive	2nd Form (Past Simple)	3rd Form (Past Participle)
let	let	let
lie	lay	lain
light	lit	lit
lose	lost	lost
make	made	made
mean	meant	meant
meet	met	met
pay	paid	paid
put	put	put
read /ri:d/	read /red/	read /red/
ride	rode	ridden
ring	rang	rung
run	ran	run
say	said	said
see	saw	seen
sell	sold	sold
send	sent	sent
set	set	set
shine	shone	shone
show	showed	shown
shut	shut	shut
sing	sang	sung
sit	sat	sat
sleep	slept	slept
smell	smelled/smelt	smelled/smelt
speak	spoke	spoken
spend	spent	spent
spill	spilled/spilt	spilled/spilt
stand	stood	stood
steal	stole	stolen
swim	swam	swum
take	took	taken
teach	taught	taught
tear	tore	torn
tell	told	told
think	thought	thought
throw	threw	thrown
understand	understood	understood
wake	woke	woken
wear	wore	worn
win	won	won
write	wrote	written

self-assessment and exam tests answer key

self-assessment test 1

1 2 bring, 3 huge, 4 down, 5 nagging, 6 starving, 7 share

2 2 rate, 3 furious, 4 settle, 5 out, 6 breadwinner, 7 go

3 2 had/'d been digging
3 have/'ve turned
4 is/'s staying
5 were watching
6 have/'ve been ironing
7 had they been
8 ran
9 has she been learning

4 2 is always crashing
3 I often used to feel/I often felt
4 I've written
5 asking her …
6 have you driven

5 2 reasonably
3 arranged
4 dedication
5 responsibility/responsibilities
6 inspiration

6 1 Bethany, 2 John, 3 Bethany, 4 Helena, 5 Matthew, 6 Helena, 7 John

7 2 calling, 3 concerning, 4 Hold, 5 through, 6 there, 7 available, 8 popped, 9 ring

8 2 on, 3 seem, 4 like, 5 To, 6 mind

self-assessment test 2

1 2 c, 3 f, 4 a, 5 d, 6 b

2 2 qualified, 3 interpersonal, 4 motivated, 5 experience, 6 skills, 7 willing

3 2 b, 3 c, 4 c, 5 a, 6 a, 7 c

4 2 will have made
3 arrives
4 is/'s throwing
5 will never ask
6 will/'ll be getting ready
7 am not/'m not doing
8 are/'re going to crash
9 will have been

5 2 should have gone hiking instead of
3 pupils in Al's school have to wear
4 wouldn't be my best friend if she didn't always
5 I needn't have taken a laptop
6 that they won, they would get promoted

6 1 b, 2 d, 3 a, 4 c, 5 b

7 2 say/argue/think/believe, 3 that, 4 disagree, 5 Let, 6 First, 7 opinion, 8 mean, 9 What's, 10 Finding, 11 same, 12 one, 13 Look, 14 example/instance, 15 rising/increasing, 16 sum

self-assessment test 3

1 2 nightlife, 3 gig, 4 acts, 5 the contest, 6 lean, 7 beaten track, 8 suspense, 9 the dressing rooms

2 2 guided, 3 release, 4 cast, 5 location, 6 sign

3 2 the post office is, 3 which, 4 a little, 5 being interviewed, 6 who, 7 a great deal

4 2 Who did/with?
3 It is said
4 only a few clothes.
5 that/which tightens or loosens screws
6 how much you paid for
7 have been arrested

5 2 b, 3 a, 4 d, 5 b, 6 c

6 1 d, 2 c, 3 a, 4 b, 5 b

7 2 percent, 3 slight/steady, 4 prove, 5 quarters, 6 same, 7 majority, 8 more, 9 dramatically

8 2 d, 3 c, 4 h, 5 b, 6 a, 7 i, 8 g

self-assessment test 4

1 2 d, 3 a, 4 b, 5 g, 6 e, 7 c

2 2 afford, 3 multi-tasking, 4 empathetic, 5 jingle, 6 details, 7 keep

3 2 the, 3 managed, 4 the, 5 a, 6 be able to, 7 –, 8 was able to

4 2 Robert suggested going out/that we should go out/that we went out on Sunday night.
3 My sister denied taking my money.
4 The airline representative asked (us) how many pieces of luggage we have/had.
5 The teacher reminded Carla to hand in her history assignment on time.
6 Jessica's father refused to let her go to New York on her own.
7 Ian apologised for not coming to the meeting.

5 2 the, 3 was, 4 surgery, 5 badly, 6 account

6 1 c, 2 g, 3 a, 4 d, 5 f, 6 e

7 2 thing, 3 Let, 4 What, 5 that, 6 really, 7 sounds, 8 exactly, 9 why

8 2 true, 3 agree, 4 say, 5 Surely, 6 know, 7 Sorry

self-assessment test 5

1 2 do, 3 forged, 4 pretend, 5 parole, 6 accused, 7 trial

2 2 sense, 3 plead, 4 litter/rubbish, 5 facilities, 6 mortgage, 7 commit

3 2 were/was, 3 would/might go, 4 hadn't lost, 5 wouldn't have made, 6 have seen, 7 had done, 8 knew

4 2 refused to do it
3 must have been tired
4 suggested going
5 encouraged me to work
6 learning English is easy
7 can't be true

5 2 imprisonment, 3 robbers, 4 thieves, 5 Burglary, 6 criminals

6 1 ✗, 2 ?, 3 ✓, 4 ✗, 5 ✓, 6 ?

7 2 According, 3 suggests/states/says, 4 topic, 5 explains, 6 means, 7 implies

8 2 mean, 3 Would, 4 kind, 5 treat, 6 Can, 7 love, 8 fancy, 9 know

exam test 1

1 1 B, 2 C, 3 C, 4 A, 5 B, 6 D, 7 A, 8 D, 9 C, 10 B

2 1 ✗, 2 ?, 3 ✗, 4 ?, 5 ✓, 6 ✓

3 1 mentally, 2 motivation, 3 thankful, 4 exhausted, 5 enthusiastic, 6 arrangements, 7 inspiration, 8 energetic

4 1 a, 2 b, 3 c, 4 d, 5 c, 6 a

exam test 2

1 1 b, 2 a, 3 g, 4 e, 5 c, 6 f

2 1 d, 2 c, 3 b, 4 c, 5 d

3 1 stressful, 2 miserable, 3 constructive, 4 impulsive, 5 unpredictable, 6 amazing, 7 exhausting, 8 starving, 9 historic/historical, 10 memorable

4 1 c, 2 a, 3 b, 4 c, 5 c, 6 b, 7 d, 8 b, 9 c

exam test 3

1 1 c, 2 d, 3 c, 4 a, 5 b

2 1 c, 2 e, 3 a, 4 b

3 1 us from getting
2 I hadn't borrowed so much money
3 she had been warned
4 in finding
5 his lawyer comes up with
6 have been built
7 so daring that
8 has gone
9 he hadn't chosen
10 us of damaging

4 1 of, 2 but, 3 in, 4 on, 5 unless, 6 on, 7 that, 8 to, 9 However, 10 before, 11 forward

Pearson Education Limited
Edinburgh Gate
Harlow
Essex CM20 2JE
England
and Associated Companies throughout the world.

www.pearsonelt.com

© Pearson Education Limited 2011

The right of Patricia Reilly with Marta Umińska and Dominika Chandler
to be identified as author of this Work has been asserted by him/her in
accordance with the Copyright, Designs and Patents Act 1988.

First published 2011
Second impression 2012

ISBN: 978-1-4082-3948-3

Set in Myriad Pro
Printed in Malaysia, CTP-PJB

Acknowledgements

Patricia Reilly would like to thank her family and friends for their
support, especially Ivana. She would also like to thank the team at
Pearson for all their hard work.

The publisher and authors would like to thank the following people
and institutions for their feedback and comments during the
development of the material:

Argentina: Claudia Marchese, Carolina Osa, Liliana Mabel Nasazzi;
Czech Republic: Hana Hrabovska; **Hungary**: Nora Horvath; **Italy**:
Franca Barnabei, Mirella Cusinato, Chiara Bellegamba; **Poland**: Marzena
Chadryś, Beata Zejnijew, Bogusława Skiba, Sylwia Węglewska, Wiesława
Sawicka, Ewa Gutowska, Inga Dawidowicz, Hanna Lipińska, Krystyna
Zebala, Magdalena Macioch, Małgorzata Abramczyk, Isabela
Zbrzeźniak, Joanna Frankowicz-Rowe, Magdalena Loska, Ewa Pilarska;
Russia: Angela Lezgiyan, Elizaveta Youshkina, Ianina Gennadievna
Barskaya, Gaulina Dokukina, Evgenia Burkinskaya; **Spain**: Beatriz
Chavez Yuste, Herminia de Juana, Darío, Hernández; **Slovakia**: Marian
Marticek; **Turkey**: Secil Guvenc, Evrim Tanis, Sevilay Ozpinar, Alper
Darici; **Ukraine**: Irina Olkhovska, Anastasia Volvin

The publisher is grateful to the following for permission to
reproduce copyright material:

Extracts on page 17 adapted from Holy Cow!: An Indian Adventure by
Sarah MacDonald, published by Bantam Books. Reprinted by
permission of The Random House Group Ltd. and copyright ©2002 by
Sarah MacDonald. Used by permission of Broadway Books, a division of
Random House, Inc; Extract on pages 64–65 adapted from Bicycling in
Africa: The Places in Between, International Bicycle Fund (Mozer, D.
1993) pp. 76–79, ©David Mozer; Extracts on page 86, page 114 adapted
from Welcome to Your Brain: The Science of Jet Lag, Love and Other
Curiosities of Life by S. Aamodt and S. Wang, published by Rider.
Reprinted by permission of The Random House Group Ltd. Copyright
©2008 by Sandra Aamodt and Sam Wang. Reprinted by permission of
Bloomsbury USA. Levine Greenberg Literary Agency, Inc.

In some instances we have been unable to trace the owners of
copyright material, and we would appreciate any information that
would enable us to do so.

Illustrations acknowledgements
(Key: b-bottom; c-centre; l-left; r-right; t-top)

Nick Brennan: pages 12, 76, 78; Joanna Kerr: pages 24, 56, 61;
Julian Mosedale: page 91; Kath Walker: pages 14, 80

Photo acknowledgements
The publisher would like to thank the following for their kind
permission to reproduce their photographs:
(Key: b-bottom; c-centre; l-left; r-right; t-top)

Alamy Images: ACE Stock Ltd 106l, Andres Rodriguez 10tc, Ashley
Cooper pics 102, Corbis Super RF 95, David Taylor 10tl, Derrick
Alderman 106tc, Glow Images 43t, Justin Minns 82, Photoshot Holdings
Ltd 108, Radius Images 43b, Silver Image 42; **Camera Press Ltd**: Debra
Hurford Brown 70b; **Corbis**: Bettmann 73t, 73c, Bettmann 73t, 73c,
Chris Livingston/Icon SMI 70tr, i love images 20, Ikon Images 28, Kathy
Willens/POOL/epa 6tr, Luc Gnago/Reuters 7; **Floodslicer Pty Ltd**: 105;
Getty Images: Chris Stein 87, Don Farrall 73b, Gary Miller 48; **Ronald
Grant Archive**: 5; **Robert Harding World Imagery**: Marco Cristofori
106r; **Photolibrary.com**: A. Demotes 64-65; **Rex Features**: John Dee 92,
Sipa Press 70tl; **Science Photo Library Ltd**: 39

All other images ©Pearson Education

Cover photo ©Getty Images/Jamie Grill

Every effort has been made to trace the copyright holders and we
apologise in advance for any unintentional omissions. We would
be pleased to insert the appropriate acknowledgment in any
subsequent edition of this publication.